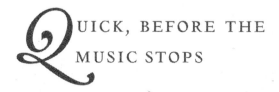

QUICK, BEFORE THE
MUSIC STOPS

For Joan,
who is Everywoman,
and yet no ordinary woman

QUICK, BEFORE THE
MUSIC STOPS

How Ballroom Dancing Saved My Life

With gratitude,

JANET CARLSON

Janet

BROADWAY BOOKS

New York

BROADWAY

Published in the United States by Broadway Books,
an imprint of The Doubleday Publishing Group,
a division of Random House, Inc., New York.
www.broadwaybooks.com

BROADWAY BOOKS and its logo, a letter B bisected on the diagonal,
are trademarks of Random House, Inc.

The names of certain individuals and their identifying characteristics
have been changed in order to protect their privacy.

This book is based on the author's article "Lift Off," which was published in O, The Oprah Magazine in September 2003.

Book design by Cassandra J. Pappas

Library of Congress Cataloging-in-Publication Data
Carlson, Janet.
    Quick, before the music stops : how ballroom dancing
saved my life / Janet Carlson.—1st ed.
        p. cm.
1. Carlson, Janet. 2. Dancers—United States—Biography.
3. Women dancers—United States—Biography. 4. Ballroom
dancing—United States. I. Title.

GV1785.C338A3 2008
792.802'8092—dc22
[B]
                                              2007051309

ISBN 978-0-7679-2682-9

PRINTED IN THE UNITED STATES OF AMERICA

10 9 8 7 6 5 4 3 2 1

FIRST EDITION

To my daughters,
Alden and Erica,
and to Wild Woman

CONTENTS

QUICK, BEFORE THE MUSIC STOPS

Prologue: Cherry Hill, New Jersey, 1978

I WATCHED THE REIGNING U.S. champion approach our banquet table in the Grand Ballroom as the music started and panicked when I realized he was coming for me. I wanted time to check my makeup, wished I were wearing a slinkier gown like Sandra, his professional partner, instead of this conservative beige sheath my mother and I had pulled out of the closet and reconstituted with sequins. *I'm not good enough.* But here he was, offering me his elbow. Me! A twenty-four-year-old amateur. I looked at him and rose with a smile disguising the state of high alert that tightened my chest and dried my tongue against the roof of my mouth.

It was a waltz. We joined the Saturday night crowd on the dance floor at the Hyatt in Cherry Hill, New Jersey. He was taller than my coach, John; that was the first thing I noticed as I lifted my upper spine to create an up-and-outward curve and then placed the fingers of my right hand on his left, which he'd outstretched as an invitation to come to him. He enfolded my hand and cradled my back with his right arm, and I let my left forearm come to rest, my wrist finding his deltoid under the sleeve of his dinner jacket.

Maybe it was postcompetition fatigue (my partner, David, and I had taken first place in the amateur open that day, and John and I got six golds, three silvers, and a bronze in the Pro-Am open gold division), but I couldn't attain my usual peak of nervousness as this champion and I began to move now. I felt a surge from him when the melody swooned, the singer's sad voice saying something about love lost. The sweet music now filled my head. I tried to flatten the small of my back, to arch without sticking my ass out, tried to get my heel leads on the forward steps. We swung among the other dancing couples, elegant in their long gowns and dinner jackets, and when a space opened up down the long line of dance, we took flight with some simple figures—I don't recall the specific steps, maybe a Double-Reverse Spin, a Whisk and Chassée, a Weave. I do know he led us into a Spin Turn in the far corner. I stepped forward on my right foot and turned nearly a full circle clockwise, rising up to my toes, feeling the centrifugal force through my upper body as we turned around each other, pausing for an instant at the peak of our rise, and that's when something changed. The commotion in my head and in the room stilled. I felt a quieting. Our movement seemed to slow, like a dream sequence in a film, only we were still perfectly on the music. The connection between us—at the triangle of flesh just below the ribs—softened, and my tension fell away. At the height of our rise on three is when I stopped working, stopped managing body parts. I felt safer for the first time in the big, luscious curve from toes to fingertips that had always been my nemesis because I have a tendency to hyperextend and pull the man off his feet. My head and shoulders were in a layout nearly horizontal to the floor. Merged at the torso, legs dovetailed, we floated now. The effortlessness was brand new to me. The beauty and smoothness of this ease overpowered my habit of resistance. I was in a state of surprise. I had no thoughts, and all my thoughts were clear. So this is how dancing is meant to feel—this is it!—like butter.

He probably had us in a Reverse Turn before I snapped out of it.

We danced until the song ended, and I remember nothing more, not the other figures we did, not how we ended, not what we said, if we spoke. I remember only the Spin Turn with its feeling of weightlessness and ease. And even though I gave up dancing a year later, I have recalled that figure now and then, for all these years, always with a jolt of longing and awe. I didn't see it for a long time, but that Spin Turn had become my gold standard, and after a while, I knew it wasn't just about the dance.

INTRODUCTION: SITTING THIS ONE OUT

MY HEART HAD gone cold by April 2000. I remember attending a bar mitzvah with my husband, Peter, at a temple in our small town, a suburb of New York City, and as I listened to the rabbi, my gaze drifted to the window through which I saw the trees, their eager, new green leaves dancing energetically, illuminated by the gentle spring sunlight. What life out there, I thought, as the rabbi spoke of the journey ahead of the thirteen-year-old boy we were honoring. And that was the moment I realized I was dead.

I was only forty-five, and to be precise, I was half dead. And I felt a mix of shame and guilt at that. Shame for my weakness, for my failure to be more exuberantly alive despite my full life and all its blessings. And I felt guilty for thinking such dark thoughts instead of celebrating the boy's good fortune and promising future (and my own). Now, looking back, I feel sorry for the woman I was then, that she experienced shame or guilt, and that she had gotten to half dead without even putting up a fight.

How did it come to this? Why had I allowed things to unfold

this way? And what does it mean, anyway, to be dead in the midst of life? The answers—I've found one or two so far—probably help to explain why the experience at the bar mitzvah did not really serve as a wake-up call for me. I remember clearly the utter sadness and helplessness I felt in recognizing my lifelessness, but there came no determination to do anything about it. *What a pity,* was my weak response. Part of being dead is the acceptance. Oddly, I'd never felt depressed. I'm much too cheerful and optimistic a person to be depressed. Half dead was rather about not taking care of myself; it was a state of mind that allowed me to push myself beyond reasonable limits to accomplish everything I believed I had to accomplish. Half dead was unconsciously giving up any expectation of real happiness.

I accepted the bar mitzvah moment just as I had accepted my lot in the eight years before, when having children changed my life—granted, in many extraordinarily wonderful ways—and I lost track of myself somewhere between keeping up a full-time work schedule as the beauty and health editor of *Town & Country* magazine (and bringing home a paycheck and medical benefits) and being more or less in charge at home, with a husband who could be described as pathologically mellow. I did whatever it took to keep the machine oiled and running; I knew how blessed I was on the face of it. I complained at times, but never questioned the need for me to shoulder the responsibility and sacrifice my comfort, peace of mind, or physical health in the name of getting it all done. I didn't see martyrdom or even sacrifice; I saw duty. And over the years, I gradually forgot what it's like to have fun. Intimacy came to seem a kind of burden. I transmogrified like a sci-fi character into a hyperfunctioning creature, part human, part robot.

It wasn't until nearly a year after the bar mitzvah that passion, the soul oxygen that I'd been lacking, took me by surprise and began to refuel my spirit. I received a supremely generous gift from my husband, who must have somehow sensed what I desperately needed (though he never seemed to realize I needed him to take out the trash). We rarely spoke about the bigger picture, the emotional landscape of our relationship. We were struggling in our marriage, trying to talk through some of our problems, and failing pretty miserably. His gift was an action, not a thing: he took me to a ballroom dance studio and in doing so set me free. It was a brilliant gift from a man who in many other ways was not able to be a good partner for me; it brought me back to life, led me to myself and to my senses.

I've been dancing steadily since that Valentine's Day. I have taken countless lessons and classes, passed a professional certification exam, done several shows and a competition—yes, dressed in those outrageous gowns and false eyelashes—and then gone back home to the kids, the soccer, the housework, and to work the next day. It hasn't been easy to make room in the schedule for my passion, but I have done it, because I'm certain now that it is necessary for life. This new period is rich—as rich in some ways as having my two children, because it has been a kind of birth—but it has also been painful thanks to the self-examination that dancing has provoked in me. And so, because of dance, I can say, unequivocally and gratefully, that I am alive at last.

I'm still trying to understand how the darkness gathered. As I said, it didn't preexist in me. I'm a Sagittarian! I always look on the bright side. The darkness accumulated somehow, despite my cheery circumstances: great job, two healthy, happy children, nice house in a lovely suburb, handsome, easygoing husband. What on earth did I have to complain about? Was I wallowing in my abundance? It didn't feel like I was. It felt like some invisible and critical underpinning had given way, and the center had fallen out. For a long time, I acted as though nothing had gone seriously wrong—and then, all of a sudden: this.

1   A Cold Day for Marriage, February 2001

IT'S A BITTERLY cold morning in Hastings-on-Hudson, and I can see my breath in the car as I say, "Seat belts," and listen for clicks in the backseat of our gold Buick LeSabre sedan (not exactly our vehicular style—we try to be much more modern and hip as a rule, but it came cheap). Our two daughters comply. Peter backs the car out of the driveway.

"Did anyone feed the rabbit?" I ask.

"Yes, I gave him hay and pellets," says Alden, only eight and so responsible. I glance back at Lucky's hutch by the trash bin. "I hope his water's not frozen." We drive the two blocks to drop off Erica at Hillside Elementary School. I watch as she climbs out lugging her turquoise backpack that's almost as big as she is. "Remember, number one rule at school, don't have any fun," I tease.

"Ma-a-a," Erica groans as usual, fighting a smile as I look into her blueberry eyes, and she slams the door as hard as she can. I see the window frost splinter.

"These brakes suck," Peter says as we drive down the hill to the middle school. "You should have Tom check them. This car has to last. We can't afford two lease payments."

I think of several responses, but don't feel like wasting the energy it would take to choose between them and deliver one. The silence doesn't feel awkward anymore. Though I'm wearing my heavy sheepskin coat, the cold has seeped into my bones and I tense against it as if I can fight it off. I slowly inhale as deeply as I can but an involuntary shudder interrupts the breath before it can find its way in.

"Mom, we have to go to the library tomorrow to do my research on Ecuador, don't forget," Alden says sternly. I hear the worry in her voice and want to reassure her.

"Okay, honey. When is the project due?"

"February twenty-sixth."

"Odie, that's two weeks from now," Peter protests, using his affectionate nickname for Alden. To me he says under his breath, grinning in my direction, "She's not my daughter." I look at him in his black shearling, thick and worn almost to gray. His hair is mostly black, but I can see a few more grays at the temple now—still, not bad for forty-seven. I notice he isn't wearing a hat or gloves. He holds the steering wheel like a teacup, elegantly, with just his thumbs and pointer fingers.

In a couple of minutes, he pulls to a stop in front of Farragut Middle School, where Alden will meet her class for an orientation meeting. She'll be switching to this school next year. Alden steps out and turns to utter her usual blasé good-bye. I can tell from the tiniest difference in her voice that she's battling some nerves. Then I notice she is dressed only in a pullover and sweatpants, and no hat, her light-brown fusilli curls pulled back in a tight ponytail as usual.

"Take your jacket, honey; it's really cold today," I say, passing her puffy red ski parka through the open window.

"I hate wearing this," Alden says, taking it from me anyway. "I mean, it's a nice jacket and everything, I just feel big and fat in it. I'll carry it." I wonder how painful it is for her to be so cooperative and concerned for my feelings—I chose the jacket at the Gap and clearly picked the wrong one.

"Will you be home at the regular time?" she asks before turning to go.

"Yes," I answer. "Actually, I'll pick you up from horseback riding."

"Oh, yeah, good." She looks over. "Bye, Dad."

We head up Farragut toward the Saw Mill Parkway. Peter turns on the radio and jabs a button just as I feared. I hear Howard Stern's voice, my cue to get out my headphones. I like driving in alone, I think, feeling a little guilty. I flip through my CD holder and choose Frank Sinatra, Shania Twain, and the new Norah Jones. Howard is asking some bimbo about her breast implants, so I move faster with numb fingers trying to get the headphones on without messing up my hair, determined to prevent the shock jock from contaminating my hard-won and fragile morning peace.

The old Buick, still cold, protests metallically as Peter accelerates onto the parkway southbound toward Manhattan. I look out my window at the geese on the bank of the Saw Mill River and let Norah Jones's voice locate my secret life. *Come away with me . . .*

Norah is just one of my escape hatches. I don't see it yet, but I will find several other escape hatches for myself over the coming years. I didn't always escape; I used to have a knack for facing things head on. But I guess I've lost my inclination to stand and fight, or stand and defend, or stand and care, love, challenge, implore, believe. I escape—into Norah's world for the moment, lulled by her voice. I wriggle out of the predicament. So much easier than persisting and declaring, "Peter, stop—let's stop this nonsense. Let's *be* together. Let's love each other."

But it all started so promisingly, as most marriages do. And sweetly. Do you know? That sweetness? The story of Peter and me meeting is nothing if not sweet and promising.

I WAS THIRTY-THREE and sick of being alone in my austere apartment on New York's Upper East Side. Sick of waking up on a Saturday morning and tidying up and going to the gym and taking extra long in the shower because I had nowhere to be next. Sick of eating alone in my apartment: round food—bagels, oranges, hard-boiled eggs (everything round, a random and meaningless coincidence or symbols of my ovaries ticking, urging me to find a mate?).

One Friday evening in April of 1988, wiped out from a full week's work, I forced myself to go to Donna's cocktail party. Hugh, my ballet date, my gay friend, said he'd go with me. Donna was a magazine editor; she worked at *New Woman*. Peter was dating Ellie, a sex therapist who had her own radio show, and she was a friend of Donna's. My sister, Alison, was invited, too.

When Hugh and I arrived at Donna's apartment, we chatted together a bit, then mingled separately. I spied Ali in a corner of the living room, and I went up to say hi. "Hey, Janet," she said. "This is Peter. Peter, this is my sister Janet. I'm prettier and younger, but she's smarter." That was part of our sister act. I smiled. Peter tilted his head to one side, lowered his eyes in a kind smile, and extended his hand to shake mine, and I fell into a deep crush right then and there.

We talked, Ali, Peter, and I, and we monopolized the crudités tray. Ali and I were a little silly and shamelessly flirtatious; whenever my gregarious kid sister and I had a chance to perform socially, we'd be unabashed and our chatter and repartee would get more outrageous as we worked our audience. Peter seemed to enjoy it, and he played right along, nonplussed—or as he would say, non-pulsed. At some point, he let us know he was a photographer. His client list was impressive: *New York Times, Business Week, Newsweek.* Later, he introduced Ellie. I found her intimidating. Ali and I left together at midnight. On the street, I said, "Wow, he was cute."

"Who?" Ali asked. She had a boyfriend at the moment, so I knew she wasn't interested herself. "Oh, Peter? He's not your type."

Well, that's for sure. Because of my job at *European Travel & Life* magazine, I was used to dating suave European men in shiny suits, some with names like Count Gelasio Gaetani Lovatelli d'Aragona. Actually, he was a friend, not a date, but you get the idea of the crowd I'd been hanging out with—wealthy, sophisticated, worldly, treacherous men. French, Italian, Austrian, didn't matter, they were all dangerous, and invariably neglected to mentioned that they were married.

Meeting Peter, my radar immediately detected his nice, safe American aura. He was a trustworthy, manly cowboy in black Levi 501s, black Reebok sneakers, and a blue denim shirt with mother-of-pearl snaps, with a beeper on his belt. God bless him, I thought, he looks like the messengers who show up at my office. But so hip, and very attractive! What a refreshing change from the guys I usually picked. I liked that he was tall, in great shape, and he had really black hair a little wavy at the back where he'd let it grow to just below his collar. I also liked how laid back he seemed, and smart—though unpretentious about it.

We exchanged business cards at Donna's party. Peter called me the next day to ask me out, and we agreed to dinner the following Thursday. Dinner at my place. I didn't think he'd show—I was used to men making excuses, having a change of plans, or just not showing—so when my phone rang at six that evening (I'd left work early to dress and prepare penne alla vodka and salad just in case) I assumed he'd say, "Sorry, I can't make it" or "Oh, was that tonight?"

Instead, he said, "I'm about to head uptown from Canal Street. Is seven okay? Should I bring bok choy or asparagus?"

By seven-thirty, I was watching him prep the asparagus in the kitchen of my one bedroom on East Fifty-second. I poured two glasses of Pinot Grigio and offered him one. He took it and started chopping. He chopped with an elegance that took my breath away. He chopped the slender asparagus on the bias. *The bias!* I stared at these lovely diagonals of spring green and swooned.

"Where'd you learn that?" I asked.

"I was a chef in Switzerland," he answered.

And that was that. I had to marry the guy. Of course, it turned out he'd worked in the kitchen of an inn in the Swiss Alps where he was a ski bum in his twenties. But still, he had a way with that knife, I tell you.

FOUR MONTHS AFTER we met, we went to Anguilla, the little Caribbean island where my family had spent summers for years. After a day of swimming, sex on the deserted beach, picking coconuts from the tall palms, windsurfing, and dining on lobster and snapper at a waterside restaurant, he proposed to me in bed, in the dark.

"Janet, I want us to spend the rest of our lives together," he said.

That was a declarative statement, I noticed, not a question. So I said nothing in response, just let his statement hang there in the heat of the night air between us while my mind raced. I should say something, I thought, because, I don't know, he might have just suggested marriage.

"Okay . . ." I started. "Um, is that a question?"

"Yes, it is," he said. "Geez, you had me nervous there. Were you just stuck on the grammar? Was that it?"

"Yes," I said. "My answer is yes."

He could have killed me, he told me later. And this became one of our cherished stories, me leaving him in the lurch of silence there, and the silliness of grammar getting in the way of romance.

THE EARLY TIMES for us were filled with magical moments, and if I squint, I can still see them forming, feel the superb weight of them anchoring us. Like the first time I brought Peter to Gloucester, Massachusetts, to visit my mom and stepfather at their sprawling harbor-front home. One afternoon, I was on a beat-up old bike, barefoot and wearing a floaty, pastel summer skirt, and he was on foot, camera in hand. As I rode ahead down the dirt path, he started shooting, and I remember hearing the automatic shutter firing away and feeling a rush of desire because of his manly competence with his equipment. Halfway down the path, I lifted both legs up and out to the side, flirty show-off, in a sort of gymnast's pose, and heard his camera rush to capture the kooky moment. At the bottom of the hill, I stopped, put my feet to the ground and turned to look back for Peter. He was approaching me, camera lowered now to his chest, tears in his eyes. As we walked back to the main road, he told me that it was my playfulness, a quality of little-girlishness, that had moved him.

We got married at my family's home in Hastings, the suburb of New York City where I grew up. Many of our friends observed that we were a Barbie and Ken couple, which I took to be a comment about our appearance, mostly—Peter being tall and dark, and me being tall and blond. But I suppose it meant even more, something about us belonging together like the dolls, a magazine editor and a photographer, a fetching couple. We bought a co-op in Chelsea when that neighborhood was still a drug dealer's haven but on the verge of becoming chic. On the weekends, we shopped for art deco finds at Depression Modern on Sullivan Street, went Rollerblading in Central Park, made dinner together for friends. Then we bought our own home in Hastings and moved out and started having kids.

There is a photograph in our album of Peter holding Alden, just moments old, in his two palms, bending over her, marveling, already loving her.

That could be called our midway point, our turning point. Because after that, things happened that didn't seem so Barbie-and-Ken idyllic.

I BELIEVE (not just because I've done this) that when two people meet, feel an attraction, and start to get to know each other, they often are in a rush, greedy to fully know the other right away, and because they begin with a sketchy picture of the brand-new person, they fill in the blank regions with their own fantasy details of the ideal mate. So in the beginning, as they fall in love, it's with a composite of real and imagined aspects of the other person. Slyly, the imagined ones become assumptions. That's a gigantic but undetected pitfall in the process called getting to know each other: two people operate in their relationship based on their pictures that are part real, part fantasy. Part of the fantasy, naturally, is that the other person is going to complete us or rescue us, and this gets us into really deep trouble.

As time goes on, reality rudely interferes and more true aspects of the other begin to emerge, elbowing out the fantasy aspects and upsetting the dreamer. Thus originates a disappointment and a sense of betrayal too vast and amorphous to comprehend— so I was told by Steven Goldstein, a New York psychologist I once interviewed for a story. We harbor the bad feeling deep down without knowing it, and then we pin our vague discontent on something else, something immediate and concrete—like the dishes or the finances or the TV remote.

Many marriages thrive despite some unspoken disappointment, but I'm talking about the ones that don't. I'm talking about those of us who allow the little annoyances to accumulate and get in the way.

It's hard not to. One of the reasons is that we get comfortable. In a way, it's unfortunate that, in the safe emotional surroundings of an intimate relationship, we can let our hair down and loosen up on our manners, because it's the caring gestures and some degree of formality that can help sustain a relationship. They ritualize our compassion in tiny, important ways. Once we get comfortable with our mate, it's not much of a leap to becoming intolerant and critical. We can start to nitpick, complain, blame. The remarkable qualities in the beloved that initially seemed so alluring we now find irritating. And because we haven't recognized the powerful undertow of that Big Disappointment, we allow the steady drip of the little, quotidian disappointments to erode our love.

NORAH'S VOICE TRAILS off and I lean forward to put Frank Sinatra in the player. "Try a Little Tenderness." I think back to the early years when Peter and I were like an average couple speaking up to each other about our minor grievances and trying to sort them out. We never really succeeded in this: I'd initiate a conversation, and then I'd use it to make my own case; he'd reluctantly allow himself to be dragged into the conversation, but then he'd shut down. I was righteous; he was passive-aggressive. Very bad combo. Ever so gradually, we settled into a perpetual state of alienation. That's how our story turned from sweet and promising to sad. Is it true for all couples that the momentous interpersonal issues are rooted in banal domestic chores like the laundry?

Over time, Peter demonstrated that he had not much memory for household tasks and precious little desire to perform them. He bristled at my constant reminders, and he tried to train me to not nag. Okay, define nag: is it saying or asking more than once? Or would that be merely reminding? In which case, nagging would be after two times? Or is it more in the tone of voice? No matter, it all felt like nagging to Peter, I guess. So I took to scribbling Post-it notes and leaving these around the house, on the bathroom mirror, the kitchen counter. "Please pick up your dirty underwear off the bathroom floor." "Your mom called again; call her back today?" He hated this even more. Who wouldn't? However, he made it clear that on Saturday mornings, cleanup time, he preferred a written to-do list to me following him around telling him what to do next.

I didn't enjoy feeling like a nag or a shrew. I tried to accommodate his communication preferences, but his touchiness had me hamstrung. We talked about this when we started marriage counseling, how we'd agreed that the recycling, which was picked up on Friday mornings, would be his job—but he always forgot. "Oh, shit," he'd say in bed Friday mornings at the sound of the sanitation truck cresting our hill. Our therapist told me not to put it out myself. "Let it accumulate until he finally does it." I tried that. The bottles, cans, and newspapers accumulated for weeks on end, until my parents or someone would come for a visit and ask how I could let it be so messy there by the side of my house.

I walked on eggshells in those years, afraid to provoke Peter's shoulder-hunching anger, asking if he'd mind . . . would he possibly . . . But I always knew he resented the interruption. Still, I wouldn't give up. I noticed Peter never forgot a photo shoot, or to pick up the film, or other things having to do with his work. Speaking of which: we both were working parents, but somehow it developed that I handled 90 percent of the household and children stuff. I simply refused to accept that "husbands are like that" and I should accept good enough. Because it wasn't good enough; it wasn't fair. Saying "Oh, well, that's men for you" was not any consolation. Maybe I had grown up during a time of liberation for women, but my liberation was not only about being able to work and be economically independent; my liberation was in expecting more from my partner.

One beautiful Saturday morning, I got out of bed and wandered into the bathroom and saw his dirty underwear and socks on the bathroom floor yet again. This incensed me—not only because I found it gross and inconsiderate, but also because our shy, polite, tidy babysitter, Kumarie from Trinidad (where the custom is to take off one's shoes before entering a home to not drag dirt and germs in, so she always did this at our house), would see the foul things— and it might be highly offensive to this lovely woman. After asking Peter nicely that morning as he was preparing to get out of bed for his weekly tennis game if he could put his things in the hamper, I went downstairs. Soon, he left with his racquet. When I went upstairs to dress, there was everything where I last saw it on the bathroom floor. BAM! That's it, I've had it, was my red-hot reaction. My anger finally erupted like a volcano and I took action. I picked up the underwear and socks, and then I picked up the dirty clothes he'd left on our bedroom floor and I lugged that armful of laundry to our bedroom window, flung open the window with one hand, lifted the screen, and tossed all that laundry out the window. It landed on the roof of the front porch below. All morning, neighbors passing by would ask as I worked in our garden, "What's that up on your porch roof?" and I'd say nonchalantly, "That's Peter's dirty laundry." When he came home from tennis, he parked his car and said hi to our neighbor, John, who was walking his dog. They came across the lawn, and John asked about the rooftop decor. "Peter's dirty underwear," I said. John smiled. Peter was not amused. "You are out of control," he said sharply as he marched into the house, leaving a trail of Har-Tru tennis court granules on the carpet.

WE KEPT UP the marriage counseling, but it wasn't really helping. It led us to try date night once a week, but neither of us really took to it, and it was frustrating to pay a babysitter so we could go out and spend the whole time talking about our daughters, antsy to get back home to them. But a bigger reason therapy was a flop, from my point of view, was that there was never anything that Peter could

own up to. I did—a lot, because it was in my nature to blame myself. But almost never did he say, "Gee, I didn't realize I was doing
that, let me think about that." Or, "Yeah, I'm sorry." In our sessions, for a whole year, he was Mr. Teflon. Blame slid off of him like
fried eggs off a greasy skillet. But it takes two, as they say in the
tango business. That would have been good to say in our session,
but I wasn't wise enough to the Teflon phenomenon then. I did assume that Peter was right; something in me needed fixing. And now
here we are, years later, the two of us in this Buick together, traveling silently, grimly in our separate compartments of the heart.

It kind of sneaked up on us, the separateness of us together,
and the crazy busyness of working and raising children conspires to
keep it that way. But every now and then, one of us will do something or say something in an effort to break our unspoken pattern
and resuscitate our moribund marriage. We aren't totally hopeless
quite yet.

IT'S VALENTINE'S DAY, and as usual on Thursdays, I'm up early to
get the kids ready for school, but because I'll be working at home, I
don't need to shower, dress, and do my hair and makeup, so I can
sleep an extra forty-five minutes. I always enjoy this little treat in the
middle of an exhausting work week. Valentine's Day is usually a non-
event in our marriage; we don't celebrate the Hallmark holidays in a
big way. But this year, in a sort of last-ditch effort to do something
nice for Peter, I went with my friend Lisa to Eve's Garden on Fifty-
seventh Street, a sex shop for women. We went together because we
were both too embarrassed to go alone. It was her idea; some editor
friend had told her about a nifty gadget, and she called me.

"It's a black leather panty with a vibrator in it, and a remote-
control device," she explained. "I'll come to your office in half an
hour and we can look at it together. Can you leave work early so we
can walk over before they close?"

The remote-control device, we learned, was good at up to twenty feet. "You have to be careful in a restaurant," the saleswoman at the shop explained, "because you can set off someone else's panty."

Perfect for Peter, I thought, who spends most of his time at home reclining on the big brown leather couch with the TV remote in his hand. Perfect, also, because he's always complaining about not getting enough sex. So now, on Valentine's morning, before he leaves for work, I give him his present, which I've wrapped in shiny red paper with a red bow. He opens it and smiles, as if appreciating that I can do the Howard Stern thing when necessary.

"Hey, I made reservations for seven," he says on his way out the front door. I assume he'll be taking me to one of our local restaurants. Later that day, I think of taking a shower and dressing up nicely, but I still have so much editing to finish that I decide just to brush my hair, forgo the makeup, and put on my mustard leather Gap pants, a black cashmere sweater, and boots.

Betty arrives to babysit. Peter says, "Let's get going, we can't be late." Hmm. He's never cared much before about being late for a dinner.

"Where are we going?" I ask, but he won't say.

He drives north. He has the remote in his pocket and tests it on Route 9 and I hit the roof of the car at the sudden buzz in my panties. I don't find it particularly pleasant. He continues past the intersection where I expect he'll turn left to go to Irvington. Instead, he continues straight and puts on his blinker by Monarch Deli. I look up to the second floor above the deli and see the neon blue sign: BALLROOM ON HUDSON. I saw an article in our local paper about the new studio some weeks ago and wistfully imagined checking it out, but haven't gotten around to it.

"What is this?" I ask. "Oh, no—you didn't!"

He leads us around back to the entrance and opens the door. We go up the stairs and find the door to the studio. He precedes me in and asks for Yuri.

"I'm Yuri," says a handsome man with a Russian accent, about forty-five. "And this is my wife, Olga."

"I'm Peter. Here, take my wife," he jokes. But it's no joke. I discover that he has made a reservation for an initial complimentary lesson with Yuri, the dance director of the Ballroom on Hudson Dance Studio, and that he told them, when he phoned, that I was the New York State champion in the late seventies but haven't danced since.

"I'm in leather and boots," I protest in a thin voice.

Olga brings out some worn pumps for me to try on—unfortunately just my size—and so I step onto the dance floor wearing her shoes, my cashmere sweater, the mustard leather pants, and the remote-control panty device. Peter sits in the chairs at the side of the room. Yuri puts on a foxtrot and a pang of nostalgia grabs hold of me and makes my legs know what to do. I have just enough time to worry that Peter has his hand on the remote before Yuri switches to tango and I forget all about it. I am moved being on the floor for the first time in twenty years. It feels like I never left. But the dancing isn't exactly like getting on a bicycle again. The feeling and the fantastically old-fashioned music are the same, but my technique is rusty. Rumba, cha-cha, Viennese waltz, we do them all and after a half hour Yuri pronounces me "quite good."

Peter takes out a check and signs me up for a package of twenty lessons. Then we go to dinner at Off Broadway down the street and I scan the restaurant from time to time to see if any other women are jumping out of their seats.

BACK ON THE BOARDS, FORGETTING THE GROCERIES

D ANCING AGAIN AFTER all this time, I am out of breath during my lessons after one cha-cha or waltz—three minutes of intense aerobics—but it feels great, the windedness. So does the soreness in my calves and my upper back muscles, which I haven't used in years. Best of all, I've found my hips again. Since childbirth and the mudslide of my marriage, they've been frozen, locked in one position, like the creaky joints of the Tin Man in *The Wizard of Oz*. Now I'm obliged to use my hips again in sultry Latin dances like the rumba. No matter that I'm quite inhibited by my rustiness, the gyrating really oils them and gets the stiffness out, with that figure eight sort of movement, front to back circling on one side and the other. But even in the more restrained and elegant waltz, the hips need to be fully engaged.

I start going to Ballroom on Hudson on Tuesdays and Fridays, the days I don't commute to Manhattan. I go at lunchtime for an hour's lesson before I pick up Alden and Erica at school. At first, Yuri teaches me both Latin (rumba, cha-cha, samba, jive, and paso doble, the bullfighter's dance) and Standard (waltz, foxtrot, tango, quickstep, and Viennese waltz). The kind of dance we do is called International Style; the strictest form of competitive ballroom dancing, it's technically very difficult, both for Latin and for Standard. I trained in International twenty years before, with John Nyemchek and his wife Cathi, when John's brother David and I were partners, and we would go to competitions up and down the eastern seaboard. The hallmark of International Standard is, I think, its constant and precise connection between partners through the arms and hands, and at the pelvis. All the athleticism and artistic expression have to happen within this nonnegotiable connection. International, which is defined by the Imperial Society of Teachers of Dancing in England, also has a strict syllabus of steps divided into levels of difficulty, along with its highly defined and disciplined technique.

American Style is the other method of ballroom dancing taught in the States. It came out of the Arthur Murray and Fred Astaire studios, where the idea was to get people into dancing with a simpler, looser, more flamboyant, and thus more immediately accessible and satisfying way of dancing. Many American Style and social dancers find International stuffy or boring, particularly Standard—but Standard's stalwart cult following finds their dancing far more challenging and rewarding than the sloppy and, to us snobs, rather dumbed-down American Style. Those of us with a cerebral appreciation of dance tend to gravitate to International Style, whether Latin or Standard; I love the elegant expression of Standard—it's so pared down and essential. Pure isn't exactly the word because, to me, pure could be a reference to street dancing—spontaneous, uncontaminated, uncodified. Standard is as far from the street as you can get. It's greenhouse dancing.

As soon as Yuri and I start comparing then and now in terms of ballroom dancing, I learn that our art has been renamed: dancesport. Evidently, the change was intended to counteract an old-fashioned image and to attract a wider following in America. And I guess it has worked; membership in the main dance organization, USA Dance, has doubled over the last decade. I also learn that the International Olympic Committee is considering dancesport for recognition as a sport—maybe one day a medal sport. I'm happy that the status of my beloved ballroom dancing has been elevated from tacky, eccentric, and pretty much unheard of in the 1970s to a mainstream pursuit in the twenty-first century. All this, even before television shows like *Dancing with the Stars* and *So You Think You Can Dance* have gone on the air and become big hits.

After only a week or so, Yuri introduces me at the start of our lesson to a young couple who arrived days before from Kiev to start teaching at Ballroom on Hudson: Sergei, a protégé of Yuri, and his dance partner, Katya. They speak barely two words of English between them. Yuri tells me that shy Sergei will be my Latin teacher from now on. Okay. Whatever you say. I begin taking weekly lessons with this gentle young man, and find that it really doesn't matter we can't speak much; in fact, it's probably an advantage. Without benefit of language, we just dance and use a lot of body language instead.

Dancing sure does whip you into great physical shape. I'm naturally slim and in decent form, despite having young kids and only walking around my neighborhood for exercise. But over the next few months, dancing three or four hours a week, I become a lean mean dancing machine. The activity burns anywhere from 250 to 400 calories an hour, and I lose twelve pounds right away because I'm suddenly exercising more and eating less due to my excitement and lack of time. Soon I discover I'm too thin, and have to make an effort to eat enough to keep up. I start to crave meat; I think my growing muscles need the protein. I don't want sweets or carbs as much, except for potato chips, which I have always adored for the salt.

One day, I look down and see how carved my calves and quads have become. My butt, which had gotten flabby in my years of motherhood, is suddenly tight and high again. Dancing tones everything, even the backs of your arms. After having two kids and hitting forty-something, it just feels so damn good to be stronger and faster. My posture has improved, and when I sit at my computer at work, Mike, the men's fashion editor, says I look like I'm playing the piano at Carnegie Hall. It's a hoot when the spring days turn warm and I go sleeveless: people stare at my biceps and ask, "Are you a marathon runner?" or "Do you lift weights?" and I smile and say, "No, I just hold up a hundred-and-ninety-pound man when I dance."

But I can be quite insecure about my looks. I'm not a beauty; my face is just okay. I was once considered attractive. I say *was* because when I started facing the inevitable signs of aging in my forties, I stopped looking at myself in mirrors because it was too disappointing. It's especially difficult because my work as a beauty editor means I focus on appearances all day long, and I hear regularly in meetings with plastic surgeons about how I could add volume to my narrow face or lift my eyebrows just a tad or correct my upper lids. It's hard for anyone to believe she's attractive in the midst of perfectionists with scalpels. But dancing has begun to suggest a more balanced view that occasionally comforts me: that a woman—a person—is beautiful in *doing;* her beauty is in the movement, not so much in the static face, or the dress, or the hair. It's what she does with herself, it's who she is. Beauty is an action verb—and a few crow's-feet are meaningless in the context. It's what I do; it's who I am. I keep telling myself that.

Getting into good physical shape and enjoying the psychological boost and the confidence that come with it mean that I'm starting to get more attention from men. Out on the street, I get more glances and comments. In my twenties I hated it, but now I love it. One fine spring evening after work, for instance, I try to hail a taxi on Fifty-fourth Street to get to a business cocktail in midtown. It isn't easy at rush hour to find a cab. There I stand curbside wearing a tight pink-

and-white skirt and pink cotton cardigan with my arm extended skyward in the I-wanna-be-your-passenger salute. No taxis in sight. I watch absent-mindedly as an example of New York's latest transportation phenomenon, a nifty bicycle-drawn rickshaw, draws near on Fifty-fourth, backlit beautifully by the setting sun. It carries a male passenger; he's wearing a suit, talking on his cell, and looking at me. He's attractive as far as I can tell, but it happens fast, so I'm not sure. Without ending his call, he gestures to me and pats the space on the seat next to him, moving his briefcase aside, as if to offer me a ride. I smile, enchanted. I've never ridden in one, but I'm not quite ready to hop on. I let him pass by. *Ooh-ha, I feel sexy again! It's not over just because I'm almost fifty.* A witness next to me on the sidewalk seems enchanted too. He says, "Only in New York." I do love New York. But this probably wouldn't have happened to me before dancing changed my outlook. Literally, I'm looking *out*; I'm less withdrawn.

My older sister, Anna, however, sounds like she disapproves of my dancing. One day, we're on my front porch chatting, and my new hobby comes up. She says, "It's over for us now that we're pushing fifty. We're meant to live vicariously through our children." Her comment makes me feel defensive, like this new joy of mine is just an ego trip. God, I hope not. Then she adds, "Their lives are what's important now, not ours."

I couldn't disagree more. Maybe Anna wasn't being totally serious, but I rant anyway to my best friend, Julia, knowing she'll sympathize because she's a yoga devotee as well as a mother juggling plenty and she always takes time for her classes, at-home practice, and weekend retreats. What kind of example would I be setting as a mother, I preach to my converted audience of one, if I gave up my own life, or my own joys and passions? Is that what we want to tell our kids, that life ends at fifty? After all, I dance while my daughters are at school; I make a point of not taking time away from them. I've simply stopped doing errands and cleaning the house. And I've learned how to take a lunch hour like many people do, to squeeze in a workout—only mine is a good, sweaty Viennese waltz, and then I'm back at my desk.

Alden and Erica see me becoming happier because of the dancing. I'm more playful and silly. Instead of dressing for success, I start dressing like a dancer, more provocatively and expressively, and they're my eager and wide-eyed fashion consultants. The fun of this makes me realize that some ten years earlier, I'd bought into the shabby, dowdy working mother attitude. And despite being told over and over that I look much younger than my years, I had come to feel a bit over the hill. Now, thanks to Yuri and Sergei, I'm shedding years at a fast clip.

There are other subtle changes, too, just little things that I privately notice. I start listening to dance music instead of sad ballads by female vocalists or Frank Sinatra. One of my favorite tunes is Ella Fitzgerald's " 'S Wonderful," which immediately captivates me as a nice foxtrot. One day, when I drive alone, dancing to it in my head, my thumbs tapping the steering wheel, I get swept up in the rhythm during the instrumental bridge. *Oh, listen to those horns and the percussion build! This reminds me of sex.* The instrumental crescendo describes the orgasm, and then comes a release and resolution. Beautiful. I even find myself listening to the Eagles differently—"Take It to the Limit" is a waltz! What a weird and wonderful blending of generations and styles; waltzing to the Eagles, that kind of says it all about me. I dance to that song in my head and feel a euphoria I never knew when I listened to the band in the 1970s.

Everything looks sharper and more brilliant now; everything sounds more immediate and beautiful. I start whistling. It's been years. I am out of practice, and my whistle isn't pretty, but it doesn't matter, because I'm not even aware I'm doing it. Peter points it out. And maybe the kids imitate me. I start liking scented candles, which up until now have struck me as cloying and unnecessary. Every evening when I come home from work, I light one on the windowsill by the sink to keep me company and remind me of something— what?—while I go about the mundane business of dinner and cleaning up.

I dance at home, in whatever small space amid the furniture beckons to me. The kids think I am nuts, wiggling my pelvis like that, moving without inhibition. If I do this even just a little outside the house, they are mortified. "Mom! Stop!!" Alden will command. Or Erica will grab my hips to make me stop. But I can see she is fascinated, too. What's up with Mommy? Nevertheless, I make sure to rein it in when I walk them to school. That's a firm rule for mothers: never embarrass your kids in front of their peers.

One night, we go to see *The Lion King* on Broadway. I bought the tickets a year ago, right after I saw it as a guest of Elizabeth Arden. This time, I want to watch my kids watch it, so I can get a vicarious thrill. I love seeing their spines long and their eyes in rapt attention through the entire show. The live orchestra performing the "Circle of Life" completely undoes me, for the second time, the way the music swells to fill the place. When we stand up to go at the end, inching our way toward the exit sign, I am boogying in the aisle to the music still playing.

"Mom! Stop!!"

AND SO I EMBRACE my giddiness, which lasts many months. Because of it, I unwittingly allow dance to become the light of my life, while my marriage by increments becomes the darkness. And although a more enduring and blessed contentment is also a product of my return to dance, I still face some ups and downs that inevitably result from this contrast. Meanwhile, dance becomes a mirror for me—the just-me, unmasked, unpackaged—and what I see in the mirror is not wholly easy or beautiful to see. I'm not referring to how I look on the outside, but to what I discover on the inside, the hidden-away aspects of me that I haven't yet realized I will have to bring into the light of day if I am to become whole again.

OTHER CHANGES OCCUR as I get more and more into dancing. For one thing, I stop doing the weekly grocery shopping. No time! I've been in the habit of shopping during my lunch hour on Fridays when I work at home. Now, I drive to Ballroom on Hudson instead. One Sunday evening, Peter opens the fridge, saying, "I think I'll cook tonight." But the shelves inside are nearly bare, if you don't count the fourteen bottles of half-used and wholly forgotten, expired salad dressing and barbecue sauce. "Well, I guess I'll do a shop," he says, staring at nothing to eat, and I nearly fall off my chair in the living room.

Hallelujah! I refrain from shouting, in spite of an inner wave of celebration impelling me to make a noise. Not that Peter never shops for groceries, but it certainly isn't a regular occurrence. He'll never, for example, remember on his way home to ask himself, "Do we need anything? I think we might be running out of milk; I'd better get some."

Finally, I understand what a wise woman, a career counselor named Renée, advised a few years before this when I was complaining that Peter didn't do enough around the house. She said, "Take care of yourself and the rest will take care of itself." I never bought it. That sounded not only selfish but also unrealistic. *I can't stop taking care of all the rest—our life will fall apart.* But now that Peter has the bright idea to go grocery shopping, I get it. Her message wasn't "every man for himself" or "let go of the details," or even "grab your oxygen mask first." It was "take responsibility for yourself, your own needs, and things will work out from there." Peter comes back humming and eagerly unpacks his favorite comfort foods (B&M Baked Beans and hot dogs, the kind of things I usually forget) along with some healthier stuff for our children, and a new day has dawned at the Freed house.

I look back on the logic and verbal admonishments I doggedly used on my husband for years to no avail—and all it finally took was a tango. I was so clever, so adept in conversation and argument, and I always won with my impeccable logic. I was always right. And yet I failed to get what I wanted, failed to come to an understanding with Peter, failed to improve our marriage or even to engage him in finding a solution to its problems. I was telling, reasoning, talking tirelessly, working out of my brain—without result. "Peter, we both have demanding jobs, we're both tired at the end of the day, but why do you get to lie on the couch and watch TV while I'm doing the dishes, cleaning the house, and spending more time with the kids at bedtime? It's not fair. You should help more." It was my taking care of myself that led to the result—Peter getting the groceries. And it was not a punitive action; I haven't been dancing three times a week to spite Peter, but because it has made me happy and I'm so ready to be happier. I've been a walking time bomb of productivity and accomplishment, the steam of my suppressed anger whooshing from my ears. Lucky for me, dancing stopped me cold in my tracks.

Normally in my marriage, in managing household and children, I lead. It's our tacit agreement. So I've tended to plow relentlessly forward all these years, unconsciously hoping Peter will take over and change our direction by stepping forward himself, so I can step back. Maybe deep down, I've wanted to share the leading, but I haven't known how to tap into that desire or speak up about it. He doesn't step forward, which frustrates me, so I push harder—forward. It hasn't occurred to me to change direction myself. And as would happen if we were literally dancing, we finally hit a wall.

Looking back now, I can appreciate how unpleasant the experience must have been for Peter. The grocery episode is a new dance for us. I just took one step back. In response, Peter stepped forward.

Eureka! In dance, there's barely a split second between the action of one partner and the reaction of the other. The better the dancers, the shorter the reaction time. For us, in our grocery dance, the action took me, oh, about eleven years; Peter's reaction, only a matter of weeks.

Everyone always asks me if I dance with my husband. No, he doesn't care to dance. Well, occasionally, at a Saturday night party in our town, but he much prefers mountain biking and tennis and kayaking and skiing and boating on the Hudson River. I've resented it deeply for some time—not that he doesn't want to dance with me, but that he somehow has all the time in the world to play while I'm insanely busy. Once during an argument, while Peter was reclining on the couch and I stood nearby interrupting his TV show, he looked at me with the cold, beady eyes of a shark and said, "Your problem is that you don't know how to relax." I could have killed him. Here I was busting my butt at work, giving up my play time, so that he could relax and enjoy his sports. What was I thinking?

Now, with the groceries, begins a new phase in our marriage. Not a total cease-fire, but we have resolved one conflict at least, and my heart lifts.

3 DELIRIUM IN THE ARMS OF OTHER MEN

THERE ARE TIMES I wish I'd chosen my sport, or my passion, more sensibly. Why couldn't it have been tennis or running, something less intimate? Could there be meaning in the fact that I chose partnership dancing? Is this where my fate has led me, like a smart bomb, with some kind of inevitability? Ballroom dancing sanctions—no, requires—two people touching each other in a way that, if they weren't lovers, they wouldn't dream of doing on the street, in the office, at a dinner party. It is not always easy, in the midst of such formalized touching—of hands, ribs, breasts, inner arms, pelvises, thighs, *inner* thighs, bellies—to keep one's distance, to remain indifferent to the person pressing himself to you. I'm sure it is more challenging for the man—the poor guy can't exactly hide an erection. I never can tell for sure, but when in doubt, I assume it's his wallet or his cell phone.

No matter how comfortable with their bodies and nonchalant about contact dancers appear, believe me, the touching is a big deal. It can be sporty or artistic one moment—nice and neutral—and then erotic the next, charged with positive sex ions, even though nothing in the physical contact has actually changed. Perhaps more significant is the way you are *not* touching. A powerful eroticism ignites in the space between you, between his ribs and yours, his belly and yours, his mouth and yours. The far-from-innocent but exceedingly respectful Sergei put it eloquently to me the other day, in his much improved but still halting English, in a way that would make any woman melt: "Dancing is better than sex because of the mystery, the holding back. Being one and one-half inch away, a breath away only, is the most sexy." Amen to that. And I defy you to look at a handsome twenty-six-year-old man with a square jaw, clear blue eyes, perfect biceps, a keen mind, and a pure heart saying that and not feel a twinge of something and then swiftly agree with him. This may seem hard to believe, but I have no secret urge to have sex with Sergei; first of all, neither of us is available, and second, we are like brother and sister—maybe more like mother and son. And he really truly is golden, devoted to his dancing and dedicated as a teacher.

But since Valentine's Day, I have gotten quite carried away by those one and one-half inches, I think because my libido was rather parched by the time I was delivered to the dance studio by my husband. "Here, take my wife." Only half joking, I'm sure. But, amazingly, like someone in a coma whose family is about ready to pull the plug, I've come back to life—in the arms of other men. Is ballroom dancing wrecking my marriage or saving me from the wreckage of its demise?

My thirst for dancing is unquenchable, and I don't care that I am making a dent in my savings to pay for three lessons a week at seventy-five dollars a pop. I'm due; I haven't had much exercise or creative escape since Alden was born, now nearly a decade ago. And at first, during the early weeks, I was the good student, paying no attention to the fact that Yuri is so attractive, well built, and athletic, and that our bodies touch so completely on the dance floor—on a warm day, even our sweat commingles. I was focused on the work.

Although there are plenty of codes and taboos to keep people in line in our modern society, there is no sexual code in ballroom dancing. Because creativity knows no taboos, and great dancing requires moving with abandon and passion, it would be counterproductive to have rules to corral all that free expression. And besides, in the ballroom world, people kiss and touch each other a lot. They dress provocatively; it's part of their exhibitionism. Beyond that, "touchdancers" (partners dancing in contact) can feel each other take in a breath, feel their partner's belly expand with the air; it is truly possible, mid-dance, to lose a sense of where you leave off and the other person begins. During a turn, dancers can feel the other's exhale on their cheek or their neck. One body, breathing. No wonder they say ballroom dancing is the vertical expression of a horizontal idea. Even the language is erotic: the "rise and fall" of a waltz, "body rise," and such. And the innuendos are endlessly amusing. A teacher will say, "Open your legs for me." It's very different from going to the gynecologist. How can you not tune in to the eroticism? The touching can be comforting, annoying, teasing, unremarkable, or excitingly intimate. And it can get complicated.

ONE FRIDAY NIGHT, I go to the studio's monthly social. Okay, I'm not the sort of person you'd imagine would go to something called a "social"—that sounds so dully old fashioned and conservative—but if you're a dancer and you want to dance for fun with other dancers, socials it is. I am shy about showing up at Ballroom on Hudson alone, so Betty, our seventy-five-year-old Canadian weekend babysitter, says she's game to go; she hasn't danced since her husband died years ago, and they used to "cut the rug nicely," as she puts it in her mellifluous Canadian voice. I wear my new skintight black pants with flared legs and drawstring crisscross tie at the front, and a lacy white top. I dance with lots of different men. In between, to catch my breath, I sit in a cluster of chairs and strike up a conversation with two young Dominican girls who've been watching, too shy to dance. Funny, I think, they're the *Latinas,* and I'm the one who's not shy here? One of them asks me if I'm an instructor, which flatters me immensely. When I stand up, I see a neighbor whose name I can't remember, but she is a regular at our tag sales. "You are beautiful to watch," she tells me. "I'm in awe." I flush, and thank her, feeling a rush of happiness on account of all the attention I am getting.

Then Yuri takes my hand and pulls me to him for the fast Viennese waltz. We spin around the room like a top, and such is our speed that I can't tell there are eyes on us, but at the end of the song, when Yuri spins me under his arm to finish with a typical flourish and bow, the crowd bursts into applause. I am confused, not expecting to have had an audience, and then I am beyond myself with pride. I *am* a dancer still.

Meanwhile, Betty has been having a blast, doing a lindy, and a foxtrot or two. I drop her off at 10:30—"Good night, dear. Thank you, I'm so glad I went. It was good to dance again, though it did make me miss my husband. He was a fine dancer!"—and I drive home, staying in the car in our driveway to listen to Marvin Gaye singing "Let's Get It On." I am overwhelmed with emotion that doesn't seem either happy or sad, just full. I hear Gaye's words: "Since we got to be here, let's live," and know this song isn't just about sex; it's about life. Sex isn't just about sex—meaning intercourse—sex is life bursting forth and lifting us up. My new joy is life. I am noticing it in everything lately, in a plant in my garden, in the perfect skin of my daughter's behind—all of it the heartbreaking beauty of living things. In the car, I wish I were younger; I feel a reverse greediness about my years, but I know this moment to be a gift and I am glad at least to be alive again.

The following week, during a lesson, when Yuri leads us in a slow-waltz step called the Wing, in which I step around to his left side for a bit, I am surprised to find this old, familiar step coming back to my muscles; my brain registers recognition. "I feel like I've been asleep for twenty years, and I'm just waking up and remembering my dreams. I'm like Rip Van Winkle," I say to Yuri.

"I feel like the prince who kissed Sleeping Beauty and woke her up," he says. "But I haven't kissed you." Well, he doesn't need to qualify. I'm not going to go there. Not that I'm not starting to want to.

By now, I am generally in a state of swooning, and it is beginning to affect my performance around the house. It is shocking to me, especially one night when I am cooking rice. I can make rice with my eyes closed, and I always time it perfectly: eighteen minutes after the boil. But this night, I drift around, stop paying attention, and after a time, I smell something burning. The bottom of the pot is crusty black. I have burned the rice! What's wrong with me? I wonder. Alden wonders. Peter wonders, though it doesn't seem to bother him. It feels absolutely weird to be so out of control. But, on the other hand, I notice my TMJ jaw pain from grinding and clenching in my sleep has disappeared.

IT'S ABOUT TEN days later, and this time I am dancing terribly because I'm upset—about what, I can't quite tell. Something tells me it has to do with the fact that I am dancing again. It's a big change in my life, and as wonderful as it feels, it's also cataclysmic. Life was so nice and regular, moderate, even tempoed until now. It's not easy for me to interpret the new ups and downs, the rushes of emotion— they feel tempestuous and threatening. I suppose if I were a great and experienced performer, the soup of my feelings wouldn't interfere with my dancing. I would know how to put them aside or use them to enhance my dancing. But I'm a mere student and I bring the soup onto the floor. Today, I am escorted by my usual anxiety; it lives with me always, a low hum of dread that I'm quite used to. In addition, I seem to have some excitement—that's a new feeling, or, rather, an unfamiliar one, and I haven't identified it yet; it feels no different from anxiety and it's adding to the low hum. There's also something else: a sadness that I gave up dancing so long ago, mixed with a thrill to be dancing again. The power of my newfound passion is bowling me over physically, making me hyper during my lesson, perhaps because I'm totally unaware of the new ingredients in the soup. I don't feel any strength in my legs as I try to move smoothly through a Spin Turn; I can't make them obey me. I feel stiff. And I'm frustrated that I can't be consistent. Why don't I have more control over how I dance from day to day? On top of all that, now I'm mad at myself for being skittish and clunky.

Yuri, of course, has no idea what nonsense is going on inside me. He just knows I'm struggling with myself. I can tell he knows I'm upset because he's being solicitous and complimentary. I'm embarrassed that he's even seeing me like this. Maybe he thinks it's PMS. Oh, please, I hope he doesn't think that. I don't even get PMS. I'm not a victim of those forces. So why can't I get a grip? Well, for one thing, because I'm about to cry. Crying saps my power. Now I'm in major trouble, my red-rimmed eyes glassy with tears, my voice cracking.

At 2:30, when our lesson ends, Yuri asks me to go have coffee with him. He holds the door for me as we leave the studio, then holds the car door open for me. He is more animated than usual as he talks, and he's smiling, as if to say, there, there, everything's going to be all right. Along with the welter of perplexing emotions, there's an excitement in me, as if I were sixteen again, and a boy is showing an interest, choosing me. We go to Starbucks in the nearby hamlet of Ardsley, sit knee to knee at the high stools by the counter at the windows, and we don't talk about me, but about him. His life before this, how he decided to come to America, leaving behind his country and relatives and friends forever. He tells me his six-year-old daughter, Valentina, has a compromised immune system because, according to the doctors in Kiev, Olga had lived so close to Chernobyl. Yuri says, "I was a famous dance artist in my country, ballroom champion, television personality. Here, in this country," he goes on, putting his thumb and forefinger together to make a circle, "I am a zero. I made only eight thousand my first year here. Fifteen my second." I'm amazed to think this ballroom champion makes less than my babysitter.

"But I've told you my story not to talk about myself, but to show you something about your chances," Yuri says. I get the point. He's had real hardship, having changed his life so drastically in hopes of helping his daughter get well. Am I a whining, privileged girl, sniffling because her life feels gloriously out of control? I had everything just so—my schedule, my household, my work, my marriage—and although my life was lacking warmth and joy, it functioned well as a sort of corporate arrangement. Maybe I don't yet know how to read my tears. Maybe something beyond tears is flowing, something bigger, life-giving and miraculous, and I just don't see it. I am comforted and thrilled to have Yuri sitting next to me, *seeing* me, accepting my murky upset, showing a polite keenness to console. I sense that I have found my tribe again. For so many years, I'd been wandering far from them, always in community, but far from my tribe. It is good to be back. At the same time, it feels weird to be turning so eagerly away from my husband, the man whose bed I share, the man with whom I've made children. It is undeniably odd that he is not of my tribe.

"You know," Yuri says, "you are a better dancer now than before, I am sure of that, even though I have not seen you dance before, twenty years ago. It is because you have lived. You are like a fine bottle of wine that has gotten better with age." I smile. Yuri and I are the same age. He must know. I think I am beginning to like him in a way I shouldn't. But there is nothing to stop me.

As we stand up to toss our cups in the trash can and leave, I ask Yuri about my potential as a dancer at the age of forty-six. "Where can I go from here? What choices do I have? What can my goal be?"

"U.S. champion," he says, as if that's that. Not a chance, but anyway, I am over the moon that he said it, although I suspect it's merely to ensure I'll sign up for the next package of twenty lessons.

THAT WEEKEND, on Sunday evening, there is a plan to meet up at the Terrace Club, an old dance hall in Stamford, Connecticut, where Wednesdays and Sundays are dedicated to ballroom. Olga and Katya bow out of what would be for them a busman's holiday, and I am the only student for the first hour or so, lucky me. After a few tame foxtrots and waltzes, Yuri invites me to do the mambo. I want to, but I feel panic in my belly. We haven't done any Latin together since I started working with Sergei. Too many unknowns. I don't do the mambo. I barely remember it. It's just like a rumba, though. He's got me by the hand—I like the way this feels, being possessed—and he's heading out there; I can't say no now. How bad could it be?

The floor is crowded, the lights are low, and the music is so loud I can feel my sternum vibrate. Yuri wraps an arm around me and I see the rhythm in his legs, animated in a way they can't be in our usual Standard dancing. His knees are pumping, his shoulders barely moving. You know a good Latin dancer when you see his shoulders moving subtly, barely at all, compared to his hips. Oh, he is good, and I am moving with him. Our upper bodies stay close, elbows bent, our forearms aligned, our faces inches apart. With impressive economy, he moves me into an underarm turn and does his own spin. The insistent mambo beat drowns out the policeman in my head, and we dance on and on. I am disappearing in the dance, in the music, in the beauty of Yuri's fluid pulsating and circling in the dark. He and I, immersed in the throbbing crowd, are undulating in sync, virtually making love in upright motion and I am on the verge of erupting, out of my mind, like an animal—then, suddenly, something snaps me out of it: the danger! I'm dizzy. My knees are wobbling—or they're loose—either way, I can't go on; this is too much. *I shouldn't be here in this wildness. I have to come back.* And just like that, I stop our dance before the song ends. That's as far as I'll go in playing with the fire.

There, I'm vigilant again.

"COULD WE START with mambo?" I implore at our next lesson. Then I tell Yuri that the dance at the Terrace Club was way too hot for me; in other words, I am like the coy damsel in distress who cries cryptically, "Please! Don't! Stop!" What does she mean? It could be: Please don't stop! (Keep doing that.) Or: Please don't. Stop! How's a man supposed to know? I think I've made it clear I like the danger zone, I just can't take too much excitement all at once.

"Standard dancing can be just as sexy as Latin," Yuri tells me. Oh, that's reassuring.

We do start with a mambo, and while I don't feel the same mystical and threatening force from the dance, I enjoy its erotic nature by the light of day. Is it the dance? Is it the partner? We switch to the waltz. I am remarkably comfortable being completely in contact, not holding myself away from Yuri as much, and I am learning to be more assertive in a few small ways, like in using my left hand to grip his bicep, or the middle fingers of my right hand to clasp his. But at the same time, I remain soft and delicate, as I am accustomed to being. We do a Contra-check, a pose in which the man stands still for a couple of counts, with his left foot braced slightly forward, his back leg bent, and his arms inviting the woman to blossom backwards over the top of her spine, hips pressing up to the man for stability, his hips pressing back . . .

Later, Yuri says, "You're dancing almost like a professional. We did good work today, didn't we?"

"Yes," I reply. "I enjoyed that."

"So did I."

FOR THE KIDS' spring vacation, Peter and I pack up our Mazda minivan, buy a video player for the car, and drive our family to Pawleys Island, South Carolina, to visit my dad and stepmother. They are spending the winter down there instead of in the lonely cold of Millbrook, New York. During our thirteen-hour drive, when the kids nap and Peter and I have run out of things to talk about, I stare out the window and escape into my fantasy. I am in my studio, being held, being touched. I am dancing so well that Yuri asks me to train as his professional partner, since Olga has retired in favor of motherhood. Sometimes I remind myself not to daydream too much, to try to be with my family. I talk and play with the kids easily. But Peter has been mostly rude and impatient with me lately, so I give in to the temptation of my imaginings. We have very little physical contact in these awkward days—made more awkward, I suppose, because of my body's reawakening and readiness on the dance floor. When we do touch, it often feels intrusive to me. But maybe that's because I've stopped showing him any affection, stopped touching him in the ways he likes.

It's too bad. I wonder what's possible now between us. Peter does have a way of being affectionate and of demonstrating that he gets what's going on for me. It's nice, but at the same time, I'm getting a sort of emotional whiplash. Just a few weeks before, when we were driving somewhere and I was minding my own business, listening to my music, rocking out in the front seat next to him, dressed in this new way I'm dressing, in my bubble-gum pink tight Prada pants with zippers up the back of each leg and a black cashmere V-neck, he looked over at me and asked, "Who *are* you?" I knew he knew, and he knew I knew he knew. That kind of thing is important between two people. But how much of the *us* of Peter and me can it conceivably revive?

AS I HEAD OFF to my first lesson after our vacation the following Tuesday, I am afraid that I'll have forgotten everything. I feel restless. I haven't danced in a full ten days, except for practicing in the pool, on the beach. I am skittish for the first fifteen minutes or so. Yuri is patient. I am determined not to permit the static in my head to interfere, and gradually I settle down for some decent work. It feels good to hear him say, "Perfect" or "That was it exactly." But there's still much to learn. My head position is still not right, and I'm not big enough with my upper-body curve. One thing that surely slows me down is our simmering chemistry. My nerves fire when he puts his hand on the skin of my lower back, which is exposed by my untucked shirt, and again when he touches my tummy while referring to the importance of muscle tone—I recoil with shame at my wrinkly mother's-belly.

A few days later, on Saturday morning, I mention to Peter as he makes his favorite breakfast, a frittata with all the leftover vegetables from the refrigerator, that the studio's monthly party is tonight. He says I should go; he'll stay home with the kids. Wow. I'm suspicious. Is he trying to get rid of me? But then I realize this is my sport, like he has his weekly tennis game, so of course I should go. At seven-thirty that evening, I head off to the Ballroom on Hudson social all by myself. I am wearing my sky blue bell-bottoms slit at the back from ankle to knee, and a pale yellow crinkly blouse. I walk in to warm greetings from all the teachers and the owner, and I write my check out for twenty dollars. As soon as I change into my dance shoes, someone asks me to dance, a cha-cha, and from then on I dance ceaselessly, loving every minute. In this setting, I let go the pressure to be an excellent student. Most of the men I dance with aren't as experienced as I, so I can relax and just enjoy trying to follow their lead. Later in the evening, Yuri gathers some visiting dancers from a ballroom show he recently directed; he arranges them in a circle and they start taking turns dancing in its center while the rest of us watch. It is fantastic. Yuri isn't expecting it when they push him to the center, but he gamely dances solo, and it takes my breath away, his freestyle blend of jazz and hip-hop. The room and Yuri's dancing get hotter, and he unbuttons his long-sleeved white shirt. I can't take my eyes off him. I think I shouldn't see this, his chest, his perfect muscles, his chest *hair*. His turn ends to a burst of applause. He smiles in appreciation and rebuttons his shirt. Later, when he passes by, I say, "Wow, Yuri, that was really good."

I stay to the end and help clean up the refreshment tables after most of the guests have gone home. Olga and Katya are in the back room putting food away. Yuri and I end up alone in the main room cleaning the detritus: empty bottles of cheap wine, discolored cheese and stale crackers. As I walk toward a table, he suddenly walks straight to me. I make an attempt to navigate around him, but then realize his intention; this is no fumble. He is in my way on purpose, standing close to me. He leans in slowly and kisses me on my lips, then again, more lingering. I wobble in my three-inch heels, try to recover, but I am dizzy with a desire I haven't tapped in years. I speak in order to disguise my awkwardness, but I say something really dumb like "Is it okay if I lean on you?" He is startled. "No, only in the Spin Turn, in the quickstep." But that makes no sense. What is he saying? It may be that someone has entered the room; he is pretending to have this conversation with me. And then he is gone to take out the trash.

But it was a real kiss, I'm nearly certain. As I drive home to my sleeping family, I am overcome; I have to stop the car by the high school track and sit there for a while, taking it in, replaying the scene. *Was it my imagination?* So what? Dancers kiss; everybody kisses. It doesn't mean anything. Over the weekend, I become less and less sure that it happened. It is probably only my fantasy. It doesn't bother me at all that we are both married—and that really bothers me. I am, however, slightly troubled by the absurdity of the compartmentalization of the men in my life: here I am living with my husband with no physical contact between us, and dancing quite intimately with a man I'm attracted to, but who is completely unavailable to me. And I shuttle between the two, carefully keeping up appearances but privately feeling like a giddy woman in a state of temporary insanity who doesn't quite know what it is she's so desperately looking for, let alone where to find it. I don't have a sense of disintegration so much as isolation, belonging nowhere.

Yet I feel more and more like a goddess exulting, too, moving seductively and elegantly in the arms of a man to beautiful music. My dancing has unleashed some feminine powers in me, and I'm really into it for the first time since the 1970s quashed all that for women. Finally, though, I am only a human being finding my way in a sport that has a gigantic pitfall: the touching feels good. And I have a dawning awareness that life will have to get a lot messier before it will be set straight again.

FUN AND PUNISHMENT IN COMPETITION

SOON AFTER THE flummoxing kiss, Yuri starts showing signs of wear and tear in our lessons. He gets grouchy and impatient, snippy in his criticisms of my dancing. He is mercurial. He'll compliment me: "If I seem to be pushing you too hard, it's because you are not the kind of student who comes to pay the money and just do a little bit of moving around for fun. You are a top-level student. I think of you as a sportsman." Then he'll ridicule me in front of other teachers or students: "Look, seven songs have played and we're still on the basic Right Turn. Do you want to spend the whole hour on it?" As if I were an idiot, a waste of time. I want to believe both in my ability and in his goodwill. But this new unpredictability is a kind of torture.

The problem is, I believe him, that my dancing is terrible, and that I'm incompetent. Why do I not believe in myself? And why do I not see the connection between his attraction to me and his recent whimsical meanness? Isn't it obvious that he's punishing me for his uncontrolled desire? Not to me it isn't. For now, I only see that he's grouchy and impatient, and I have to stop screwing up. But the snippier he gets with his criticisms—and sometimes it's just in the way he exhales sharply, or takes my hand roughly—the more I screw up. Take my Right Turn in the waltz: a basic, easy step and I can't do it. That's why he's fixated on it, making me do it over and over again, like a kid having to write her punishment on the blackboard after school. And he's always letting me go at the end of the step kind of roughly.

Unfortunately, Yuri isn't the sort of man I can talk to about such things—he's so terribly Russian and strict, and he even criticizes me for being too sensitive and wanting to talk and make a big deal of things I shouldn't. It's confusing, because this Yuri is so different from the endearing Yuri I sat knee to knee with at Starbucks. Now, I see I've been ignoring a bit of a hint: in the way he treats Olga—he's pretty harsh with her—it's clear that he thinks of women as subjugated creatures. Well, no surprise. And you'd think that would piss me off sufficiently that I'd manage to get out from under. But no. I naively take his new penchant for anger and nasty remarks at face value and little by little, as the weeks go on, I begin to think less of myself and my capabilities. In lessons, when the color rises in my cheeks and the tears well, I lambaste myself for not being tougher. He's just a typical coach, I tell myself. And he's right, you do need to focus better. I become stiff and weak with the humiliation of my own mediocre dancing. I knew all the praise in the beginning was too good to be true. I feel battered, pelted, raked over the coals— and completely devoted. I am still thrilled to feel "chosen" by Yuri, and I am enslaved to his anger: two aspects of one close bond. His anger doesn't diminish the thrill for me but, ironically, makes it even more urgent to be chosen, to get it right. And so it doesn't occur to me to walk away or get angry back; I only want to assuage his anger by dancing better.

And I'm also doing my damnedest to be irresistible. I press back with my hips. I flirt. I am by turns the brazen hussy, the vixen, the innocent princess, the geisha, exploring all the roles that push the buttons of excitement for me, for him, for me, for him, for me, and it's headier than twirling at top speed in a Viennese waltz.

Many wise and experienced teachers, I'm told, can handle the feelings stirred by physical contact so as not to cross that crucial boundary between teacher and student. What a huge responsibility the teacher has: not to violate the student's trust. It's up to the student to recognize the—what should I call them, troubling?—feelings and to practice various ways of channeling them back into the dance, or into her marriage or another intimate relationship, or into a creative pursuit. But here I am dancing with Yuri, and I am too needy and my marriage too far gone to take that wise and proper course.

I'm not sure how I came to agree to enter a competition, but I've done it. Yuri, Sergei, Olga, everyone at the studio more or less assumed a few months back that I would sign up because, I guess, they had other students signed up, and they expected me to join in. It's sort of what you do if you're a serious dancer—you enter comps. I competed so much years ago, and it was glorious and exhausting. Maybe it'd be good to try again, only with a different spirit this time around. So I signed up and paid the fees in April; I stepped up the lessons to two or three a week with each teacher in the last few weeks, and I attended the rehearsal on Friday evening last week. I canceled our family's annual trip to Gloucester to celebrate Independence Day, and instead left Peter, Alden, and Erica at home in Hastings while I practiced in the studio. I've sweated, fretted, and memorized the routines for ten dances: waltz, foxtrot, tango, quickstep, Viennese waltz, rumba, cha-cha, samba, paso doble, jive. And now it's time.

At six a.m. on a hot July morning, I leave my house, my family snug upstairs asleep, to drive into New York, to the John Sahag Workshop, where I'm getting my hair styled for the Manhattan Dancesport Championship, the biggest, most important comp in our area. I will be on the floor in a matter of hours. Jutta, a slender, hip, slightly high-strung German woman who dresses all in black, is there waiting for me at 7 a.m. She creates an architectural wonder out of my fine, barely-still-blond hair, John himself inspects and approves it, and off I go to the Sheraton Hotel on Seventh Avenue to park my car and register for the Latin division. My first heat is late morning, about 11:30. It's too early to check into the room I'll be staying in overnight, so I head for the lobby to wait for Jacquie, a makeup artist I'd met through work who'd offered to do my makeup. I am running on adrenaline, unable to eat, so I force myself to drink a smoothie I bought at the deli across the street. Jacquie comes through the revolving doors with her black case slung over her shoulder and her coffee in hand.

"Hi, Janet. Wow, your hair looks great! How do you feel? Are you so excited?"

"You could say that," I answer, unable to chat due to my nerves. I want to save my energy for dancing. "Thanks for coming."

Jacquie follows me to the escalator and we go up to the ballroom floor one flight up. We find the ladies' changing area and she sets up her wares. There are a few women changing in the corners. Gowns in bright colors hang on dress racks. Dance bags stuffed with shoes, water bottles, Advil, bras, hairpieces, breath mints, and other paraphernalia lie all around on the floor. A man walks through freely, probably looking for his partner, but other than me, nobody notices. It's so funny how ballroom dancers have no shyness about flesh—they'll show themselves half naked, even fully naked. Jacquie is about ready to start. I hand her the Swarovski crystal tattoo I brought for the occasion, and ask her help in applying it to my lower back just above my butt. It should sparkle nicely while I'm dancing. I like the raciness of it.

My makeup done, false eyelashes like awnings blocking the bright fluorescents of the changing room, I go to the ballroom to find Sergei and practice. I feel pretty good, though nervous, and my hands are cold. We dance, not full-out, but halfway, just to warm up and run through our routines. Sergei will also be dancing with other students competing in other divisions, so I leave him to warm them up. I stretch on the carpet before going back to the changing room to put on my tiny, sparkly, light green dress. This dress could fit, as Peter has said, in his shirt pocket. It has no back, just a flesh-tone strap to secure things, and the hemline is way up by my hip on one side, down to my knee on the other; the skirt acts like a sort of whip when we dance. The air-conditioning is too strong for me; I put a jacket over my shoulders and head back to the ballroom. The announcer's voice makes my heart leap to my throat. Heat 372. Only three heats to go. Sudden dread. My hands are trembling. But I don't want that. I went through all that in my twenties: unable to eat or sleep before competitions, dancing in fear like a zombie, forcing myself to perform as if I were relaxed, faking it. Why am I doing this today if not to enjoy my dancing? It has to be different this time around. Sergei is such a sweetheart; I'm in good hands. My family will be here. I want them to see how good I've gotten. I want to be good for Alden and Erica. And even for Peter. I inhale deeply and push my nervousness out on the exhale. Okay, good.

I am standing in the on-deck area when they arrive.

"Mom, you have so much makeup on," Alden says, checking out my dress. "Let me see your hair. It looks cool."

"Hi, Mommy. Hey, turn—you have sparkles on your butt." Typical Erica, she has found the glitter right away.

"Hi, Alden, hi Eri," I say, not able to manage much more. "Thanks for coming."

"How do you feel?" Peter asks.

"All right, I guess. Nervous. So where do you want to sit? Over there?" I point to where the other people from our studio are sitting around a table on the far side of the vast room.

"Sure." Peter has brought his camera gear. I watch my family make their way over. Then I glance to the right and see my coach from the old days, John Nyemchek, approaching me. I haven't seen him in all these years. We hug, and he asks me what I'm doing, though I suspect he knows. "I'm about to compete, Johnnie, what do you think? Hey, how's Cathi? Is she here, too?" He nods in the direction of the judges' table and I see his wife. I'm embarrassed that John might see me starting over, after he'd groomed me so well ages ago, but I guess it's unavoidable. If I'm going to do this he may as well see me. He hasn't gotten any younger either. I notice he's put on a lot of weight, and I wonder how his dancing is these days.

"Hi, Janet." My friend Julia has arrived, toting a backpack so she can spend the night with me here at the Sheraton. We call her my ballroom doula because, like the woman who assists another woman in childbirth, she's going to help me through the competition. We embrace, and she knows to leave me alone and find her seat. I need to focus. It's time.

"Heat 375, dancers, if you please," croons the master of ceremonies. That's the call for all the couples entered in this division of the competition to take the floor from the on-deck area where we have lined up. A competition of this size will have dozens of heats over the course of several days, building in level of difficulty and culminating in the finals of the top professionals in International Standard and Latin and American Smooth and Rhythm. This is a Pro-Am Open Bronze Latin heat, meaning each couple consists of a teacher and a student, and we're all going to dance our different routines using specific steps in the Bronze syllabus for rumba. Years ago, I'd worked my way up to the Open Gold level of the Pro-Ams as well as the Amateur division, in which I danced with my amateur partner, but because I haven't competed in decades, we're starting me off at a lower level to see how it goes.

Sergei, wearing our number, 216, on the back of his costume, lifts his hand, palm up, and I place mine on it. We do not talk now. After the couple ahead of us moves forward, he starts to walk. I walk beside him. I survey the floor, and I see John Nyemchek out there with his clipboard. He is going to be judging me! If I weren't so nervous, I'd think that was funny. Here I go, I am moving my legs, and I am breathing. The rest is a blank. Am I crazy? How did I get myself into this?

"Ladies and gentlemen, the rumba."

The DJ starts the music, and all the couples begin swaying to pick up the beat in their hips and launch their routines. I don't see them, however. I see only Sergei, and my own limbs. I feel the familiar tightness in my chest. But now, I look over to the tables and I can see: my girls! They are standing, toes at the very edge of the floor, to get a better view. I'm doing this for them. I'm doing this for me. I barely notice Peter's flash. (Later I will see seven rolls, 250 shots of our dancing.) I have started kind of stiffly, but Sergei gives reassuring smiles and gentle hand signals that we are fine. I smile back and begin to relax. I may as well, if I'm going to have any chance of impressing the judges. Then comes the cha-cha, a much faster dance that gets the heart pumping. The speed of this dance brings the risk of dancing too high off the floor, especially if you're tense, so I concentrate on staying grounded, letting my weight drop, pressing my shoulders down. I look at Sergei, and there he is, dancing for me. He seems so relaxed. What a guy.

Often, if you look at couples on the ballroom floor, their dance technique and expression are fantastic, but there's no connection between the partners. He's not looking at her, inviting her to each next step, caring for her, but instead is looking off somewhere, enjoying how great he is. And she's pretty much doing the same thing—being quite seductive, but really making love to herself. I think this brings their performance down. If they want to dance alone, they can choose jazz or ballet. So I appreciate that Sergei is being so gallant and solicitous. It's his manners, but it's also his kindness. I feel good. We are in our own little bubble. I scarcely notice the other competitors. I can breathe now.

Next, we do the samba, which may be my favorite Latin dance because the music has several rhythms going on simultaneously, so this Brazilian-African dance employs multiple body actions: an up-

and-down bounce through the knees, hip rotation, and a bit of for-ward-and-backward motion in the ribcage. It's fun to try to get them all going at once. We start off fine, and when we get to the tricky part I am focused, but flub one part anyway. Twenty years ago, I would have been distraught, distracted by that failure, tense for the rest of the dance, but now I actually laugh and look at Sergei as if to say, "Oh, well, hope the judges weren't looking then." Getting past the mistake this easily gives me a boost, and I begin to move with more vigor and confidence. For the jive, I'm practically sassy. Another misstep, though—this one in a figure that in practice always caught me by surprise. I knew I didn't quite have it down. I cover it over without hesitating. Peter gets a picture of the moment; it captures me smiling at Sergei, his hand at my forearm to help me get back on track, a fine memory.

Now that I'm warmed up, we go on to do all five dances in Pro-Am Closed Silver, the next higher category, and my happiness, along with a little muscle fatigue, brings me a kind of calm I never had as a competitor before. So after all these years, there *is* a differ-ence. I am having fun. And I know it makes our dancing more satis-fying to watch. I hear a familiar voice shouting my name; it's John, the deputy editor of *Town & Country*. Between dances, I glance over and there he is standing with Tracy, the research director, and a few others from the staff. They are cheering and yelling our number. "Janet, you are a goddess, an absolute goddess!" John will later pro-claim before rushing back to the office.

For the awards, I stand with Sergei on the floor near Alden and Erica. They will start with the rumba and announce the third-place couple first, then the second, and finally, the first. Then they'll do the same for each of the other dances in order. I don't know what I'm expecting; I'm just glad to be done and to feel such a rush of ac-complishment. I hear Peter saying to Julia, "That's my wife. Not bad for a forty-six-year-old lady." Alden, my little straight-A stu-dent, my perfectionist-in-the-making, asks, "Mom, did you make any mistakes?" I am thrilled to reply: "Yes, I did, wasn't it great?" In the next few days, I will think about her question and my answer and feel glad to be a role model, imperfect and joyous. For right now, I'm just wondering if we placed in any of the dances.

" . . . and first place in rumba . . . couple number 216."

That's us! We've won it. We walk up and I shake hands with John, who is the designated presenting judge; he makes a wisecrack for old times' sake and gives me a kiss.

The announcer then continues, "In cha-cha, third place to couple number 225, second to couple number 176, and first place to couple number 216." I am shocked. Sergei looks at me, looking not shocked at all; he kisses my cheek and we walk up again. I have not prepared for success, so at first I feel overwhelmed by it. As the awards continue, I begin to accept that I have done well. I feel a huge sense of relief; then happiness, simmering undetected until now, starts to really bubble and foam. I am beaming with pride as I walk toward my family when the awards wrap up.

"Mommy, can I hold them?" Alden asks excitedly. I hand her the dinky medals that in the old days were actually made of metal, but now are plastic or paper disks. She takes them reverently, as if they're made of pure gold, and holds them in her lap. Erica is on the dance floor collecting stray sequins and rhinestones that have flown off of women's dresses.

When it's done, Alden counts and recounts, then proudly announces: "Mommy, you got seven firsts! Out of ten! Two seconds, one third. Mom, did you think you would do that good?" No, I surely did not. But my daughters' shining eyes as they watched their mommy dance in front of an audience, under the scrutiny of judges, meant far more to me that day than the medals I won. Nevertheless, I have boasted many times since about getting seven out of ten because that means something too.

"Thank you, Sergei," I say as we leave the ballroom. "I can't believe how much fun I had out there."

"You did really good. You should be proud."

Peter takes the kids home and Julia and I join Elaine, the owner of our studio, and a few other students for lunch in the hotel's restaurant. It is clear somehow that I am the new queen bee of Ballroom on Hudson, having replaced a good Latin dancer named Marianna, who isn't speaking to me anymore. I bask in my glory, no matter how small-pond it may be. Later, in a moment when we are alone, Julia says to me with a very serious look on her face, "Janet, you are a goddess." First the deputy editor, now Julia. I'm liking the new moniker. If I were any happier, I think I would burst.

BUT THERE IS no fun without due punishment. Julia and I spend the night in our hotel room. We bring food in, eat it on our beds, watch *Dirty Dancing* on television, and then I take a bath. We talk about how I did, and how to prepare mentally for tomorrow, when, at 9:30, I will dance with my nasty beloved, Yuri, in International Standard. Yuri and I have trained hard together these last few weeks, during which I used all the fortitude I could muster to not give up in the face of his unforgiving harshness. Only once, when he saw me practicing with Sergei, did he relent and say something nice: "Your Latin looks so good, so nice and free. You looked relaxed and confident. Why don't you dance that way in Standard?" Ha, I wonder why. At our rehearsal last Friday evening, Yuri upbraided me in front of everyone—including Julia, who'd come to watch—because I forgot one part of our quickstep and also my bow at the end looked stupid. I never bowed before, what do you want? I felt ashamed, but I showed nothing until later, when Julia and I sat in my car in the parking lot and I cried in defeat and fear of the competition, of dancing with Yuri. Julia was aghast at his treatment of me. I'd kept her apprised of all Yuri developments, but I think this was the first time she'd actually witnessed anything. "You are just going to have to dance as best you can, knowing that he is not supporting you," she said in the car. "You will pull it off. That said, it's got to be okay if you don't dance well."

Tonight, despite the day's triumphs and her encouraging words, I can't help anticipating the worst for tomorrow, and she knows this. I am grateful to have her here with me. Her presence helps calm my nerves. Julia and I have known each other for over twenty years. We met at *Town & Country* in 1980 when she was a copy editor and I was assistant features editor. Later, we worked together at *European Travel & Life* magazine, where she was copy chief and I was executive editor. One day, we talked about swimming and then decided to go together at lunchtime to join the Vanderbilt YMCA, which had an Olympic-size pool. We went two or three times a week together, walking up, changing, waiting for our lanes, stretching, doing laps, changing, walking back with wet hair, raccoon eyes and the happy fatigue that comes from exertion.

Julia soon left magazines to study physical therapy. She moved to Laguna Beach with her husband, Chris Shaida. They had two children in the same years Peter and I did, and Julia and I grew into motherhood together. We conducted our friendship mainly over the phone. Some years later, after they visited Peter and me in Hastings, the Shaidas decided to move back east, and they found a house in the next town up the Hudson River, Dobbs Ferry. Then our families started having dinners together regularly—mostly at their house, which is bigger than ours. Chris is a fabulous cook who loves nothing better than spontaneous company around the big old wooden table in their kitchen while he presides over his cherished Viking. Julia started getting more serious about her yoga practice at about the same time I started dancing again, so we've been weaving the threads of our pursuits into our phone chats. We both recently read *Women Who Run with the Wolves* and had late-night marathon conversations about Wild Woman, Wild Man. Always on the phone. Now, here we are at the Sheraton having our first sleepover alone together, and despite my dread of what's coming tomorrow, it's good and cozy.

But I don't sleep well that night in our hotel bed. I am concerned about my hair, which is still styled, and I'm trying not to mess it up. Plus, I'm scared of what I'm about to do. I wake up at five-thirty, brush my teeth, and step out into the hallway to work on my routines. Not another soul is around. It's a profitable time for focusing and psyching myself up. At seven, Jutta arrives with bobby pins to repair her handiwork and Jacquie shows up to do my makeup again. I have no appetite, but I sip some tea. Julia does her stretching and some yoga poses, sensing perfectly how silent to be.

My team of wild women helps me on with my lavender lace sleeveless gown with a Grecian neck and matching lace wrist pieces. I step into my lavender pumps. Jutta and Jacquie leave, and now it is time to go warm up. The ballroom is freezing again. I pull my fleece jacket tighter around my chilly body and look for Yuri. He is not here, so I watch the other dancers moving quietly on the floor. Things are looking very serious. I get a cup of water from the dancers' water table, and look at my dance notebook once more to study my routines. *Oh God, what if I forget this corner?* I dance the tango in my head for the last time. Then I leave to find the bathroom again. When I return, there are Alden and Erica, dressed up in their fanciest outfits, as if seeing all the rhinestones and lace yesterday has inspired sartorial splendor in them. I see Erica as she takes me in, not recognizing me at first, "Mommy, you're a princess!" she exclaims. They've never seen me so done up.

"Good morning," Yuri says crisply and cheerlessly, as if putting on his strict tux has enforced this in his demeanor. I smile. We greet with a cool kiss on the cheek. He is aloof. I knew I'd be on my own here; that's okay, but I still feel disappointed that he isn't more encouraging. It has to be okay, like Julia said. It has to be okay. Yuri says something to me about his calf hurting. He seems distressed about it.

Suddenly, it's time and Yuri sweeps me with him onto the floor. I wonder how I look. I glance to where my family is getting settled around a table. I see Julia with her daughter, Isabel. And Diane, a T&C colleague, with her whole family. Even her husband, Paul. I didn't anticipate this audience. It is touching. I appreciate that support is there, just not necessarily where I expected it.

Yuri takes me to dance position. His torso feels rigid, ready for battle. I feel shaky and my tongue is dry, which I hate, but I will fight the good fight. The first dance is a waltz, a slow dance, with plenty of time between steps for rubbery legs to buckle, for hands to tremble. I don't feel so good. I think I'm dancing thigh high in wet cement. It's such a simple figure, the Chassée: side, together, side, but my right leg gives in on the last side step and I exhale a weak apology.

"Stop saying sorry!" Yuri hisses to me in the corner after we've passed the judging table. "All the judges might hear you!" I've never before had a teacher even speak to me during a competitive dance. We've just completed our first counterclockwise turn around the room, and I can barely focus because of Yuri's ongoing sotto-voce critique.

"Come on, use your legs!"

"Sorry," I say as we continue down the line of dance close to our audience, and I am crushed to have said sorry again. I can't feel my legs. Where are they? My mind has gone blank, and my body doesn't belong to me. I can't make it do anything beautiful. My stride is short. Fear weakens my knees. I don't trust them to work for me, so I'm not bending enough. I can't tell about my head. It feels awkward; my neckline must be terrible. I force a relaxed smile.

After the waltz, we stay on the floor to do the foxtrot. I make myself breathe deep and find some resources inside to help me get through this. I picture Alden and Erica watching, though I can't look at them now. It seems to me I must be doing better. After this second dance, my mouth is so dry, I make a move for a sip of water. Alden hands me a cup, and takes the cup back after I've sipped it. She must feel so important to be helping her mommy, and that makes me feel much better. Now, tango. I am angry somewhere deep inside, angry with Yuri for abandoning me here, so this dance is sharp and strong, more like what the judges are looking for. But the final dance, quickstep, is a mess.

We leave the floor to applause and smiling faces in our corner. Probably not bad, I think to myself about how we did. But Yuri takes me aside and gives me a stern reprimand. "I can't dance with you like that! You are so heavy. If we get called back, you must use your legs and don't lean on me."

I try hard not to say sorry again. I am ashamed. What a nightmare. We have a few minutes before they call the finalists. Yuri doesn't even stand up. I forgot to check what number he is wearing, so when they call number 512 for the tango, I don't realize it's us. He looks distracted. Sergei and Olga tell us to get out there. We go. I am in a fog.

After a few more heats for other dancers during which I sit with my family and pretend to be okay, it is time for the awards to be called. I look for Yuri. He is not here. Yuri has *left* me in the ballroom right before the ceremony. But before I can even begin to worry about what to do, Sergei steps up to me and offers me his arm. I could cry. Gracious Sergei stands by me as the judges call out the awards for each dance. I receive none. He kisses my cheek and elegantly, but with warmth, walks me back to our table. Julia and Peter are enraged on my behalf; I realize they could see my terror as I danced, and during one interlude between dances, I know they heard Yuri snap at me as we walked past our table to catch our breath at the side of the room. Perhaps from where they're sitting, they even picked up on his rudeness as we danced. I'm fine, I'm fine. I hate to know they feel sorry for me. I smile, and sit with Alden and Erica, sipping more water from the plastic cup.

THAT NIGHT, DURING the formal banquet, Yuri takes me onto the floor to join the crowd dancing to a waltz. This social dancing is much less formal than competition style; the hold is close, easy. His torso and arms feel softer to me now and more forgiving. "Why didn't you dance like this in the competition?" Yuri asks. His clumsy attempt at a compliment stings. Later, we all go out, our little studio group, to a small club way downtown for more dancing. I should be sleepy, but I'm not. At two in the morning, we walk up Second Avenue for a few blocks. Yuri and Olga are arm in arm. I am a step behind and to the side, next to Sergei and Katya. Yuri lifts the elbow of his free arm, and gestures with his head for me to take his arm. I move to him and lay my wrist on his inner forearm. We walk, Yuri and his two ladies, to the subway.

It's hard to say why I'm grateful for his gesture instead of mad as hell at him. I don't identify his competition behavior as rude and unacceptable; instead, something powerful in me overwhelms my reason and makes *me* responsible for his ire. I do not feel anger, at least not that I can name. I do not want to walk away, fire him as my teacher. To be back in his good graces is all I want. Well, almost all.

LATER THAT SUMMER I am preparing for a week's visit in Gloucester with the girls and the rest of my family—Peter has begged off, saying he's a little sick of all my gang. I invite Yuri to come up with his family for a few days and see a part of America they haven't seen yet.

I would like to be able to explain why I've invited my dance teacher to join in something so private and intimate as my family's vacation, but I can't. Surely it's not possible that I'm a masochist. All I can say is I want him to come. I want his whole family to come. Actually, for my own family, this is not an unusual thing. We have always been very socially inclusive and spontaneous. Ever since I can remember, my mother has included new acquaintances at our dinner table, in our holiday rituals. Because she worked at the UN, she was always coming home with a gaggle of foreigners and announcing, "Hey, kids, help me set the table. We have company!" One time, in the early 1960s, when we were staying in a rental house on Martha's Vineyard for the month of July, she had a Russian family come for a week. I didn't understand diplomacy at the time, but I did have a sense that at any moment, the FBI could show up at our door. Mom had met Mr. Pavlichenko at the UN. His wife and son spoke not one word of English, but we managed to communicate anyway. And we played Battleship constantly with young Nikolai, sinking each other's ships gleefully and innocently smack in the middle of the Cold War. And to think all this friendly exchange happened just before that film *The Russians Are Coming* came out.

But now, in the summer of 2001, bringing Yuri and company up to Gloucester isn't just a matter of international goodwill. It's about how for me the punishment is all tangled up with the reward. What else can explain my embrace of him? I am still rewarded by Yuri's intelligence and humor (when he's in a good mood), his attraction to me, and his sporadic and sparing appreciation of my talents. Our dancing is not just a bundle of conflict and difficulties; we do have moments when we soar high above concerns about technique and correctness, and it feels stunningly beautiful—nearly enough to make the rest tolerable. And in Yuri's small pond—Ballroom on Hudson—I am a very big fish, his star student. That feels so damn good, I wouldn't dream of giving it up. And I know we have a soul connection, though he refuses to speak of it, except once, after that kiss, he did say, "If this were ten years ago, I would go for it." Which brings up another aspect of reward—if not for Yuri, if not for another man being at hand, I might not be able to so neatly and completely cut myself off from Peter. I'm not sad my husband won't come to Gloucester. I'm too busy looking for love in all the wrong places, and he'd just be in the way.

Peter has carved out something of his own social life over the years, and I more or less have left him to it. He has his weekly tennis game with the guys, his biking buddies, his kayaking group, and then in the city, his friends through work. He moves around, a free spirit, and I have no idea who he has lunch with each day. He has a revolving door of photography interns who assist him at shoots, sometimes young men with blue hair and multiple eyebrow piercings, sometimes pretty young women from NYU. They'll occasionally just show up at home before a shoot Peter's driving to, and then come back with him late that night and sleep on our couch. I try to roll with it, but it's sometimes hard. In earlier days, I'd get jealous when I saw the cute female assistant in tight jeans in the passenger seat of his car, or the Polaroids of models half undressed he'd shot that day. Or the women in his black-and-white nude series. Now, I'm finished with caring that much. Peter's casual and mum about what he's up to, and I don't like the feeling, when I ask about his day, that I'm checking up on him. I doubt he likes it either. To this day, I have nothing to say about whether he ever transgressed or betrayed me. It's only important that I have suspected that he has. But for the most part, I have chosen not to play the jealous wife. I have chosen to back away. Welcoming Yuri and his family to Gloucester, to the very center of my extended family, is a big step. I am fashioning my own world, separate and apart from my husband.

IT IS STIFLINGLY hot on this August night, even though there's usually a good breeze at Mom and Joe's house on the harbor. Yuri and Olga exchange a few words in Russian, and then Olga takes Valentina up to bed. Yuri's mother has gone up, too. Mom and Joe are watching the news. Alden and Erica are asleep in our room, the studio above the garage. Peter called from New York to say goodnight just before I tucked them in. And my sister Anna drove back after dinner to the Eastern Point Yacht Club, where she and her family are staying this time because the house is full. This leaves me and Yuri to ourselves in the billiards room, where we are playing pool.

I haven't played pool in decades. Yuri has poured two small shot glasses of cognac and placed them on the shelf in the corner. He lifts his cue and bends over the table, taking aim at a promising ball. I watch with fierce hunger as his graceful body takes its position. I see the dark hair of his forearm, the curve of his bicep, and his lats, displayed so irresistibly for me by his muscle shirt. I notice the evenness of his toes pressing the floor in his black flip-flops. He takes his shot; there is a loud clap and the ball travels swiftly to its destination and drops in the pocket. He continues for three or four more shots until he misses. My turn.

I don't expect my aim to be good, but my shot is clear and fine. Down the ball goes.

"You play well," Yuri says. "You are such an athlete. Excellent." He takes a sip from his glass. When he smiles I can see a crooked upper tooth that makes him seem more boyish than manly.

I take another shot and it speeds tidily into a corner pocket. Then, with my next shot, I miss. Yuri comes over to me to show me how I could have set it up better. "Next time, maybe take it from the end of the table like this," he says as he leans forward and places his cue. I imitate him. He corrects the placement of my hand. His forearm is next to my upper arm and I feel the hairs tickling my skin. I want to stay close like this forever. The sublime closeness inebriates me and erases any memory of torture or ugliness on the dance floor. I want to touch him so badly I can't move. I am frozen in place. One of us should move. But we are alone together tonight at the pool table and it seems just right to me. Urgent, even. The force of my need has obliterated any discernment I might have exercised in choosing a man to meet it. Some weeks back, the touching our sport requires dared me to start telling myself a very romantic story in which I am the heroine, the beautiful heroine, the answer to his prayers. I have allowed myself to be swept up in my imaginings that are all mixed up with hopes, and which brook no protest or caution. And what of Yuri? He has helped, wittingly and unwittingly, standing there by my side without making his intention clear. It is such a lush, seductive heat between our barely touching arms that I don't need to forgive him his temper. It is already forgiven.

We haven't danced since we drove up here four days ago in two cars, Yuri, Olga, Valentina, and Yuri's mother, Mama, following me up Route 84 and across the Mass Pike, and along 128 to the coast. I was so proud to bring him and his family to see this cherished place, to smell the salt in the air of this historic fishing village, and I was happy to furnish his family with a little vacation experience, one of their first since they came to America. We have had meals together, our families, listening to each other's stories. We have walked along the beach, tossing stones, swimming in the freezing cold water with the kids, looking for crabs, warming ourselves afterwards on the big boulders. We have shopped for lobsters on the wharf in town. I am learning to count in Russian, and to name foods. Yuri's mother thinks I'm too skinny and cooks thick, delicious soups to fatten me up. Olga and I are friendly, but I do wonder if she has picked up any signals. I think she has, but it appears she counts on her husband. Mom and Joe see that I have come to life, I can tell, and I notice them glancing at Yuri, probably wondering what he has done that I am so lively again.

Now it is my turn to watch him again. We play until one in the morning, then we walk through the house quietly, turning off all the lights. My desire is at its peak, fed to such fullness by the game of pool, the cognac, and the impossibility of our being together. Yuri pauses close to me, then says, "Janet, our families are right upstairs." I have to yank myself away from him so that we can go our separate ways at the intersection of the hall and the staircase that leads up to his sleeping family. Nothing happens between us beyond this— not now, not in the future—but I sleep barely at all that night in the studio above the garage, on the futon next to Erica, who tosses and turns. The heat keeps me right on the edge of sleep, not able to fall. I spend the night in a dreamy doze state, listening to my children's breathing and the moans of the distant foghorn giving warning.

5 GROWN WOMAN CRYING

EARLY SEPTEMBER ARRIVES, and I am at Kurt's Gym in Scarsdale, doing a waltz with Yuri. He teaches me here because something has happened between the hotheaded owner of Ballroom on Hudson and these hotheaded Russians—disagreement, mistrust, and that was that. The floor here is a bit too small for Standard, and there are stationary bikes and dumbbells in the way, but we manage. Despite the flashes of intimacy in Gloucester or perhaps because of them, Yuri still gets cranky with me, like one of those old-school Russian gymnastics coaches who are so rough with their tender-aged little gymnasts. I am trying to do each thing he asks, pushing myself hard. It's not going well.

"No," he snarls. "Do it again."

I inhale, exhale—an unconscious effort to relax so I can do better. I lift and open my arms to him, a student surrendered to the master and to the art. The fun that dancing is supposed to be seems terribly far from my reach now. But September is a time for new beginnings. Once I feel his hand on my back, I let my left arm rest on his right. I try not to weigh him down; a lot of women dancers do that, burden the man with too much weight through their arms. We start again. Now Yuri huffs sharply, abruptly takes his arms from me, and stands away, annoyed. He is suddenly angular and unkind. I must have done something, but what? My brain fogs. *What did I do?*

"I told you so many times, when you tilt in the Fallaway, it pulls me right off my feet! Come on!" Then he berates me for not knowing the footwork; for my right elbow poking back too far; for my head position, for not practicing enough. For so many things.

His irritation fills my chest with a searing fluid and my breathing is labored, but worse even than that is the thick lump in my throat. It hurts, like when I was a little girl about to cry. I press my lips together as hard as I can as if it will push the lump back down. But there is more to manage: my eyes glisten and redden with tears and now on top of shame is the mortification that my teacher might detect my childish upset. I get down to the business of hiding these signs, first turning to look for my water bottle, faking thirst. I walk five or six steps with my back to him, using the time to blink my eyes back to normal. I swallow the lump with an ice-cold gulp, shocking my body into obedience. Or anesthetizing it.

I come back toward Yuri, composed, hiding everything successfully. Or maybe not. It is possible he saw perfectly well, but he, too, prefers the ruse. We begin again. It must be because I am completely discouraged and spent that my malleable, softer body moves in a way that satisfies Yuri. Does it mean all the hard work the good student does only serves to stiffen her body, betraying her and frustrating her teacher? The irony, when it occurs to me later, really pisses me off. And why can't I tell for myself when I'm dancing well or poorly? Why is this not clear to me? At any rate, he gives up picking on me for the time being. We switch to a figure called the Bombshell, which I only started to learn last week, a tricky figure with twirling and rondés, both partners swinging a leg in a wide circle. Every brain cell is intent on the pattern and the job of each body part, hoping for the smallest affirmation. *I have no idea if I'm doing this right. Don't panic. Keep it up. But, oh, God, please don't let him yell again. Please let me get it right, so he won't be mad.*

That night, after I put the kids to bed, I take a hot bath. I draw the water extra hot to soothe my sore leg muscles and ease the pinch in my lower back. The water's heat melts the stoicism that got me through today's unpleasantness and I allow the dammed tears to flow in my privacy. If the faucets are running, no one will hear me cry. This is different, this crying—not like what I do on the floor with Yuri; it's more healing, an acceptance of my feelings denied by day. As the water cools—faster now with the too-early autumn chill—I am wondering why that painful lump comes to my throat. *I am a forty-seven-year-old woman—why am I crying in my lessons? I should be able to take it. Shouldn't I? Could it be him? Maybe he's not the right teacher for me.* Still, I want him, want him to want me. I think about his arms and how it feels to be in them, cradled by them. I picture his legs, his nice, athletic thighs, not too skinny like some male dancers', but strong, powerful, and sexy.

I drape a steaming, wet washcloth over my face, and suddenly I am transported back to late August 1968, and I am sitting at the kitchen table with Anna and our brother, Robbie, while Mom loads the dishwasher. "Come on, you four, clear your plates," she says without conviction. Alison, our younger sister, is on the floor, trying to tie a bell on the cat's collar. It is a sweltering night, no breeze coming through the wide-open sliding glass door or the windows. Bugs smack the screens; moths flutter stupidly up and down them, and from further outside in the dark of mid-evening, the full chorus of cicadas screeches.

I am thirteen and already I hate August. I hate the cicadas taunting: "School starts soon." Summer has evaporated too quickly. The fun is over. The days will get shorter, cooler now. I hate August.

The phone rings. It's Daddy. I can tell from the tone of Mom's voice. She pulls the long cord around the door to the cellar and goes down the steps part way to talk where we can't hear. We stay put. We don't want to hear. They may be arguing again.

Daddy is calling from New York City, where he lives with his second wife, Nancy. He is furious with Mom and she is furious with him; the way they talk, it sounds like it's because of money, but I know that it's actually because they can't stand each other. He pays her $125 per child per month, which she says is not enough. She can't pay our doctors' bills but she cheerfully takes us to our appointments anyway and somehow pulls it off, gets the secretary to let her pay later, in installments. She tells us Daddy is bad, because he holds on to his money to punish her, but she says it ends up punishing us.

Now Daddy doesn't want to pay for private school even though Mom got us some kind of scholarship, which I later learn is an unofficial deal offered up by the sympathetic head of admissions, who also endured an ugly divorce and sustains a pretty good head of anger toward deadbeat dads generally. Anna switched from our public school to Riverdale last year, and I'm supposed to switch this year, ninth grade. But we don't know if we'll be able to start there in mid-September because Daddy doesn't think we should, doesn't have the money. Mom says not to worry, it'll work out. But we need to know soon because public school starts Tuesday, the day after Labor Day. I hate August. I don't know what school supplies to shop for, or what to tell my friends, if I'll seem them anymore. Maybe I don't want to change schools.

Mom's muffled voice becomes more audible as she mounts the stairs and emerges from the cellar, untangling the cord from the door knob. There's an odd look on her face, one I recognize. She says Daddy wants to speak to us. Anna takes the phone from Mom and I go upstairs to the front bedroom to get on the extension. I lie tummy down on the bed.

"Hi, Daddy," I say, a little nervous, though I'd just spent, with my siblings, two weeks with him up in Old Chatham, where he has an eighteenth-century farmhouse on two hundred acres, and played tennis, went for ice cream at the general store, played Clue. I don't hear Anna's voice. Did she hang up already?

"Hi, Janet. Listen, I told your mother and I just told Anna this, but I'm not paying for Riverdale. Your mother is being completely unrealistic and unreasonable. I can't talk to her anymore, so I wanted to tell you directly."

"But Daddy, it's a better school, and they said we could go for less money."

"I don't give a good goddamn what they said!" he screams at me. "You're so fucking brainwashed by your mother, it's impossible to have a conversation."

I'm not positive he used the F-word, but I know he swore. It's not possible for me to dredge up with any clarity how it felt at that moment to have him swear at me with so much vehemence. My daddy who once stood in the freezing cold Vermont brook and caught me in his arms when I jumped off the high rock; my daddy who let me fall asleep on his chest when I had the mumps, and then he got the mumps. I have tried for years to remember, but amnesia is a stubborn trick in my clever psyche's bag. I can only remember how hot the night was, how loud the cicadas' screech had become, and Daddy, my daddy, so mad at me. I am startled. I am crying. I thought he loved me. I am bad. *What does he mean, brainwashed? What have I done wrong? I have to be better. I will be better.*

Soon, it is October, and I'm still struggling to make it work better with Yuri, but by now my children have started expressing their opinions. Alden sees me one night in the kitchen tearing up in frustration over the day's lesson. "Why are you crying, Mom?" I tell her a little bit, a light, nine-year-old-appropriate version, about my disabling fear of getting out on the floor with my teacher. Of course, I tell her nothing of my bizarre attraction to him, but kids are wise; some things don't need explanation.

"If you don't like dancing, don't do it. It's your choice. You're doing it for you. You're throwing away money, giving it to people who make you sad." Then she sits down and draws a picture of Yuri as a "short bull" and Mom as a "skittish thoroughbred" and writes a poem:

> *Mom loves dancing,*
> *And prancing.*
> *Yuri makes her sad*
> *Then she gets mad*
> *Then she thinks more*
> *About it and*
> *Goes on dancing and prancing.*

It strikes me as perfect, that with all the training a therapist can draw upon to give advice or feedback, sometimes it's a kid who says the most helpful thing. The wisdom of her uncontaminated perception follows me for weeks, until, finally, I understand how ridiculous I have been and start taking action to protect myself. It is time.

"You've done the Slip Pivot right a hundred times," Yuri complains at Kurt's Gym some weeks later. "Why can't you do it right now?" Then, "You're not concentrating. You're being too tentative, checking for my reactions. Just dance." Huh? I have a fuzzy sense that maybe he's describing himself, but still I feel chastised.

"Is this the kind of lesson we're going to have?" I ask, looking him squarely in the eyes. "Because if it is, let me go get a box of Kleenex."

He goes over to an exercise bike and sits down, saying nothing for a time, then quietly asks, " 'This kind of lesson,' what does that mean?"

"It's the kind in which you criticize me instead of my dance steps. When you beat me up, I dance worse, not better."

"I can't think of one thing I said . . ." More silence. Then, "Are we going to talk or dance?"

"Dance," I say crisply. "But not if you punish me."

"That sounds like something a married couple says," he snaps. "I already have a wife at home who talks to me that way. I don't need another woman to speak like that to me."

I am stunned. I think of how Elaine, the studio manager, told me a few weeks ago that Yuri and his wife had to stop dancing together professionally because he kept making her cry. It's not just me. So I turn around, walk to the corner, gather my things, change my shoes, blow my nose, take out cash, walk back toward Yuri without saying a word, and drop the cash on his jacket draped on the stool. And I walk out.

But this is not the end. I am not ready yet to let go completely. I will dance for the next few months with two teachers at once: a new teacher at a studio in Manhattan, in order to see if removing all the static of chemistry and punishment will allow me to dance better, and one lesson a week with Yuri—once we've patched things up again—sometimes in Westchester, sometimes in Manhattan. At one of these lessons, he curtly instructs me to leave my feelings at the door when we dance. "The lessons shouldn't be mixed up with our personal feelings. Dance at our level is a sport. Treat it like one." I'm not sure I can obey.

A FEW MONTHS LATER, on a Monday at 1 p.m., I gather up my courage and leave the office to walk over to a dingy building on Fifty-fourth Street between Broadway and Eighth Avenue, to the Dance New York Studio on a mission. When Yuri and I came in to the city once to try out the studio and do a couple of lessons there, I saw someone I recognized from the old days of my dancing. Someone who might be able to help me. I don't know why I thought he could. Intuition perhaps. I walk up three flights, step inside timidly, and say to Karen at the counter in the entrance hall, "I'm just here to see if I can talk to Bill Davies."

"Go ahead."

Bill Davies is a former U.S. champion, older now, and a legend in the business. He used to own a studio on the Upper East Side. When I danced in my twenties, I would occasionally go there with Johnnie and David Nyemchek. I am nervous to approach this famous coach because he teaches top couples, and who am I? But something tells me to go ahead. I must rescue myself somehow from Yuri—from my attachment to him and our destructive partnership.

I walk into the main area and see Bill leaning against a column, watching the couple he is teaching as they move across the floor. He is thick around the middle, his hair is white, and his face has fallen since I saw him twenty-some years ago.

"That's better, Irina," he calls over to them as they execute some heavenly foxtrot sequence. "Sasha, try to not interfere with her when you do that."

I walk to the banquette by the windows and sit near the table and chair that Bill claims as his own. The lesson ends and Bill walks over. He sits and takes the stylus from his Palm Pilot. I stand and approach. *I am not good enough, but here goes. I can't believe I'm doing this.*

"Hi, I'm Janet," I say, extending my hand. "I wonder if I could talk to you for a moment?"

"Of course," he replies with a smile. His hand is huge. His eyes are bright blue. They immediately remind me of my grandmother's—Swedish eyes. Familiar eyes. "I'm Bill Davies."

"I know. I recognized you. I used to dance with John Nyemchek and his brother David."

"Sure, the Nyemchek clan. I trained John and Cathi. When did you dance with them?"

"In the late seventies. I saw you win in Cherry Hill a few times with Sandra Cameron."

I don't tell him (not yet) that he and I danced together once, one Saturday night at a competition banquet. This doesn't seem like the time. But I think it's partly because we danced that once, and I never forgot, that I have approached Bill rather than, say, go back to dance with John or find a teacher who's still actively competing with students in Pro-Am competitions.

"Well, that goes back a ways. What are you doing with your dancing now?"

That's when, to my consternation, tears fill my eyes. He handles it well, very well for a man. He is not the least bit flustered while I explain through sniffles that I've been dancing with Yuri, it isn't working, my confidence has been eroded.

"I think we can do something about that," he says. I feel huge relief in his calm response, and I will remember forever his use of the first person plural. "Can you stick around for a bit?" he asks. I nod, sit back, and then watch him teach his next student, an older woman. After half an hour, he comes back to where I sit and leans on the chair next to me. We talk more about the past, then book my first lesson for Wednesday.

WHEN I RETURN for our first hour, I have the jitters, but they dissipate as soon as we get started. Bill seems so calm and in charge, and the soft, yellow Ralph Lauren cable-knit of his chest feels like a safe place for me to perch. I'm tense by habit, but with every inhale I remember to take, my muscles relax a bit more. He tells me to be a lump, which surprises me. It sounds so ungraceful, but I get his point: I'm supposed to be more of a piece. And he tells me to break at the hip joints instead of scrunching my butt and pressing my hips forward at him. This will help me to be on my own two feet rather than literally perched on him.

The hour is over before I know it and I'm overjoyed to have had such a fine time. I'm also happy not to have bumped into Yuri, who now and then teaches other students here. Bill offers me a three-hour-per-week deal, which will save me a few dollars, and I accept.

THE GOLDEN RULE OF BALLROOM DANCING

6

YURI KNOWS I'M dancing with Bill. I told him that I had to find out why we've been struggling so fiendishly. I said I couldn't learn the answer in the vacuum of our lessons, had to see what it would be like to dance with somebody else. He asked, "Who?" When I told him "Bill Davies," he sneered and walked away. The Russian snob—he doesn't have a clue how major Bill is in this country. Yes, Yuri is unhappy about this development, but in truth, he's the one who put the idea in my head. It was his attempt at rapprochement after I suspended our lessons that day I stormed out. "You could try dancing with two teachers at once," he said some days later. "It will help you be a better student."

IT IS ONLY my second lesson with Bill, and already I can tell I am in the arms of a master. He may be big—he's built like a football player, stocky, barrel-chested—but he is so amazingly nimble and comfortable to dance with, "more comfortable than any other man you'll ever dance with," Ariel, his longtime student, told me when Bill introduced us earlier. Randy, a cute young teacher who passed by a few moments ago as Bill and I were getting ready to start, wrapped an arm around Bill's shoulder and said to me, "He's our national treasure." It crosses my mind that this elevated status is fair compensation for the insult of growing older in the dance world.

We start the lesson and Bill takes me into dance position right away. No warm-up. We move down the line of dance in uncomplicated foxtrot steps and then he stops to instruct.

"Would you open your legs for me?" he asks. An abrupt, nervous laugh escapes me, but I see in his face he is perfectly serious.

"You mean, stand with my feet further apart like this?" I ask, looking down and plunking my feet shoulder width apart.

"I mean *move* like that," he says, and he comes at me, looking eager, as if he were about to test-drive a car. This feels really strange, my crotch so exposed, especially because today I'm not wearing a long, full dance skirt but tight black pants, and with my legs opened, I more plainly feel his pelvis on me. But we're moving along now, so I'll just shut up and go with it.

"There, that's much better," Bill says after a bit. "Now there's room for my right leg between yours, so I can move forward and you're no longer an obstruction."

Oh, good; I wouldn't want to be an obstruction. Nor, I realize, is my inhibitedness of any use. Good dancers aren't reluctant. They're show-offs. They love an audience. In my deep recesses, I'm desperate to be seen and appreciated, but when the moment presents itself—when I'm trying something new and I'm clumsy—I feel like hiding. I don't want to be seen until I'm perfect.

Now Bill is doing a familiar, basic sequence: a Reverse Turn, a Three Step, a Natural Turn, into an Impetus Turn. Very simple steps really—simple and languorous enough that I become stymied; my low hum of anxiety escalates to high pitch, and my mind is racing.

Don't hyperextend. How's your neck line? Don't cock your head in that weird angle. Ignore the pain in your right foot. Keep your ribs in.

I am like an airplane pilot checking the instruments incessantly during flight: throttle, trim, altitude, recheck.

Bill stops again and we stand aside to talk. I'm relieved as always to stop and talk.

"Do you know what your job is when we're dancing?" he asks. I notice he peppers our lessons with these pop quizzes. He's smart, and I like these amusing interludes.

"Well . . ." I'm thinking fast, wanting to get the right answer. "I'd say my job is to pick up on your lead as quickly as possible, and to be light and get out of your way and look good doing it."

"NO!" he bellows. My shoulders scrunch at the volume and I look around the room to see if other people have been startled. But no one is paying any attention. That's the beauty of a room full of narcissists busy watching themselves in the mirrors. Or maybe they're just used to his bold theatrics.

"I don't want you to get out of my way. I want you in my way. And being buoyant is a good thing, but light can be a problem. At times, you're . . . let's see . . . you're ethereal, like ether, and it's uncomfortable for me to dance with you because it's as if you're thin air—I can't get a hold of you."

He's perfectly kind in the way he delivers the critique, and I'm enjoying the logic of it all. My body may not be cooperating yet but my brain is right with the program. Then comes the clincher:

He says, "In our partnership, as we dance, your job is to think about my comfort and my job is to think about your comfort."

I swoon over the implications of this metaphor. And instantly, I regret not having danced like this more in my marriage. But here on the floor, I'm excited, I get exactly how to do what he's talking about. My mother raised me and my siblings to "think of the other person, not yourself."

"That's great," I say to Bill. "I can do that. I know it's selfish—

I'm only thinking about my own comfort and my footwork and various body parts the whole time we're dancing."

"Do you think it's wrong to be selfish?"

"Yes."

"I don't agree. I don't think we can be good and generous to other people unless we accept our own selfishness. Our basic human drive is to get pleasure and avoid pain. Nothing wrong with that. We're animals."

I am tempted to get into a whole discussion, but that would take up the rest of the hour. Bill goes on, "The ultimate selfishness is getting what you want by taking care of the other person's comfort, their needs or desires. If I make sure you're comfortable while we're dancing, I won't be interfering with your beautiful movement or your expression of the music, and if you do the same for me, we each get the ultimate payback, we get what we want—to feel good."

Dancing again, I try thinking of Bill's comfort. I decide that this means sensing with my body and mind what's going on with him. I'm not sure at first if I'm at all successful, but I'm finding it sort of fun to quit my own body scanning, the human MRI machine inside my head, and get tuned in to his mind and body. It's one of the fantastic things about ballroom dancing: the connection through the two torsos pressed lightly together; you can feel when your partner tenses up, feel when he relaxes, feel when he is moving with pleasure.

"This is working" is all Bill says as we keep on, and I know he doesn't want to interrupt the happy flow. But here comes the Impetus Turn and I'm distracted by my old habit, my failure to execute the Three Step. *Damn, I'm so flat-footed there. And my hip is out of line.* My self-consciousness is suddenly overwhelming. Without knowing it, I've pulled my elbows back, which forces Bill off his feet into my space and now we're a mess. I am in a panic and I totally flub the Impetus, stepping on his right foot with my left. This brings us to a grinding halt. However, Bill merely tips forward gracefully.

"I'm sorry," I confess. "I panicked."

"That's selfish of you," Bill says.

Uh-oh. Usually when I criticize myself, showing that I know what I did wrong, it has an appeasing effect on people in all walks of life. It preempts their opportunity to criticize me. It's even worked once or twice with Yuri.

"Why selfish?" I ask, though I know he's teasing me.

"You weren't thinking about my comfort."

I allow the loveliness of this notion to seep in. I have been plagued all my life by self-consciousness born of perfectionism. I have tried to override it with sheer will and disguise it with brutal discipline—show no one until it's right. That's why I became an editor, I guess. But I've never stopped feeling like an imposter.

Bill has just proposed the ideal antidote, something to fill my overbusy brain when I'd ordinarily implode. Now I have a job to do. How can I be self-conscious if I'm thinking only about his comfort? It is exciting beyond words. Do unto others. I'm so well trained at that in the outside world. But when I'm in circumstances that ignite my all-consuming bashfulness, my mind's eye can see only me, and I lose sight of others altogether. I see the narcissism of my people-pleasing habit. And so has come the first major blessing of lessons with my new teacher. I am released from a stupid prison of my own making that has prevented me from staying connected. What I've just learned from Bill may be that dance isn't merely about sex, as many people imagine, but that dance has a great deal to do with love. The thing is, the thing I have not understood is that love is not a competition.

I SUPPOSE THERE was a time when Peter and I thought of each other's comfort, certainly when we were in the early stages of dizzy love. That's when it's a no-brainer, though. Much harder is to do this long after the honeymoon is spent. Then, it's a real accomplishment; it would have to be true love. Like many couples, we did things like apply sunblock to each other's backs. Or I'd fill out his passport renewal application because he hated doing forms; he swore he was dyslexic. And when I was pregnant, he'd gladly jump up to make me a five-egg omelet because I was ravenous after getting over morning sickness. But then came the days when the golden rule shifted in the direction of tit-for-tat and suspicion: *Wait, am I doing it all? Is he doing anything for me?*

There was no acute emotional abuse, just a steady drip, drip, drip of disappointment between us, until I guess I got to feeling abandoned, the way people do when the other person doesn't act or feel the way we want them to. There was a time when I was angry and could say precisely what the causes of our falling apart were, rattle off one thing after another, and then Peter'd accuse me of being like a dog with a rag in its teeth. I could spit out the vignettes to prove it: he was wrong, he was the thoughtless jerk, and I was unimpeachable.

In trying to tell what happened, how Peter hurt me or I hurt him, I'm frustrated to find that I forget the actual incidents; I can't recall exactly what pushed us to the place where we've arrived. Without the specific memories, it's as if I've spaced out, drifted here on a current. Maybe the amnesia serves a purpose, like the glass of wine at night after a hard day at the office.

ONE MORNING IN late fall when I'm on the train, the 8:21 a.m. into Manhattan, and I've been sniffling due to allergies, one of the forgotten memories comes flooding back when I reach into my pocket to pull out a tissue. As I unfold it, it's as if the story, like a delicate insect trapped in the Kleenex, flies to its freedom.

Peter and I used to ride the train together; that was until he decided to drive his car to work. We'd sit together and read the paper; I'd tackle the front section first, he the lifestyle or metro pages. We didn't talk much, unless necessary. It was a quiet time in the morning for most of our fellow commuters, too, and I always loved staring out the window at the majestic Hudson River as the train chugged south along its banks. So when Peter started sniffling (repeatedly) as he usually did on these train rides, I would notice. He didn't carry Kleenex in his pocket, but I did, and I would give him one. It became one of my wifely jobs. He didn't *want* to carry Kleenex, you understand. He must have appreciated, even enjoyed, having his wife hand him the Kleenex, taking care of him ritually in this small way. Maybe he even experienced it as a romantic gesture of love. I didn't get this at the time. No words, just the movement, my hand offering it or pressing it into his hand. "Thanks," he'd say, and blow, and his sniffling would cease.

But as time went on, I came to be annoyed by his sniffling. Or rather, by his inattention to how irksome his repeated sniffling might be, not just to me but to others on the train. Like tapping a pencil, or snapping chewing gum. Looking back, I wonder how the tenderness turns to annoyance so predictably. I'd get silently pissed that he didn't plan ahead and stock his own pocket with tissues. He seemed helpless and incompetent. Take care of yourself, that was my view. It's a tough world.

How had it come to pass that I didn't feel a gladness that Peter relished my caring for him? Where was my compassion? No wonder I'd forgotten this story: in this one, I'm the bad guy. More painful perhaps than remembering Peter's transgressions is remembering my own. I begrudged him the damn Kleenex. I was intolerant and unloving. I do remember the little things we did for each other in the beginning, when we'd just met in 1988, how he bought me a lightweight telephone headset and personally delivered it to my office so I could do hands-free telephone interviews and alleviate my neck pain. And for our wedding, I spent months secretly tracking down Dell's, the chain of fresh lemonade trucks in Rhode Island, so he and his relatives would have a familiar landmark at the reception on my family's turf in Hastings. I remember, too, how well he cared for me in the minutes after I delivered Erica, all nine pounds of her without any pain medication, at six-fifteen a.m. on May 12, 1995, and then had a massive hemorrhage. There was all this noise and rushing to the operating room and the doctor said to Peter, "I'm sorry, it doesn't look good" and Peter faced my imminent death there in the OR and made a critical surgical decision. The way I see it, he saved my life. This was about the very real love. But within a few years we lost sight of it and started keeping score instead.

By now, I realize I'd come to expect Peter to be the same as me—to cope, to plan ahead, to be self-sufficient. A minor thing, a tissue, you might say, but so are the dishes, and so is the trash, and so is everything in our little fussed-over lives. None of it is big. It's all small stuff. What's big is what we make of it.

I have just enough time, before the train pulls into Grand Central, to wish I hadn't been such a hard-ass.

ONE NIGHT, SOME years later, after we'd finished dinner, I made an effort to ask Peter to help with the dishes in a new and more sympathetic way. "Hey, Pete, how about we both do the dishes now?" Typical male, if he ever did the dishes, he'd only wash the fronts; the backs, still greasy, would taunt me from the drainer. So maybe if we did them together, he could do the fronts and I could do the backs.

"Just leave them; I'll do them before I come up." He was too comfy on the couch to get up.

"Okay." I did not do the dishes, although I sorely wanted to in order to have that sense of order a clean kitchen can represent at the end of the day. Instead, I went up to get ready for bed, which meant hand washing my blouse that Alden had thrown up on that morning, sorting my office tote in preparation for tomorrow, and picking up a few stray toys before going in to look at Alden and Erica sleeping, then getting into bed to fall asleep within seconds.

The next morning at six, I came downstairs, turned on the kitchen light to boil water for my tea, and my heart sank. There were the dishes glaring at me in the sink, still dirty; on the kitchen counter, piled with dried remnants of dinner. A few scoffed from the coffee table in the TV room. The tea kettle whistled to let off steam. I made my tea and fumed.

Peter came down at seven-thirty in his socks and underwear on his way to the basement, where he kept his clean clothes hanging on a clothesline by the washing machine. He always dressed in the cellar.

"So, Peter, you didn't do the dishes," I accused, firmly standing in the realm of my rightness, where a storm was brewing.

"Yeah, I fell asleep during Howard," he muttered.

We got into a juicy argument. In the middle of it, Peter got up and walked into the kitchen and started doing dishes. He hunched his shoulders over the sink in anger while we kept at it. "Jan, I don't think you realize how good you have it. I do more than you think. More than most husbands."

"What does that mean?" I shot back. "It would be different if you handled the trash or the recycling, and we could just agree to that, but you forget those, too." Right again.

Now would be a good place to tell you what Peter said next that provoked me beyond words, but I cannot recall. It was a doozy, a really passive-aggressive thing to say, and it set me off, pushed me right over the edge. I wish I could dredge it up; I've tried, but it's gone, totally obliterated. Maybe he didn't say anything. Withdrawal was often his reaction. But no, it had to have been something he said.

What else would possess a wife to throw a stainless steel tea kettle at her husband? I was standing a good six feet away when Peter said the thing that pushed me past my limit. I picked up the now-empty kettle and let it fly at him. It was a glancing blow to the upper arm, and the kettle hit the floor and came to rest, dented, misshapen and useless. I barely had time to see it land before Peter took a wide swipe with his right arm and swept the dish drainer and all its contents off the counter and onto the floor. A gorgeous Christian Dior gift, a French porcelain serving bowl, smashed to bits and I winced, as if that were the most important loss in this ugly scene. There, we did it. We acted like a crazy, passionate couple in a movie with subtitles. Did it feel better? No. Was it the kind of fight that made us want to have sex and make up afterward? No. It was the kind of fight that made me feel hopeless and just bad. I knew there had to be meaning in the fact that I'd destroyed my tea kettle, one of my treasures. Lucky for us we didn't wake the kids. If it's come to this, physical violence, aren't we past the point of no return? I wondered. I was never before a physically violent person. Where had this temper come from? How had I turned into someone I didn't recognize?

7   TRYING HARD IS NO EXCUSE

I AM DROPPING Erica at a Friday night sleepover at Jasmine's. She has eaten her hamburger in the car on the way here, licking the ketchup off her fingers. It is seven forty-five, a September twilight. She woke up a little while ago from an afternoon nap in my bed after a long, hard week at school, at the very exciting beginning of the school year. From our Toyota RAV4, I watch her walk toward a door on the ground floor of one of Hastings's old apartment buildings, where Jasmine's dad is the super. Erica leans sideways slightly against the weight of her overnight bag, which is slung over her beautiful, straight shoulders. I study her blond hair, pulled back into a tight bun, and think how sophisticated this leggy girl looks, except for her long, bright yellow pajama bottoms dragging on the pavement under her Tweety Bird flip-flops; she turns only her head to glance back at me to make sure I won't drive away until the door is opened and she is safe inside; I keep watching, transfixed. She does a little hip-hop jig. I flash my headlights twice in response. She does another jivey thing; my dancing daughter has impressive rhythm. I flash the lights again. The door opens, the raven-haired

Jasmine, one of five children in this family, steps out, and the light from inside illuminates the two girls as they greet each other. They are both so excited, their shoulders are up around their ears as they tilt their heads toward each other, smiling and entwining arms. Erica looks one last time and waves. Often, I don't get a wave, so this feels especially good. I flash my lights one last time. Then they turn to go inside for a delicious conspiracy of talking, playing, sleeping close.

I am in absolute total love with the memory of being an innocent little girl and I sit motionless in my car for a minute, treasuring this scene even before it has time to become a memory. I miss my early girlhood; I miss the spontaneity and innocent fun of a time too far back to recall.

I'M A RECOVERING good girl, actually. A second child. You know the type. I grew up being, above all else, cooperative and diplomatic. It was vital to me to fit in, not make waves. I loved pleasing my authority figures. Early on, I learned to apply myself. I was no trouble to teachers. I got good grades. Never pulled an all-nighter to write a paper because I worked at a regular pace. I graduated magna cum laude from Yale with a degree in history and no idea what I wanted to be when I grew up.

If I were good enough, I figured, when I was little, my mother wouldn't get angry at me. If I were good enough, everyone would like me. And maybe I'd even live up to my mother's belief that I was special. We were *special,* she said, her four children, better than everyone else. Special? Uh-oh, what if she finds out that I'm just ordinary? I was sure I was ordinary; if she found out, she might stop loving me. I decided I'd better get to work.

Furthermore, I'd better keep up the good work—indefinitely— and I did, so nobody would discover that behind the cooperativeness, the sparkly productivity, the impressive accomplishment, there was only nothing much. The more effort I made, the more effort I had to make, because eventually, as a young adult, I had myself totally convinced that I *was* my effort, and that underneath or inside was a void, an empty space of nothingness. Everything of value was on the outside. I was invisible.

This sense of an interior void was preferable to an alternate feeling I had that really got me down: I am a bad girl at the core, but I pretend quite convincingly to be a good girl. A friend who loves dogs recently told me he thinks of himself as a Labrador retriever, and then he asked me, "What kind of dog are you?"

"I'm a bad dog," I said. Ha! You can't trick me.

DANCING IN MY twenties was another way of proving my worth, earning love and adulation with all those medals. Alden took them out of the big glass vase and counted them once, when she was about five or six, and there were ninety-two altogether—mostly gold, some silver and bronze. That's a lot of love. I didn't see any expiration date on them. Back then, in the seventies, however, ballroom dancing was not a trendy, fabulous thing to do, the way it is now; it was just plain weird, and kind of tacky. I couldn't tell most people about my hobby. And yet, some recessed part of me was proud to be doing something quirky. A rebellious creature must have been in there, but I'm sure she'd have been very, very tiny and almost powerless.

When I took up dancing the second time that Valentine's Day evening, I didn't consider whether it would be different. But this time, it turns out, I am dancing just for me, for passion, for good feelings. Competitions, judges, and medals are less important because I'm reaping some inner reward. At first I don't see it as working on myself—dance lessons as life lessons. But it makes sense that now, as a more mature woman, I might be prepared to notice, for example, the good girl, and to see her working side by side with the good soldier, another character in me, hardworking, indefatigable, brave, commanding, and self-sacrificing. And then I might recognize the geisha, who is always adept at pleasing a man (she bought that remote-control device for Peter). I have no recollection of who trained her, or of how she came to be so expert. She knows how to be subtle enough with little seductive gestures, how to seem desirable rather than needy, how to let the man decide where to go for dinner, how to zero right in on the man's pleasure in bed and ignore her own. Often, I wish she weren't so skillful and sly, because when the geisha steps in, she subverts the interests of both the good girl and the good soldier, dismissing their needs in order to serve those of the man. The geisha hasn't seen much action in my personal life lately, so she seems to be showing up in the dance studio.

NOW HERE WE are on the floor, about a year after I started dancing again: the good girl, the good soldier, and me. We're earnestly dancing our damnedest. The geisha joins us in order to remind me, say, to compliment the man, or act a little delicate in a flirtatious way so he'll be captivated by me. The characters are going through something like sibling rivalry; the good girl will elbow out the geisha, and then the good soldier will command them both to get out of the way. It goes on like that. But then the foxtrot cuts in, exposes my chicanery, and suddenly I feel like the wizard at the controls when Dorothy or whoever pulls away the curtain. I suspect that Bill isn't fooled one bit; it's possible that he sees behind the curtain and still likes me. He says, "You don't have to work so hard; you're lovable just as you are." What a thought! But what does he know?

Any good dance teacher worth his salt—teaching any form of dance, I imagine, not only ballroom—will eventually get around to telling a good student to quit trying so hard. This of course would spell my unraveling. It flies in the face of the American rulebook for success. Pulling yourself up by your bootstraps or your pink ballet-slipper ribbons is written into our DNA. There I am in my lessons, task-oriented, eager to improve and win my teacher's praise; I haven't a clue that there is any other way. And I'm doing okay. But finally the turning point comes one day as I try to be lighter and softer, less like a Mack truck in Bill's arms, while executing a series of figures in the jazzy dance.

"I'm trying!" I say in a mock whine to my teacher. Trying, by the way, is the primary tactic of the good girl in good student mode; it never fails to score points with the teacher. "But I just can't get this."

"Why don't you stop trying?" he asks, as if it were the most natural request. I have nothing but respect for his teaching, so I have to take the loopy suggestion seriously. "You mean don't work at it? What would I do instead?" The room is practically spinning.

"Do nothing. Do everything wrong. Be lazy," he orders. Well, that's infuriating. Then it dawns on me, a teeny glimpse of a notion: the good student isn't all there is. I might be on a threshold here, about to enter a new place where I could meet the artist in me, who'd say to the good student, "That's okay, I'll take it from here." I really should be open to this possibility. I realize that the good-student persona has two faces; she can be a crafty dodge or more like a cozy way station along the path, the very scary path leading to discovery and ownership of one's excellence and artistry. In that moment, I see my artistry as a nebulous blob of dark shadows. If I want to become a great dancer instead of a competent dancer, I'll have to give up the hard work and allow the shadows to take a form. It might be worth it to try . . . easier.

We do the foxtrot again, and I try not to try, which of course is absurd. My muscles are practically quivering in protest, but it's a start. I feel a distinct hint of sponginess in my bones. "There, that was nice," says Teacher, and I think I'm going to throw up. "Now, try not to hold your arms up. Just hang. And let the rest of you be a lump."

I try this lump thing again. The feeling of letting go of my arms brings about an ease in them that's unbearable—I can sustain it only for a few moments at a time. But it's deliciously tempting, like being tickled softly on the sole of the foot until you writhe and scream.

"You know, you have the capacity for a lovely, crystalline lightness in your dancing," Bill tells me now, "but it's thwarted by your hyperextension. When you're as light as that, it reminds me of Bobbi Irvine." He's referring to a famous former champion from Scotland, so I'm perfectly flattered. Hyperextension, that's my nemesis. I've known about it forever. Swaybacked, it used to be called. Now I see this tendency—pushing my ribs forward, curving my lower spine—as the physical expression of trying too hard, rushing forward. I tell myself to ease off, let my spine relax, and channel Bobbi Irvine.

MEANWHILE, MY DANCING energy is showing around the office. There may be a certain spring in my step, or a different default expression on my face, I don't know, but I notice that my boss, Pamela, seems more relaxed and comfortable around me. I think happy people may project something simpler and easier to read than unhappy or more darkly complicated people. I am taking it easier at work too, because I'm spending quite a few lunch hours at the dance studio, and I have less time at my desk to prepare for meetings. So instead, I've been winging it. Now, to my dismay, it's three o'clock, time to go to the editorial meeting, and I didn't do the research, I didn't write up my ideas. No script. Just me in the moment with the boss and the rest of the staff. Panic shadows me into the conference room. I decide to keep my mouth shut and not try to entertain with my cleverness since it hasn't been properly rehearsed.

But things don't turn out at all the way I expected. I have no notes to refer to, so I am adrift as the meeting gets going. I pick up my pen and look at my blank pad. I fidget a bit. I put down my pen and fold my hands in my lap, but this feels stupid, so I pick up my pen again and look around. I listen. I look at people when they speak. Without a plan, my mind is working in a freestyle way. The inner spontaneity is an unfamiliar pleasure, and it makes me a little anxious. At first, I am careful not to say anything without properly thinking it through. Until Pamela, the editor-in-chief of this glossy lifestyle magazine for the very rich, asks if anybody has any suggestions as to the latest trend, the latest best thing (she is no doubt anticipating mention of the new sexy Italian tenor, a must-have Patek Philippe watch, or a rising fashion star or something), and I lose all self-control and say, "Wild salmon." Everybody cracks up and looks at me expectantly. I'm not convinced they are laughing *at* me, though. I smile and enjoy having provided a moment of levity.

"We've seen many medical journal reports lately," I say, "about how most of the fish we eat are contaminated with PCBs and mercury—which are either neurotoxins or they screw up our hormones." People are looking at me now with worried expressions. Good. "We have to stop eating swordfish. Tuna only once a month. No farm-bred salmon. But wild salmon, because it's out in the deep waters, is far less contaminated. It's the best fish, loaded with omega-3 oil, brain food—it helps ward off Alzheimer's. It's also beauty food, because the oil is anti-inflammatory." Now I'm going on too long, but never mind. "It keeps the lining of skin cells intact so they can stay nice and plump, which is the hallmark of cells in young, healthy skin. There are doctors who say you should eat wild salmon every day."

I glance at the editor. She is taking notes! She looks up and says, "That's great. Let's do that as a two-page feature." This is a surprise. Pamela is no pushover; she will often hold off after hearing a story suggestion, and just say, "Hm, interesting." I am reeling from having spoken off the cuff; what a rush that it actually worked! You never know what the untethered brain will come up with.

MY MOTHER, HELEN BRYAN, was born in a small town in India named Miraj, near Poona, southeast of Bombay. Her dad, Alison Bryan, a Presbyterian minister, worked as a missionary in India. He met Marion Cuthbertson, from Scotland, who was teaching there and, as he used to say, he liked the way she threw a softball so he married her. Mom spoke Marathi for the first five or six years of her life. When I was little, I thought she was an Indian like Pocahontas, with a feather sticking straight up out of her hair.

Mom always told stories about her childhood, and we were interested to hear that her first friends were monkeys. She recently delighted Erica with the story at bedtime of how she would climb into a big banyan tree to taunt the monkeys, despite the fact that her ayah, or babysitter, gave strict orders against it. One day, when the monkeys charged her, the ayah had to intervene, and the monkeys lunged at the ayah and tore her dress. But the ayah managed to prevent them from hurting my mother, who subsequently got in big trouble. She got in trouble a lot.

Erica reminds me of my mother. She has her same independent spirit and very quick intelligence, sometimes perceived as eccentricity. Neither has any intention of pleasing authority figures. I admire this. They seem quite brave to me. But they're also infuriating sometimes.

When my mother's family moved back from India to the states, they settled in Salem, New Jersey. Mom went to Sarah Lawrence College in the 1940s and graduated with a degree in international relations. During the war, she'd corresponded with a soldier named Joseph Garland from Massachusetts. He came home, and they met and hit it off. They ended up not getting married, but going their separate ways. She next met John Reurs when she was working for a student travel program in New York, but I think they only dated. Then she met and married my dad, Robert Carlson, son of Swedish immigrants who lived in New Britain, Connecticut. Armed with two degrees from Harvard, he was on the path to assimilation and making good as a New York attorney. They had the four of us, and in 1959 we moved to Hastings, the town I now live in with my kids. At the time, my parents bought a big old Victorian mansion (for a song) with ten bedrooms and marble halls through which we'd bicycle and roller-skate. It was a fantastic house to grow up in, and my mom somehow managed to maintain it after the divorce despite the financial burden.

Her second marriage was to John, the guy she met after Joe. John was a nice and generous man, part Dutch, part Danish, who ran trans-Atlantic and cruise-ship lines, also had a Harvard degree, and was a metrosexual before his time. Mom started dressing better, I remember, wearing lipstick and getting her hair done, because she had to go to functions with John. We kids joined them on their honeymoon, a cruise on the *Nieuw Amsterdam* to Europe.

John taught me how to make *blanquette de veau* and vinaigrette dressing, the latter without using measuring spoons to add the salt—just pouring it into your palm with the confident carelessness of a professional and tossing it into a ceramic mug and whisking it with the mustard and *vinaigre*, which you didn't measure either. John would sometimes drive me to school in his Porsche. When he could, he helped pay our Riverdale tuition. I think he may have also sent a check or two for Yale. He died of cancer, in the early nineties, some time after he and Mom had divorced. Meanwhile, Mom reencountered Joe, who also had a Harvard degree, and was traveling through our area to interview old buddies for a book he was writing about World War II. He called Mom. They got together and, as Joe later put it to me in the dining room, "the sparks flew," and so they married finally after all those years. I always thought my mother's marriages resembled an inside-out sock being turned right side out, because she met my dad last, and married him first; met and married John second; and met Joe first, but married him last. Mom and Joe have been married for ages now: twenty-seven years.

MOM HAD THE four of us kids in four years, and she often chirped about how clever it was to get all the diapers over with at once. No big deal, being pregnant for almost five years straight. She frequently referred to us, fittingly, as a litter. There's a cute photo of us Carlson kids, four towheads in a row in the kitchen: Robbie, the youngest, about four then, facing Alison, six, who was buttoning his vest; then next is me, eight, standing behind Ali, and I'm buttoning her dress, and our big sister Anna, nine, is behind me buttoning my dress. An assembly line, how adorable.

I always thought the litter reference was very apt, and sort of fun, but when I was all grown up, a therapist pointed out to me that our individual attributes might not have been acknowledged or celebrated, our individual needs left unmet. That never would have occurred to me; I had piano and dance lessons, and I know my mother tried hard to be a good mother, just like I'm trying hard myself. She rarely did so-called normal activities with us on the weekends, like shopping or going to the movies. Instead, she took us rock climbing on the Palisades cliffs across the Hudson River with her friend Woodrow Wilson Sayre, who had climbed Everest. We sailed along the river on the sloop *Clearwater* with Pete Seeger, who told me, when I was fretting about not getting back to do my homework, "Don't let schoolwork interfere with your education." When we were quite little still—I was maybe six or seven—Mom let us swing naked on the swing set after a swim in our plastic pool, saying nonchalantly, "What's the matter with skin?" I'm sure it freaked out the grocery delivery boy who was bringing the weekly order to my grandparents, who lived on the top floor of our house. Mom often bought us all the same outfits, except for my brother, who got his own, so we didn't express our individual fashion styles as kids. I don't think I even wanted to, though, until I arrived in ninth grade at Riverdale (after all that Sturm und Drang) in 1968; I'd buy psychedelic bright opaque pantyhose, in colors like acid green and bright yellow, and wear a different color on each leg, tucking the other leg into my underpants. Early evidence that I wanted to stand out in a crowd. There was a sign-up sheet one day on the boys' school bulletin board: "Guess which colors Carlson is going to wear today."

OVER THE YEARS, I never believed I was lovable simply by dint of my existence, nor that I was special, though I tried hard to be. Today, I scoff when I hear about elementary schools telling children that "everybody is special." Not true. Everybody is unique, but not necessarily special. That kind of thinking, in my opinion, devalues ordinary as well as my unyielding commitment to making an effort. This Protestant work ethic as applied to love: you don't get it because you're you; you have to earn it. That's what I believed. I'd worked very hard all my life to earn love and be singled out in whatever I was doing.

This hard work accounts, partly, for my being half dead at the age of forty-five—the way I felt at the bar mitzvah before I got back to dancing. Half dead was an exhaustion resulting from *both* my external goings-on and my inner life. Sure, juggling work, children, and a disabled marriage was enough to make me tired. But being driven to always be better—not to be the best I could be, because that suggests the possibility of success, but *better*, because whatever it was I did was never good enough—was an incessant, often frantic mind game that was utterly exhausting and finally led me to a state of burnout. Peter used to shake his head in mock sympathy sometimes during our conversations and say, "I'd hate to be inside your head." I think it made him nervous just being near the outside of it.

Now, on the dance floor, I'm astonished to see how striving doesn't always pay off, and can—au contraire—get in the way of success. Could I be plain me and still stand out in the crowd on the floor? Do I already? And that leads me to wonder, could I use Bill's instruction to let my arms just hang, and then apply this just-hanging technique to other areas of my life? Could I stop trying to be the perfect mom and still feel worthy of my children's love? Still give them what they need? And then, what about other parts of my life? That's asking a great deal. I don't think I can do it. Not trying hard on the dance floor in that nice confined space is one thing; abandoning the defining aspect of my identity is expecting way too much. The *idea* of actively "trying easier" is a nice one, and giving up the good-girl act *sounds* appealing. But no—it's not going to happen. Forget it.

8 DEMONS ON MY DANCE CARD

IT DOESN'T TAKE Bill long, maybe just two or three lessons, to notice the bitch nag. She is another one of my characters, and he has identified her before I have. But I guess that's not surprising—he's used to dancing with just one partner at a time and here I am with an extra in tow, and she's a noisy one.

"You do criticize yourself a lot," he says after I make one of my preemptive strikes like "I'm always losing my balance in the simplest steps!" or "Viennese waltz is my worst dance" or "I know I think too much."

He says, "I'm going to charge you a dollar for every self-criticism you make from now on."

I smile. But when we get going again, I notice the impulse and catch myself, stifle the put-down. Hmm. I guess he's right. Still, I've never thought being self-critical was a *bad* thing.

"You aren't your own best friend." Bill has stopped our dancing to make the point, facing me squarely for emphasis. "If your best friend talked about herself the way you do, what would you say to her?" I am thinking of Julia.

"I'd say, 'Hey, take it easy, you're being hard on yourself.' I'd defend her against herself, I suppose."

"Try treating yourself like your best friend."

I like Bill's protectiveness of me. It is dawning on me that we do a fair amount of standing around talking during our lessons, and clearly we're both into it. I know we should be dancing as much as possible, but it seems helpful, this cerebral stuff. Or is it that being in my brain is comfortable and familiar and I want to stay put and not challenge myself? (Oh, is that another dollar? Doesn't count if I don't say it out loud.) Bill is so mellow and accepting compared to Yuri. He has a kind of pre-forgiveness, as if he knows we're all flawed. I love that he enjoys the intellectual side of dance. We have a lot in common; we talk about things, like friends do. I feel safer entrusting my dancing to him. I think of the conversation I had with Julia the other day about how the student has to allow herself to be vulnerable, to surrender to the practice. Ordinarily, I wouldn't dream of surrender (dangerous, if not simply stupid), but standing here with Bill, my jaw softens and for a moment I stop watching my own thoughts.

"I think there are two observers of the self," Bill says. "One is a nonjudgmental observer, the other is critical. Your self-critical observer has taken over. Why don't you put her in her place? She's the brat. Call her that and tell her to fuck off."

I'd never do that. But now I'm wondering, who is this bitch, and why is she in control here? I name her the bitch nag. I see that she has no place in the dancing. She is strident, ungraceful, too angry even to hear the music. I wonder, though, since I just got wise to her, why that hasn't taken away her power. She seems to be hanging around.

AFTER TWO MONTHS of dancing with Bill, my pre-lesson jitters are gone. Ariel was right: there's no man more comfortable. The more I dance with Bill, the more I'm obliged to admit that Yuri is really the antithesis of comfortable; he certainly doesn't give a hoot about following the golden rule. Dancing with him, I had no idea what I was missing! Soon, instead of climbing the stairs to the third floor with anxiety mounting at each step as would happen before a lesson with Yuri, I come to the studio with something else; I think it may be excitement, though I still can't really tell the difference.

Today, Bill decides to start with a waltz, the hardest dance for me—perhaps because the rise and fall movement requires a letting go I'm not willing to attempt. In fact, most teachers of social dancing don't start beginners with the waltz, because they have difficulty with closing their feet and changing weight before taking the next step forward or backward. Not long into our waltz, after just twice around the room, Bill is impatient for the first time since we've been working together. I recognize it first in a sound he makes: a gruff muttering, no words. Then in his exhale, which seems to express discomfort and irritation. It is intimate, this experience of his feelings when we are dancing, because his mouth is so close to my ear, and though we aren't making eye contact, our hearts and minds are inches from each other. They transmit directly, without benefit of detours.

"Do you know why you keep doing that?" he asks. "It's like you're putting the brakes on." His words puncture me and my failure oozes onto the surface. Damn, how fragile my newfound confidence is. Then he says, "The definition of insanity is doing the same thing over and over and expecting a different result."

A lump rises, spreading pain around my throat. *Wait! The lump—why is it back? I thought it wouldn't happen with Bill. Bill is nice.* I can't speak. I try to behave, but my mouth muscles are engaged in the silly contortions common to wimps.

"What's wrong?" he asks, not unsympathetically, just puzzled, and he doesn't seem afraid of whatever answer may be coming.

I shake my head to say never mind, but I still have no voice. The lump is a stopper. I don't want to make him feel bad.

"No, what is that? Is that pain?" he asks.

What is he doing? He shouldn't look. Leave it alone. Go away.

But I am standing there with my teacher looking into my eyes, expecting some kind of response. I swallow and shake my head again. "I'm sorry. It's so stupid," I say weakly. "Let's do this." I move to take dance position again, as if being brave and private now will work to get him off the topic.

"What's it like in there?" he asks. My coyness isn't helping me out here in the face of his persistence, but part of me does want to cooperate. Okay, if he's not going to turn away, I won't either.

"I think I feel like a fourteen-year-old girl, and I'm embarrassed that she's here with us." I wasn't trying to use dancing as therapy, but it seems to be going ahead by itself anyway.

"There's no need to be embarrassed. Judging by how you turned out, she must be an awfully nice young girl." His courtliness, initially amusing to me, is soothing in this circumstance.

We dance again at last, moving silently to "It Is You," the waltz from the soundtrack to the movie *Shrek,* which I adore. I am looking at the lump from the outside, looking down from the ceiling at myself dancing here, with a lump, and I look at it for the first time without shame. As we swing around the room, I am aware of my breath in, my breath out, timed to the music, and I can see an image: a young girl, alone, her head bowed. I think I know her. Yes. She is mine. She is me at the moment in my life when the turmoil of divorce and the havoc wreaked by its aftermath got to be too much. I see dimly, but I am rapt: she is sitting alone in the corner of a dark room, crying. I think I must have stashed her away to protect her. A little girl, desperate to find safety.

For the first time in my dancing, I have been captivated by an image instead of a thought process. After this fleeting glimpse of the girl, I realize there are characters emerging from me like clowns from a Volkswagen bug at the circus. The good girl, the good soldier, the fourteen-year-old girl, the bitch nag, the geisha, and who's next? I wonder, is the bitch nag guarding the door to the dark room? I can't blame her; she thinks that's her job, and she takes it seriously. In the locker room as I change back into my work outfit, I decide I don't want her to "fuck off," as Bill ordered; I don't even want to banish her. I think she must have served me well at some time, keeping things organized and on schedule. I am grateful to the bitch nag. She can stay and watch my dance, but I'll tell her she has to go sit in the corner. And I may invite the little girl to come out and join in the dancing.

After this encounter, I think about pain differently. Yuri didn't cause mine. Nor did Bill. It exists, that's all. Whatever I felt back then is a blurry memory becoming clearer as I dance. Today, I wasn't immobilized by the lump; I danced with it. The pain is part of what makes the dancing beautiful. We don't dance only for joy; if we're lucky, we sometimes dance for pain.

ONE DAY, STARING at an old Oriental rug that my mother gave me when her father died, a rug that used to be in his study, where he wrote his sermons, and is now in my front hall, I am mesmerized by its pattern and it takes me back to a time when Mom would get mad. I hated to hear her yell. I knew as a child that she was furious with my father for all the bad things she told us he'd done to her and to us. But taking that in didn't give me distance or any kind of protection. The pattern of that burgundy and gold rug carries me back to my bedroom on the second floor of our family's house, when the voice in my head started up: *I don't know what I did, but Mommy's really mad. Whatever it was, I'd better fix it. Act better from now on; yes, no matter what, I'll be better.*

Some years later—I might have been just about ready to go off to college—I read some letters Dad had written to Mom when they were fighting about whether we kids could enroll in private school. I'd always believed what my mother said: that Dad just refused to pay. Then, standing at the dining room table where she'd spread out all these letters next to the cardboard box she used for filing correspondence, I read two or three letters saying something like "Dear Helen, I can appreciate your desire to send our children to a better school, but I cannot afford to pay the tuition at Riverdale, certainly not for all of our children. Perhaps, if you got a job, we could share the cost. My salary alone is not sufficient." Several letters pleading with her to consider his point of view. I was struck by how reasonable he sounded, and by the fact that he'd actually given the subject some thought. Could it be he was not a monster? That things were not what they seemed? There was no denying he'd caused her pain. Maybe his asking her to pitch in was designed to protect his money, or even just to piss her off. To me, it looked like my dad was proposing something at least worthy of discussion, though he probably didn't realize that whatever she might earn if she took a job would go to pay a sitter.

Still, the letters changed everything for me. I forgave my father for his misplaced anger at me that August night three or four years back. What I discovered at the dining room table was not that my dad was right and my mom was wrong, but that there are two sides to every story. *Maybe both my parents are right and wrong. Maybe I don't have to choose—I can love both.* I needed to find out more for myself. And so I contacted my father. In those days, my siblings and I had fallen out of touch with him. I let him know that I'd glimpsed his side of the story. We got together. There was a tender rapprochement, and thus I became the black sheep of the family. But gradually over the next few years the color of my wool changed back as my sisters and my brother contacted him, too. Mom was upset that I was seeing more of Dad, and I was a wreck at the prospect of losing her to get my father back, but I had to go ahead anyway.

I'M ON THE dance floor with Bill again, and I'm ready for it now. I stand up, at last. In the sweep of a simple quarter turn in quickstep, without forethought, I do something new. It is an impulsive decision to just try, because when if not now? I speak up to the bitch nag. *Stop talking to me like that. I'm not going to listen anymore.* Anger wells. *Oh, no. Anger is bad. Don't do this.* Too late. There it is, and it's driving my movement. I feel myself shift gears, pissed as hell, and I don't have any idea whether I am flying with ease, released, or leaden and sluggish under the weight of this taboo explosion. I keep going. I am hot with anger at the predator in me, and I deny her access now. *Go! Leave me to do this. I don't want you here.* I push harder, fueled by my intention to go where I will by my own dead reckoning, with no fear of displeasing anyone. No fear of consequences. Although I am dancing with a partner, I am moving powerfully forward, sure of my direction, neither passive nor afraid, not waiting for his Morse code. I am down now, bending my knees, not tentatively as usual but in a flash of certainty that this is how deep I need to be in order to use my momentum to push myself backwards for two more steps, then diagonally. It's happening so fast, we're heading into a turn, and I feel reckless, but I keep on, hypnotized by my body's determination. It's amazing all this can go on in the psyche and a dancer can still manage to move her legs properly, spin and smile and be lovely. But I guess I've done it in this crazy sequence because when we stop, at the end of the song, Bill says, "That was great. What did you do?"

"I got angry at the bitch," I say, my chest heaving as I suck air in and blow it out.

Bill had said early in our working together, "Find the power behind the tears." The tears aren't always about hurt. Sometimes they are a letting go. And sometimes, they serve as a governor, hobbling the anger. Gradually, after that energized quickstep, I can tell my dancing is getting stronger, not because of muscle tone and practice alone, but because my characters are beginning to sort themselves out.

THERE IS ANOTHER bitch nag with whom I must come to terms, a voice that isn't in my head. The voice is Yuri's. Who knows, maybe the strong connection I feel with him is through our mutual bitches. I am increasingly resigned to the necessity of ending our lessons once and for all. At least things aren't always miserable between us. Some days, our dancing is pleasant and wonderfully lilting, if not exciting, and I wish it could always be like this. Other days, he is snippy, and I am confused and mealymouthed. But every hour I spend dancing with Bill is bringing me closer to a knowledge I sort of wish I didn't have to face: that Yuri is not only a poor teacher for me, he's not a good enough dancer. Not only does he not know how to "think about my comfort," he doesn't even care to. And yet I am drawn to both teachers as if they belong together in me, two pieces of a puzzle.

9 SPRING FEVER

SPRING IS MY favorite season. I love the promise of all the rebirth. I am moved by the bright but still cool sunlight, the delicacy of the greens, the fragility of new shoots—yet the insistence of it all, the tenacity!

Shoes on, hair out of my face in a sloppy bun, I emerge from the locker room one afternoon in late April and find an empty corner to stretch in. The studio is warm on this gorgeous day. The old, iron-framed windows are propped open with sticks. The heavy burgundy drapes undulate in the breeze. Sunlight streams in on a slant and I see New York dust particles afloat in it. I bend forward and hang for a few moments, my cheeks nuzzling the fabric of my ankle-length black ballroom skirt. After my calves and hamstrings soften, I stand erect and roll my head around to warm up my neck, enjoying the snap, crackle, pop on each side, followed by a release, a minute satisfaction in the neck tendons.

"Ready?" Bill asks. He takes me by surprise because my eyes are closed as I do the neck rolls. It is one p.m. sharp.

"Ready."

He reaches for my left hand and walks me out to the center of the floor where we will start. I prepare, lengthening my spine, feeling my hip joints, my knees, and I think of last time: we left off with the Tumble Turn. Bill showed me how I was tilting, and collapsing my left side as we spun. No good. I should support myself. Tilting puts undue pressure on his right arm, which cradles me but is not meant to hold me up. All these fine points are intriguing.

But Bill doesn't start where we left off. He decides on a foxtrot. Though I'm not warmed up yet, it feels long and lazy. I wonder if I'm being remiss, because I don't feel any stress. Am I working hard enough?

"Okay, now, do you think you could bend more?" Bill asks.

"Yeah, I guess so."

"Show me."

"Here, by myself, like this?" I ask, unsure. He takes both my hands and lifts them so my arms go up and out, and he turns his feet out, for me to imitate, in second position. I do this. We are in plié.

"Bend," he says, looking hopefully down at my hips, my legs.

I bend.

"More. Can you do more?"

I do more. I feel like an indiscreet cowgirl who doesn't know how to behave in a skirt.

"Even more?" He goes around to the side of me to check me out. He is unabashed in the way he looks at my body, his long arms by his sides, his legs apart, knees locked, feet in second position, head tilted slightly to the right, eyes examining me as though I were a racehorse he were considering purchasing, or a woman he might find attractive. I get a little buzz.

"There." He comes around, opens his arms, walks up to me, right up close, to dance like that, with me deep in this open plié position. It is really comfy, and I am amazed. I hear him say softly, "That's good." Yes, it feels good, his torso so totally flat against my torso from clavicle to pubic bone, because my hips and thighs in plié are completely out of his way. When we take off, I feel him get taller and I imagine it's from the pleasure of our unencumbered movement.

"I'm going to hold your hips now," Bill says. And so he does, forcefully pressing them down as I move around the floor. It feels awkward, but kind of nice and, when I relax, more stable, too. Now, Bill touches my tummy, my navel, to adjust my alignment. I don't flinch; not so bad.

"I feel like a cowgirl," I say.

"Perhaps you can think of yourself as a crouching tiger instead," he suggests.

I like that. I saw the film *Crouching Tiger, Hidden Dragon*. I like the image of me as a deft, athletic, mysterious Asian woman who puts up with no bullshit, has eyes in the back of her head, and flies across rooftops, never losing her balance. Fierce. That's what I need to become.

"My lesson with Yuri yesterday was very unpleasant," I say before we begin again. Yesterday, during that lesson, I'd spied Bill sitting on his regular chair at his regular little round table that everyone knows not to use because it's Bill's. I could tell he was checking things out. I think I am tapping Bill's avuncular side to make myself more comfortable about two-timing Yuri. I'm not sure why I feel bad about this; all around me in this studio, there are women taking lessons from more than one teacher. What's the big deal?

"Yes, I did watch for a bit," Bill says. "It looked like Yuri was taking something out on you."

"Actually, Yuri was a real jerk. You know, it's only been a couple of months that you've been teaching me," I pick my words carefully, "and already I feel a difference happening in my mind—its ability to focus. I can't really explain . . ."

"That's because you're about to be great."

My eyes flash to his. I check for teasing in his expression, but there is none. I am floored, just momentarily, and then a liveliness takes hold of me as we come to dance position again to work on my being down—earthbound—in every step, not just the straight-ahead ones, but the turns as well.

"Oops, I lost you there," Bill says about our body contact after a bit. "Where'd you go?"

"That's all you get today," I say, putting a little syrup in my voice. His face breaks into a big smile.

And then we work on the connection of our torsos. He shows me how there are two imaginary parallel, vertical lines running down my front below each breast; these are the axes by which I connect to him. Sometimes we're to touch at just one line, at other times, along both of them, but always at least one.

I keep this image in my mind as we move in waltz now, and I feel Bill rise up tall again. He seems to be floating, expressing more. This makes me feel really good, to be inspiring a retired champion. We do an Attitude, a pose in the corner in which I lift my right leg up-side-back, knee slightly bent, and hold for a time. I should, ideally, look proud yet relaxed, and as if I'm enjoying taking a break here, but I must have telegraphed my fear of going all the way into it.

"Let me take care of you," Bill whispers. *Yes, yes, take care of me!* His words instantly reawaken an immense desire dormant for decades. *But he means just the dance step, you knucklehead, he means it'll be easier and you'll be better balanced.* We readjust and try it again. What does it mean to let him take care of me in this? I allow a little bit more of my weight to rest against his able body, settling my back in his arms, prepared to believe he'll support me.

The song ends. He has punched a tango on the music monitor, and it starts. He moves to the center line and turns, raises his arms for me to come to him. International tango has no rise and fall motion; it's a level dance, with alternating staccato (crisp) and legato (fluid) movements. It's also a dance of urgent emotion. I'm used to containing or packaging mine, so tango is a reach for me. In lessons I assume I can get away without the passion or anger that accomplished tango performers show, and instead just work on my footwork and body position. In this particular tango, the man expresses his passionate desire and the woman is aloof and resistant at first; then she, too, shows her passion, or her libido or her anger, depending on how you look at it, and they go at it together. There's some flip-flopping of ardor and anger, approach and retreat in the dance, and I like it because it recognizes that we are all bundles of contradictory emotions. Not me, though. I'm just hard at work here on my footwork and body position.

Bill and I are darting down the line of dance in a staccato sequence. Now comes a Reverse Turn, then a Lunge, in which I snap my head way to the left and backward in an enormously big, open layout of a pose that couldn't be more aloof, while Bill stands tall, looking the other way, as if he has somewhere to go despite my uncooperativeness. We are like an elastic band stretched to the max. He holds this for a time and I begin to wonder if we shouldn't be going somewhere by now, but only my eyelids are showing any signs of movement.

Then I detect something barely perceptible: I am sitting on his right leg at this point, holding my shape, except that I seem to be rocking slightly. What's happening? My pelvis is rolling back and forth on his leg, without intention or volition. He is rising subtly, holding his head up, but looking down at me now, in an arch that's like a dare to me; I detect this through my peripheral vision. My shoulders, torso, and hips are rotating sharply clockwise, then counterclockwise. He is doing this to me, faster, with bigger yet still crisp movements. In contrast to my body's movements, my head turns gradually, and I look at his nose, unable to look into his eyes, keeping my distance, still stretching my body far away from him, not willing to give him all that he wants, but then meeting his eyes. I feel myself shaking like a trout on a fishing line, except for my gaze, which is steady. Then: snap! Our heads turn simultaneously, our bodies return almost to vertical, and suddenly, it's over. We are facing the same direction, the corner, our resolution, and I am in shock and wonderment at his expertise in leading me through this electrifying sequence called the Shrug so that I don't know how it happened or how I did it. I *didn't* do it; he did it. And, God, it felt superb.

Was that "inappropriate"—whatever that means in the dance world? I don't think so. More like playful. Well, excuse me, but I'm going to go ahead and have a good time.

MOST OF THE time these days, I am feeling more confident in my dancing. Bill's way of criticizing me doesn't get me all worked up and crybabyish; it feels nice and neutral, not personal at all. This is how it's supposed to be between teacher and student. Now I know I have to stand up to Yuri. I feel a little sad about what I'm about to do. On Sunday afternoon, I decide to make the call. We are scheduled to dance tomorrow, but I really don't want to. I can't let this drag on any longer. Whenever I have to have a difficult conversation, I make notes. Today, I write out what I think will sound best, so I don't hurt his feelings, but allow him to save face. If I can't be completely honest ("You're a lousy teacher! I'm sick of your rudeness and disrespect. Where do you come off treating people this way?"), I can be diplomatic.

"Allo," Yuri's deep voice sounds so good I want to chicken out. I'm sitting on my edge of the bed, facing my nightstand, where I have spread out my notes, and I have closed the bedroom door.

"Hi, Yuri, it's Janet."

"Hi, Janet." Not icy, but definitely chilly.

"I'm calling because I'm wondering if we can . . . skip our lesson tomorrow. I don't think I can get out of the office, but that's not the only reason."

"What, then?" He sounds impatient.

"I've been realizing that I need a break, not just for a few weeks. I mean I, um, I need to be a much stronger dancer to dance with you, or with anyone. I need a stronger frame and a stronger mental focus, just like you've always said to me. I haven't managed it so far." Silence. I can't even hear his breathing. He's not making this easy. "It's been so frustrating for both of us lately. When I dance with you, I get stuck." *Get to the point, Janet.* "But the work I'm doing with Bill seems to be helping with that. And I find it confusing to go back and forth between the two of you. Plus it's kind of hard on my budget. So will you accept my thanks for how you've trained me so far, and we'll stop, at least for now? I really need to just work with one teacher. I'm very grateful, Yuri." *Please, say something, make this okay.*

"Yes, well, have a good life." He is gone. I hang up the phone, and I take a deep breath. That is that. After all the drama, it is over in a matter of a few seconds. I go downstairs to rejoin my family and pretend nothing just happened. But inside where my family cannot see, I am churning a mixture of relief and loss—loss of my dream, dancing on clouds, more than of any reality that gave me sustenance. But still, that counts as loss. Yuri and I will never dance again. We don't speak again when we cross paths at the studio, though I will try to start conversation. He will ignore me, until, one day on the floor when I'm dancing with Bill and he's dancing with his student, Bill will break the ice with a friendly comment, teacher to teacher, and finally Yuri will look at me, and speak. But it will make no difference; we are done.

I'M HOPELESSLY DEVOTED. Again. And I'm drunk from the easy admiration I'm getting from Bill. It's such welcome respite after the weirdness with Yuri, which I can't believe I tolerated. And Lord knows I don't get much admiration at home. So forgive me if I'm intoxicated, but really, it's been so long and I didn't realize how much I craved it. I'm drinking the attention in. Despite the emotional roller coaster I'm on with dance, my overall outlook is increasingly cheerful and my behavior effervescent. You might imagine that this surplus joy would lead me to shine some of that good stuff on my marriage, the poor thing, hanging on by a thread. In rare moments, I guess you could say I do make an admirable effort to share something more with Peter, as does he with me, but no way am I putting my heart into it completely. It's a mystery why not. Is it that I have made some decision, and I don't want anything to challenge it?

Once or twice over the recent years, Peter and I have talked about what he squeamishly calls "the D-word," but he has made it clear, whenever we've had a bitter, dead-end argument, that he doesn't want that. Of course not; his parents have been married fifty years. He has no reason to know that divorce isn't the end of the world. As painful as divorce is, I think it's sometimes better than the alternative, and you do survive it. I've seen three among my parents and I'm still here. But I'm chastened by Peter's reaction when, one day, I say the word after one of our disagreements and he says, clipping each word so the edges are really sharp, "Don't ever joke about that." *Okay, okay, I won't. I'll keep my thoughts to myself.* And so, occasionally, when I'm frustrated by the clogged drain of our marital life, and our inability to clear out the gunk, I do ponder divorce. I don't picture it, don't have an image of life apart from Peter, but I ponder it quietly, in solitary moments. *Maybe it's the solution, because this isn't working. But careful: it could be that you're too cold-blooded and divorce is the easy way out for you. Keep trying for now. Think of the kids.*

ONE OF PETER'S best attributes is his ability to teach himself new things. He became interested in mountain biking years before it became all the rage, and he cruised the bike stores, learned about the best equipment, bought guides to bike trails, and became proficient. Same with kayaking; he researched the sport and the vessels, drove to New Jersey to buy a kayak, took a course in the Eskimo roll, and presto: he was the first in Hastings to drive around town with a boat on his roof and put in on the Hudson through the hole in the chain-link fence by the tennis courts. When he got curious about the saxophone, he purchased a used instrument from a local musician in our town, found himself a teacher, and learned to play. Sometimes these days his incessant and loud practicing annoys me, but often I'm impressed by how beautifully he blows that horn for someone who just started. Peter got into jazz not too long ago and became friends with Michael Brecker, the late tenor saxophonist, world famous, who lived down the hill from us. I've tried to like jazz, but haven't succeeded to any real degree. The only kind I like is the stuff you can dance a foxtrot to. The other day, I bought the Louis Armstrong CD with the tune "That Old Feeling" on it because it's Bill's current favorite for when we do the foxtrot, and it's grown on me. I want to listen to it outside of the studio. I just played it as I drove home, and in my mind did our entire foxtrot routine the whole time. I see an opportunity here, begging to be grasped.

"Hey, Pete," I say later that evening when the girls are deep into their TV show, *Thornberrys*. "Want to go upstairs to our bedroom and listen to Louis Armstrong? I just got this CD."

He declines. Oh well, it was a nice idea. And I give up without a fuss. Instead, we go upstairs and argue about where we'll put the new air-conditioning unit, which window. He insists it has to go in the window near my head. I say I don't want the air blowing on me from that close, and besides, I'm a light sleeper and the noise will keep me awake. How about over by the walk-in closet? He bulldozes ahead, sure that his idea is the right one, and that infuriates me. But I can't bear to argue past this point. "You don't care about my feelings," I fling at him. "So let's not discuss it any further. I'm so sick of arguing."

That old feeling: such a marvelous one in the song about love, but a dreary one in the case of love gone bad. How could I possibly shine my precious dancing joy on my marriage when this is what happens to it? No, thank you.

And yet, I try again. One evening, we're soaking in the hot tub, Peter in his corner against his favorite jets, me in mine. We haven't had sex in ages. I float over to his corner. He says something romantic like "Let's do it," and I say, "I have an idea, how about not going straight to it, but playing a little bit, touching like this for a while. I'd like that." Couples get into their ruts, so this is a big deal for me, to be brave enough to suggest a change, particularly a change that would bring us to a place of greater intimacy, which would be alarming to both of us. I suppose like so many parents, we've gotten too busy for foreplay, which, I have been learning from the delicious touching in dance, might be the best part of sex.

He gives me a blank look. At first, I think he hasn't heard me right, or I wasn't quite clear. But then I see that he is actually looking at me as if what I suggested were a dumb idea, didn't make sense. I am hurt, but for once I'm not crying—there's an accomplishment. I go back to my corner. I'm sure I must be angry, but I can't tell. I wonder why I have given up here so easily, rather than ask again. I think Peter has made it too clear he's not enchanted by me anymore, and I am more fragile than I thought.

As high as my spirits may soar from dancing, so can they come down. I am forced to accept that dancing is not a panacea and being part of a vacant marriage is painful no matter what. How bizarre that a partnership can thrive in demise—that two people can engage so fluidly in a cycle of hurt and hurting, a darker dance, but a dance nonetheless.

10   WHY CAN A WOMAN BE MORE LIKE A MAN?

I AM TAKING Bill's professional Standard exam class on Monday mornings. The students, all professionals except me, have signed up for the class to prepare for a grueling licensing exam in all the Standard dances administered by the United States Imperial Society of Teachers of Dancing. I joined not to take the exam and become certified but because Bill invited me to and it seemed like a huge honor. "You need to learn where you are in the room, and where you're going," he explained. "This class will be good for that." In other words, it was time for me to give up relying on the man to lead. "The man doesn't lead," Bill would say. "And the lady doesn't follow. It's a dialogue, both people talking. A good lady knows what's coming next. The better she knows the routine and the directions, and the more assertive she is, the more pleasurable the experience is for her *and* for him."

The characters in the ballroom dance world are too colorful and eccentric to be real; they belong in fiction. And yet, here they are in this studio, one of New York's best. Champions and would-be champions from around the world dance and teach here, and I am standing among them. How did this happen?

There's Oksana, a Russian hottie Latin dancer who parades around in her black-and-red lingerie and fishnets and dyes her hair a different color before every competition in hopes of getting more attention (currently it's a bright red not found in nature). She prances her stuff, selling her gorgeous breasts and her big brown eyes like you wouldn't believe, and kissing me on both cheeks in appreciation of my ga-ga admiration of her theatricality. There's Pavel, a skinny little Standard dancer, also Russian, who dresses more formally than most teachers, in shiny button-down shirts and conservative trousers and calls home all the time to talk to his mom about his nutritional needs. Bill once made him dance with me, and it was like floating on a cloud, he was so light and breathy. The other Pavel, the U.S. Latin champion, is dark, swarthy, unbelievably buff, always in muscle T's and tight Lycra pants, and completely full of himself. He was in that film *Shall We Dance* with Richard Gere and Susan Sarandon, and I was kind of glad when his part turned out to be cut to one tiny scene. Tomas, who will later be a teacher on *Dancing with the Stars,* is softspoken and kind, and one of the least flamboyant dancers. Some of the colorful characters are American, like Harry, the partner of Bill's longtime student, Ariel. Harry is tall, lanky, and very moody, but a fine dancer, and he is the ballroom deejay of choice in the area. Danijel is from Croatia, and he has ballet training and thinks he is God's gift to women ballroom dancers, but he pushes too hard and has bad breath; nevertheless, I've enjoyed dancing with him in figures class, Bill's other pro-level class. Danijel has a student, Caroline, who dances stiffly with a frozen, scared expression on her face, like a deer caught in the headlights, while he barks at her; she takes it, and that bothers me. I want her to rebel, walk away, something, anything. But every week they are there, working in the corner with her near tears. And she *pays* for this. Somehow, I fail to see the irony of my outrage on her behalf.

In our Monday exam class, the group is equally colorful. Kristy is such a hoot. She has the mannerisms of a show dancer, so I'm not surprised when I learn she is a Rockette at Radio City Music Hall. "I'm the shortest of them all," she says with a heavy Massachusetts accent. "So I'm all the way at the end of the line." Kristy segues easily into sexy jazz or honky-tonk moves whenever inspiration strikes. I envy her freedom, her lack of self-consciousness. You would not call this woman coy. She has a strong, mellifluous voice and sparkly dark eyes and dark brown hair that she wears short and sassy. And she has the most gorgeous implants. "All the girls have to get them," she says nonchalantly. "It's the way the business works. You have to have tits." She is totally irreverent in class, cracks everybody up, and she laughs at her own jokes. I like her tremendously. We are very different. For one thing, I could never pull off implants (she let me touch hers once, right there on the dance floor, and I was shocked at how *hard* they are). And while I learn by studying the textbook, *The Ballroom Technique,* and using my semiphotographic memory to store information visually, she learns by stepping out there and trying it with her great sense of timing, without shame or apology, and she fits her body movement deftly into the music. Her command of the beat is impressive. She doesn't rely on memory of a figure's steps or the amount of turn or the rhythm as they're delineated in the book; she can work it out in the moment with a dancer's reasoning.

Today, we're continuing with foxtrot and Bill calls upon me first: "Janet, give me please the man's foot positions and alignment for the Open Telemark, Natural Turn to Outside Swivel and Feather Ending." I have spent hours this weekend memorizing both man's and lady's parts, which have eleven steps each. In class, we must stand up, speak the words and demonstrate the steps at the same time.

"Okay," I say, inhaling, nervous, because I so want to be perfect here and don't imagine I will be. Just as the edges of my mental screen start going dark, I call up the image of page sixty-one in my dog-eared book. I stand at the ready position in the corner of the room near where Bill sits with his book propped open on his belly, his glasses way down on his nose. "One, left foot forward, facing diagonal center," I begin. *Is that right? I think so.* "Two, right foot to the side, backing diagonal wall. Three," *careful, this gets tricky . . .* "left foot sideways in promenade position, facing diagonal wall against line of dance." And on I proceed through all eleven steps without a slipup.

"Very good," Bill says. "What a memory you have."

"Wow, you're amazing," says Kristy. "You should be an examiner." The praise is a warm bath of wonderful, and I smile in relief, slightly exhausted from my effort that used up so much adrenaline.

"Kristy, give me the rise and fall please."

"Oh, I knew it. I reviewed this on the train in, but not enough. Okay," she says, standing ready and looking like a jazz dancer. Her voice alone is convincing enough. It almost doesn't matter what words come out.

"One, rise at the end of one. Two, up. Three, up. Four—"

"You left something out on three," Bill interrupts.

"What? No I didn't. It's up! That can't be wrong."

"Ariel, what is three?" Ariel is a pediatric surgeon with a Mensa IQ who teaches dance in her spare time. She's an old friend of Bill's and never hesitates to tell him what she thinks or to sit on his lap to get a hug. She's one of those people who don't treat their opinion as opinion, but as fact, and they're so intelligent it's hard to argue with them.

"Up, lower end of three," she answers without a second's hesitation.

"Well, that was implied," says Kristy with an insolent shrug. Bill laughs. He gets a kick out of her balls.

"Implied? Nothing's implied in the book. It's all spelled out. That's a good one, Kristy. Try saying that to the examiner when the time comes. Okay, please continue."

A FEW WEEKS later, it's time for us to start dancing the man's part, because during the exam students are tested on their ability not only to dance with their instructor but also to recite both the lady's and man's parts, as well as to dance as man with another woman. This is necessary because in a lesson or class, a dance teacher has to do the man's part while saying the lady's part out loud for the student— and vice versa. No small feat, believe me. It's a little like patting your head while rubbing circles on your tummy. To my mind, dancing as man requires the ability to see a pattern in your head and flip it to its mirror image, and then to execute that, despite your muscle memory of the exact opposite begging you to flip-flop. Many female dancers will tell you that's nonsense; they just become a man. They get into that head. More power to them. I find it immensely challenging.

When we divide up into couples for this exercise, Kristy and I pick each other. Ariel, who is on the short side, also wants to have me be her lady, because she likes how light and cooperative I am. She's a great man, so I'll do both happily. Kristy and I practice in the main room. We start out with the simplest sequence of the foxtrot. We're a good match heightwise. I'm her lady first. For me, this is the easy part. I'm relaxed, able to enjoy how Kristy feels: slight compared to a real man, with skinnier arms, but strong and plenty forceful, with her hard breasts, pointy like torpedoes, steering me around the room. There is some awkwardness between us in the lower regions, however. I'm not exactly floating; it feels more like drowning.

"Kristy, stand up," Bill shouts and I glance to the other end of the room, where he's working with Ariel and Mark, a husky, earnest guy who's struggling at the moment to be a girl. He looks cute, crouching down like that with his head way over, his elbows fully bent, and a thick hand resting delicately on Ariel's upper arm, his chunky pinky raised in a most feminine way.

"What am I doing, Bill?" Kristy shouts back.

"You're pushing Janet off her feet, that's what you're doing. Are you thinking about your partner? Where's your center? Where are your hips? Bend, feel that hip angle and stop coming over the top."

That does it. Much better. She gets us around the room twice in a halfway convincing transgender foxtrot.

Now it's my turn to be man. I'm nowhere near as good as Kristy yet—not being ballsy by nature, I guess. We attempt to assume dance position. Bill comes to help. He lifts my left elbow up and back to a place that feels in violation of all the principles of my ballet training from childhood. Then he places my right hand at more of an angle on her back, and he presses it flat. I will use both hands for steering. Next, Bill takes my neck in both of his mighty hands and turns my head to the left side, bringing me more upright. A man has to be able to see where he's going, to navigate successfully around the room among the other couples. In contrast, a woman needs to be less upright, her head held quite a ways out there at the end of her upper spine and neck, her beautiful curve originating from the perfectly vertical lower spine—so she sees the ceiling mostly, the danger here being that she appear vacuous, smiling into outer space, not looking where she's going. Well, in any case, she's going backwards a fair amount of the time, so her head really only serves as decoration.

Okay, we're off. I'm upright, my chest pumped like a gorilla's, my arms in a functional, protective cradle formation, and I get to decide where we're going. This doesn't feel right at all. I am normally not very assertive or intrusive, and in fact, I tend to confuse the two qualities in real life. Our first few steps of foxtrot are so-so, but as soon as it's time to make a turn in the corner, I get flustered and immediately give up, taking my arms from Kristy, abandoning her.

"Don't stop," she whines. "That was going fine. You need to be more of a *guy* is all. Channel some macho man. Come on, you can do it. I'll do it, too. I'll be a black dude named Rufus. Who are you?"

"Let's see. Oh, I know. I'm Sly Stallone."

"All *right*," she trills, ready to go. And so Sly and Rufus become dance partners. We try again, my limbs in position, my psyche summoning Sly. Rambo. Rocky. What is it like to be a man? Not know-ing how else to impersonate, I simply start *pushing harder*.

"That's great," Kristy says in a high-pitched girlie voice. "Oooh, now you got me. Don't stop, now, don't giggle, don't you *dare* giggle now. Keep it up, Sly, keep going. Yes, push, go, go, go! Make me do what you want!"

I'm getting the physical side of the man, and I like the small taste of testosterone I have for a minute, but the floor craft and cho-reography stump me. My brain feels fried after only ten minutes. I know the woman's steps in the waltz figure called Weave from Promenade. What I can't keep in my head is an image of the couple moving across the floor in a weave pattern. The big picture eludes me. My mind is not ambidextrous. My brain doesn't feel flexible. I cling to my own lady's part. I feel like one of those drivers with a lousy sense of direction who relies on instructions like "go two blocks, turn right," eschewing a map because she can't grasp con-cepts of east and west.

So here at the fourth step of the Weave, instead of stepping for-ward on my right foot, I need to go back on my left, turning left, and then back on my right, not forward on my left. Got that? The frustrating thing with this step is that you can so easily turn from man to lady, or vice versa, because it weaves inside out. It's almost an invitation to cross paths and change gender roles. My body is doing what it should some of the time now, but haltingly, without grace or confidence, and all at once I notice that my consciousness is with Kristy. I am her. In my head I am dancing as lady. My body is moving in the mirror, who knows how, and I am seeing with my mind not what I am doing, but what she is doing.

At the end of the hour, I am exhausted. "This is not fun; this is work. I hate this," I announce to our small group. I have a headache.

"That's why you need to keep doing it," Bill says. "You will get better at it."

Pretending to be more assertive is good training, though, and after a few more classes it leads me to a better understanding of how I behave as a woman. How I've taken some things about being a woman for granted. We have some exceptionally useful, albeit quieter traits. From these traits, exercised with a certain wiliness, comes our strength. A woman may appear to be a doormat, when in fact she is merely waiting for the right moment. She may seem soft, especially on the ballroom floor in her feathers and pastels, while she is in actuality tough as nails. It's not uncommon for the woman to be the driving force in the partnership on the floor.

I know how to get my way, and it's not with physical force. I call what I do at times—at work, socially, interpersonally—manipulation. No negative connotation there—it's just getting what you want without force, discreetly. People who use the word with only its negative connotation are simply revealing that they feel stupid for having been duped. Another word for this skill is diplomacy. For many years, I've treasured a saying: "Diplomacy is the art of letting someone else have your way." Diplomacy in ballroom dancing could translate as "back leading," through which the lovely woman gets the man to move where she wants him to, when necessary, by a sort of trick of reverse control, which looks of course like she's doing absolutely nothing. And he is putty in her hands.

I have a profound respect for feminine wiles (another term whose connotation undercuts the accomplishment). I remember using them when I worked in a magazine job with two men. I was the female in the triumvirate, and starting from down inspired me to use what strengths I had. This meant, for example, taking advantage of the fact that at an important black-tie dinner, I'd been seated, because I'm a woman, between the two most powerful men at the parent company. I had their attention; I was noticed, always a good thing for a career. My ambitious and competitive colleague Craig was insanely jealous, and you'd better believe I worked that angle. Despite coming of age during women's liberation, I am proud of my survival skills, the kind that are activated when I'm in a midnight blue Armani sheath and stiletto heels.

There surely must be some Darwinian function to the captivating feminine traits like elegance and glamour. Elegance comes easy for me. Bill has actually told me a couple of times that I've got elegant down, but it's time to learn glamorous. The latter is more overtly seductive. When I extend into a pose, I should milk it fully, in every inch of my body, from the way I arch at midspine to the length of my neck and the angle of my chin. I'd like to be overt, but something inhibits me. "Think Grace Kelly versus Marilyn Monroe," he suggests. "Elegance is a whisper; glamour is a shout." I think of my secret fear of Latin dancing that's intensified since I've been concentrating strictly on Standard. My confidence on the floor is specific to Standard; I know how to project a cool elegance and to operate pretty well with a partner. Latin requires a woman to be much more out-there sexy as she writhes and undulates in the open. A successful ballroom dancer must command attention with her outrageous glamour and her unquestioned belief in herself. The very idea scares me. I'm hesitant to make that much noise or take up that much space—in all honesty, to be unabashedly womanly—but I'm hoping one day to get over my inhibition, and to not be laughed at when I try for Marilyn.

A COUPLE OF months ago, I was on Anguilla, the tiny island in the Caribbean, researching a story for *Town & Country* about luxury hotels. My mother discovered "the least of the Lesser Antilles" in the 1960s, before it became chic and overrun with luxury resorts—in fact, before it had electricity, running water, or paved roads. We've always stayed with family friends, the Gumbs, at their Rendezvous Bay Hotel. This time, I was staying at the incredibly luxurious, private, and romantic resort called Cap Juluca. One afternoon, I tried a session with Dana, a yoga teacher from St. Bart's, called Coming Home Transpersonal Therapy. Dana's report, after holding both my hands in hers through the session and going into her transpersonal trance, was this: "I don't know why, but I saw TR and the Rough Riders. You know, Theodore Roosevelt. In your past life, you were a Polynesian princess whose beloved was a diver with beautiful hands, and one day he dove down and never came back up." What the hell was she talking about? "You have a beautiful bliss body as surely as you have a flesh-and-bones body—you have a beautiful woman in you, but she is in disguise. It is as if you are in drag." She said this without euphemism or tact. At the time, I was kind of shocked and I dismissed it as an out-of-left-field comment from a flaky yoga quack. But over time, I came to see what she meant. I was relying on my masculine qualities to manage my household and the exigencies of my working life, and letting some of the feminine qualities fall by the wayside. I'd become a tough, self-sufficient, I-can-handle-anything kind of guy. So the question is: how come I've had such trouble channeling the masculine out on the dance floor? Why am I such a girlie girl out there?

WITH MONTHS OF practice at our Monday class and during practice sessions with Rufus, I see some improvement, but I never come to like being the man. But learning to dance as man has made me more conscious of the fact that we all have some combination of masculine and feminine traits in us. And in class, I need to call up more of the masculine in myself. I am Sly, see me dance. I think of it like using two hands on my backhand in tennis. Why use just one when you've got both? Why not use straightforward force on occasion, as Sly does? I *can* be more like a man. And being able to be more manly, I relish more than ever being a woman.

Soon enough, it's time to decide about taking the exam. My fellow students refuse to let me skip it. In a private moment after class one day, I go to Bill to talk about the test. "I really hadn't planned on it," I remind him.

"Yes, you know, at first, when I recommended you take the class, it was just with the idea that it would help you get oriented in the room, and more familiar with patterns and technique. But now," he says, "it turns out you're the best in the class. You show that you have a very good mind. You're inquisitive. You study. You're serious. I think you'd do very well."

ON EXAM DAY in early December, I punch the off button on my alarm clock when it rings at 4:30 a.m. I shower, do my hair and makeup, dress, and head downstairs to leave in pitch darkness. As I reach for my dance duffel, I find tucked in it a note from Peter, who is fast asleep upstairs. It says, "Enjoy the fruits of your labor." I am too pressed for time and too keyed up to feel the full effect of this unexpected and sweet missive, but I am touched fleetingly as I grab my gloves and the car keys and head out into the cold.

It's barely light outside when I arrive at the studio. We all prepare in nervous silence. I change into my black dance skirt, a moss green velvet top, and my pale lavender ballroom pumps, and I walk over to the benches and sit by my dance bag to take one last look at my notes. I look up and see that Bill has finished scraping the suede soles of his dance shoes with a little metal-bristled brush. He looks cute, if old-fashioned, in his navy cashmere V-neck and red bowtie. I make a motion to borrow his brush, but he gallantly scrapes my shoes for me.

The dancing part of the exam takes twenty minutes. First, Bill and I dance together—we do our waltz, foxtrot, tango, quickstep, and Viennese waltz routines—and then I dance as man with Kristy while the examiner, Peter Billett, a coach I know from the old days, stands watching and making notes on his clipboard. My nervousness has converted to a sharp focus as I execute figures. Sure enough, I turn back into a lady during a Weave, but overall it goes well. Then I dance as lady with Ariel. My oral exam, behind closed doors in one of the private rooms with Peter Billett, takes three hours, longer than for most students, I'm told. I feel sheepish—it's because I like to talk. He does too, evidently. The geisha shows up and distracts him for a bit, but then the good student takes over and shows her stuff. When I'm done, just after noon, I sit with the others while Kristy is in the private room. Later, she and I fall asleep together on the benches along the wall of windows, waiting for the others to finish. We wrap ourselves in our coats because the wind whistling through the old windows is frigid. At the end of the day we learn our results and receive carbon copies from the examiner. Everyone has done well. I have passed with highest honors a test I never intended to take, and I feel a rush at being part of an elite corps in the ballroom.

"HOW'D IT GO?" Peter asks when I walk in the door. It's late, 10:30 or so. The group of us dancers had a celebration dinner at a nearby restaurant and then I drove home, utterly exhausted.

"I passed. Highly commended." I kick off my too-high heels and walk to the living room in my fishnets.

"Good for you. Now you can relax. Man, you worked hard on that. You're a pit bull."

"Yeah, I know. I'm glad it's over. Thanks for your note, by the way. How are the girls?"

"Fine. They wanted to stay up but I wouldn't let them. You can tell them in the morning. You didn't dance in those, did you?" he asks, glancing at my fishnets and tight black faux-leather skirt.

"No, I changed for dinner."

Maybe he was judging me for dressing provocatively, or checking up on me. Clearly I have caught his attention. It's possible he's jealous—I don't dress like this for him anymore. And I have my private life now, my separate friends. I have taken my lead from Peter, who's always drifted off without saying where he's going, always had things going on I don't hear about. Maybe it's my turn. Even so, it's awkward here at home.

A FEW WEEKS after the exam, on the morning of December 31, Peter and I awake at the same time and speak about household matters. I mention the new cleaning woman, whom Peter will be responsible for paying. We've always kept our finances separate and I've paid most of the bills, but I refuse to cover the cost of a cleaning woman because housework is the big issue for us. It would be nuts for me to settle the argument between us by hiring a cleaning woman and then also paying for the services, letting Peter off the hook in both regards. No way.

"I'll be able to afford it if I stop seeing my shrink." He lays that on me casually like that, I assume to make a point about how little I know about him these days, how abandoned he feels, how little he thinks I care. I am surprised, shocked even, and maybe a little angry that he's kept a secret like this from me, but my pride makes me hide my reaction, and I ask him how long he's been seeing a shrink. "A year." It's telling, a moment like this, of the distance between a couple in a king-size bed—that they can know so little about what's going on in each other's lives. Partly to deny Peter the satisfaction of having put me off my balance, I tell him that I think it's good he has an outlet, an advocate. I don't know how to say, "Oh, God, Peter, I'm so sorry I didn't know, I'm sorry you felt like keeping this to yourself. What's become of us?" That compassion is not within reach.

Then I start talking about us: "We've tried, and nothing's worked. It seems pointless to me to keep trying." He's mum. I keep at it. I mention the possibility of joint custody and what might work for us. It's possible that this is my unconscious surprise tactic in our volley. I know he hates talking about the D-word, and in this conversation a part of me enjoys taking him aback with my candor. It's not just wanton meanness spurring me on, however. Up to now, we've had just a few incomplete and rather too casual conversations about splitting up. Now that he's set a new tone by revealing himself, I'm up for letting down my guard and saying it out loud: "I'm tired of living like this. I want something more, something . . . that feels better."

At last, we openly discuss other possibilities rather than pull the veil over them. I say I'm not happy. I don't want to sustain a life of tension and dishonesty anymore. I've suddenly realized I don't have to. But Peter says he can't afford his own place. And with that, we both seem to sense it's time to get out of bed to face the day. I feel some relief. Even though nothing has been decided, this feels like a breakthrough, because at last we're not ignoring the bedraggled entity known as "us." In retrospect, the pretending has exhausted me. I feel dazed at the prospect of mammoth change, but now it's time to make pancakes with Alden and Erica, and the topic goes out of my head for the day.

Paradoxes, Ambiguity, and Separate Bedrooms

I DIDN'T USED to like paradoxes. They annoyed me. And I was always trying to unravel the contradiction to find the absolute truth, as if such a thing existed. In dance, I bang into paradoxes regularly. For instance, Bill might tell me to let go completely, but survive. He'll say, "Be light, light, light," but at the same time I'm supposed to be "a world-class lump," a solid blob, not something ethereal that he'll have a hard time steering. Try your utmost; don't try at all. Anticipate; but be in the moment. Stay on him and fly backwards.

Until recently, I would look at him and say, "That's impossible." He'd smile at me, as if I were the grasshopper character in a kung fu movie, a young neophyte, and say, "Just give it a try." His knowing amused and frustrated me. Obviously, you can't execute opposites simultaneously. I can't let go completely without falling down and becoming a puddle on the floor. I can't stay *and* go.

Nevertheless, the music starts and off we go one fine day, me with two opposite instructions in mind and Bill in no rush to show me the resolution. He knows I have to find it myself, the bastard.

This is where faith comes in. It has taken me a really long time, almost a year of gentle urging from Bill, to get what "letting go" feels like. I've been bracing and holding on tight to my own self for so long that I don't know any other way. The muscles haven't had the experience of releasing. Now we're waltzing and I don't know when or how it happens, but I give up. It is not intentional or conscious. There just arrives a split second when, inexplicably, I let go of my weight between the three and the one counts, let it drop into the floor without deliberately putting it there. I feel like Jell-O, all wobbly and rubbery, and I make a loud whooping sound. But my body is too quick for disaster to befall; it knows what it's up to. Before I can end up a melted blob on the floor, it has me up perfectly between the one count and the two. Oh, what a rush—the inside of me is like an amusement park ride, but I've done it! I committed to giving it up 100 percent, not 75 or 80 percent, trusting in something to pull me out, and it worked. This first time has sapped all my energy. But within minutes I do it again, at less cost to myself, and I manage the lilt of the waltz, the letting go and surviving, without screaming or giggling. The paradox has resolved itself through my body, as opposed to by some exercise of logic in my brain. There has to be some intelligence in the body that the brain doesn't manage. It hides in me. Counting on its being there, that is my faith.

Eventually, I start to meet new paradoxes with delight instead of consternation. "Stay and go" is less scary than letting go, but equally puzzling. Staying means I must alight like a bird on a branch—my arms, torso, and thighs on my partner—and remain there in a reassuring way for him. It's an awful feeling in dance when your partner pulls something away, a hip, the rib cage; you feel like part of you has abruptly collapsed. Bill says it can also feel to him like being smothered, which I find surprising; if I take myself away, I smother him? The worst part is, when you pull away, your partner has no reference point, and the couple loses its bearings altogether; you are adrift on the floor. But it's quite tricky to "stay" while you're propelling yourself around the room. Imagine trying to breathe in and breathe out at the same time. When Bill instructs me to stay but fly away, I meet the task with what I now know to be the only reliable tools: a shrug and an "oh well." I don't know what to do to accomplish both things, so I just give it up, as they say, to a higher power. *Oh well.*

Meanwhile, I of course have to tell my brain it isn't going to get any satisfaction for now. Poor thing, it's programmed for resolution, isn't it? I don't think my heart or my soul or my gut cares much one way or the other about paradoxes, but the brain is compelled to eliminate inconsistencies, the stuff that doesn't conform to the logic of its software. At least *my* brain is. It's the bully, and it has subjugated the body, imprisoned the heart, and tied the gut in knots. But slowly, dancing is standing up to the bully. That is, by dancing, something in me is called upon to stand up. What is that mysterious and invincible thing, not quite the psyche, nor the heart nor gut, but something that intersects all of those, perhaps the soul? All I know is, it is a wild thing.

I don't get to see the wild thing very often. When it makes one of its rare appearances, it blows through like a gust of wind. I saw it once during a tango with Bill, while we were working on my getting fierce after Promenade Position in a forward-moving stretch of figures. The wild thing is like a cross between a flight of fancy and a Navy Seal. The wild thing knows, trusts, and accepts, while the brain is suspicious, guarded, and domineering. The wild thing can dance without looking; it sees and feels the floor with its soul, whereas the brain scans constantly in all directions via the eyes. Bill and I are standing in Promenade, both of us facing the same direction in order to move forward in a kind of V formation, touching on only one side with the other opened wide. He has told me I need to be less passive and take each step with more hunger. Of course, my socialized self has been trained not to be that imposing. But I'm torn. I want to please my teacher. I want to be great. Inhale. This is when the wild intelligence takes over. "Allow me," it says quietly. I don't make a conscious choice so much as I just observe. My quads now push hard, using the floor as leverage, and my ankles flex quicker and more deeply than ever before. We press forward with a burst of power and we cruise across that floor. I see nothing; I feel everything. Ordinarily, my brain would be running through its checklist but the wild thing is so flashy that we—my mind and I—have no choice but to go along with it. The brain tries to interrupt like the robot in *Lost in Space*—"Hey, this goes against regulations. This isn't logical!"—but nobody listens. The wild thing in flight is so lovely and inspired, it's undeterrable. When we arrive at the far corner, I am even more amazed than Bill, who says, "Good. Do it again."

SOONER OR LATER, if I get out of its way, the underlying lesson of a paradox reveals itself. Once I stop demanding explanation from the universe, I am able to stay and go simultaneously. It happens when I stop thrashing about mentally. Hush—now, go! Like the wrist slipping itself out of the knotted rope, it is magic. To start with, I focus on staying—but not weighing Bill down, just being constantly there, my arms on him, light but definite, my ribs at him but not pushing at him, my hips and pubic bone settled with his without blocking his way. We cruise along and I sustain my position. It's a subtle, internal thing. An onlooker would detect nothing except ease or fluidity.

Now that I know not to use my brain to command my legs, or my feet to propel me backwards in our foxtrot, I only ask to fly. I hold an image of me in my imagination, and she is in flight without effort. And as I do this, I never quit staying; this is not so hard, because all I need to do to accomplish it is to change nothing about my presence. I remain still in both senses of the word—I am serene and I have not yet departed—and I fly, holding two opposites in the air like delicate soap bubbles.

How do I know I have succeeded? There is the reaction from Bill, a "Yes," or "There, how did that feel to you?" He is always clear when I do something more excellent than what I have done before, and I invariably do something more excellent when I least expect it. In such instances, though, I know, even without my teacher's approval, because of the stillness in my head and the ease and simplicity of my movement. I am getting the hang of inviting the magic into my dance. I call up images of birds, soap bubbles, a woman in flight, and respect the power of these childlike pictures. My executive brain has to sit quietly and twiddle its thumbs. It is a big change in corporal management for me, and I don't want to jinx it by being too self-satisfied. I remind myself that this magic will take constant practice.

More confirmation that I am getting the hang of it comes from the audience. People in the studio have started to watch Bill and me fly around the room. Bill is dancing with more energy and expressiveness, he says, because of me. Another top teacher, Paul, has been telling Bill he should dust off his tux and get back into competition, with me. In the locker room one day, when I am changing back into my street clothes, Anne Marie, a shy woman and a beautiful Standard dancer, says, "Janet, you are looking really good out there. Really good. I've been watching you. You're a lovely dancer." I pause in putting on my tights to look her in the eyes and say thank you.

The beautiful paradox in dancing and in life that has taught me the most is that my strengths are my weaknesses. Physically, I am a very flexible person. As a young girl, I could do splits in all directions. This was an advantage in gymnastics and dance; it was even handy on the tennis court. But my orthopedist told me that it made me more vulnerable to injury on the ski slopes, because I could fall in a distended position and blow out a knee. I never have, but maybe I owe him thanks for the warning.

The first time Bill danced with me as my teacher, he identified this flexibility and told me he used to be flexible, too, and it was his nemesis. The downside of my flexibility is a kind of amorphousness as a partner. I tend to be wiggly. My partner needs me to be predictable and constant in his arms, and instead, my natural inclination is to be too flexible, giving way with an elbow here, a shoulder there. Wiggly is very bad.

It's not enough to recognize my weak points. I must accept the strange duality: weaknesses lie on the flip side of strengths. They come as a package deal. I know that if I don't honor this duality, the weaknesses will rise up and bite me in the ass. Another strength, my self-reliance, is an all-American trait, good as apple pie on the surface, but it can be a detraction in partnership. And my brain itself is both a strength and a weakness. Knowing that is big.

An author I met at a workshop, Dani Shapiro, told a story about when she was first getting started writing her novel. She'd written thirty pages at one point, and when she later reread them, she decided they were terrible. So bad, in fact, that she tossed the hard copy up on a shelf with the dust and other discarded things, and she deleted the file from her computer. She continued writing. One day, Dani told her close friend who reads all her writing about these pages and the friend asked to see them. Dani climbed up and rummaged around the high shelf, found them, and gave them to her friend, who read them and said, "This is the best you've ever done." And this writing became the opening to her novel *Family History*. "What I learned from this," Dani said in this workshop, "is that what you think about what you are doing is none of your business."

Get out of your own way. To stop my brain's meddling, I sometimes do a body scan to see what feelings are happening around it, like in my jaw, in my belly, my knees. I deliberately focus on these feelings. When I'm dancing, I make myself listen better to the music, so that I am experiencing music instead of thoughts in my head. I keep at it, doggedly, but the brain is sly, and it quickly moves front and center again.

"Try letting the thought in and leaving it at that," Bill has said when I've protested that I don't know how to let the brain participate without dominating. He insists that you don't banish the brain on the dance floor; you let it do its job.

Well, good. I'm fed up with trying to get out of my brain and into my heart. Balance in dance isn't just physical: it's even more about using both the brain and the heart, the mind and the body. In order to be successful in dancing, says my teacher, I have to name my feelings (a hard task), then sort them out; otherwise, "they obstruct clear behavior and forward movement. There is no excellence with muddled or unexplored emotions." Okay, back to the fourteen-year-old girl.

But hang on a second. No excellence with muddled emotions? Isn't that idea a little too neat? Tempting in its tidiness? It would mean that artists like Jackson Pollock, Van Gogh, Mozart, and Balanchine had their acts together, wouldn't it? I'm not buying this yet. What if, instead—despite my teacher's pronouncement—excellence bursts through *despite* the muddle, indeed is born of the beautiful mess of human emotion, like a plant of the dirt? Can we really hope to ever fully sort out our emotions? Personally, the more I try to do that, the less I know for sure what's going on. Lately, I'm convinced that wisdom lies in tolerating the ambiguities and contradictions of life. Of myself.

ONE DAY IN early spring, Peter and I are driving to work in our new minivan, minding our own business as usual. It has been a few months since our last conversation about our marriage and we've settled back into our comfortable distance, with no mention of divorce. But somewhere between Ninety-sixth Street and Seventy-ninth, he brings up the subject of us. This is rare. Peter doesn't usually launch this topic, so I know I'm in for something major. All of a sudden I'm tense, and paying close attention. *Man the torpedoes.*

"Hey, Jan, I've been thinking. Neither of us is happy, and we both deserve to be. There's no affection between us. It's really sad." A strange relief has replaced my trepidation, but I still somehow fear what's coming—the unknown. I'm not in control here. *Is he about to ask me for a divorce?*

Despite the fact that we've talked about our unhappy situation before, tackling the subject head on now makes me jittery. I am my own best paradox. I can be so competent and assertive at the office, and even in our conversation a few months back—and I can be a diffident blob of wiggly Jell-O. "Alden and Erica are what's most important," he goes on. "I'm awake at night thinking about them. It would just kill them if we split. I want us to stay together, for them. But between us, we'd have an understanding. I'm not ready to give up on getting affection and giving it. I want an intimate relationship. It's pretty obvious you and I aren't going to have that again." We exit the highway at Fifty-sixth Street and head west.

Suddenly, I get where he's going. Bizarre, but this could be good. I'd be off the hook sexwise. I wouldn't have to feel guilty anymore. I've felt responsible for our lousy sex life and his not getting any, at least not from me, for so long.

"Do you mean, like, seeing other people? An open marriage?" I ask, half in disbelief, half intrigued.

"Yeah."

"I guess that could make sense. But I'm not sure how it would work, practically. I mean, I don't want to know . . ."

"There'd be nothing to know. We keep our private lives private already. Hey, we don't even socialize together now. Nothing would happen close to home. We'd just tell each other what the other needs to know, you know, like, I'm going to be out tonight, know what I'm saying? That's all. I don't see any other way to handle it without ruining the kids' lives."

I flash back to my parents' divorce. Did it ruin my life? I didn't think so; it had only brought some bad times. I knew at the age of nine that my parents didn't belong together. But I guess that's not the same thing as wishing they'd split up. I don't think Alden and Erica are fully aware of what's been going on. They don't see us argue much, but they know we don't see things the same way often enough, and we sometimes indulge in disrespectful sarcasm toward each other in their presence, which we both regret later, but that's really all they see. More important may be what they don't see: affection, intimacy. But they probably assume that their parents are together forever, and friction is part of the deal. Us separating wouldn't kill them, but it would crush them.

"I agree with what you're saying, Peter," I say, and I notice I'm feeling better than I have in a long while. "You deserve to be happy and to have what you want. This is weird, but—I think it's okay. I dunno, maybe it's best for now at least."

Peter pulls over to let me out on Ninth at Fifty-fourth. I look at him. He looks at me. We haven't looked at each other directly a lot lately, so this feels ticklish. Although I'm surprised by what we've just agreed upon, it seems right. As big a deal as this would probably seem to most people, to us, in the little private world we've created as a couple, Peter's suggestion seems logical given the persistent alienation we've both been enduring and our mutual devotion to our children. For us, this is a moment of real gravity and meaning, not because of the scandalous idea of us coexisting in a house and dating other people, but because here at last we are being open, honest, and, ironically, intimate with each other. In considering this solution, we are finally coming toward each other with compassion. We both want the other's relief, and release. And we have given these to each other here in the car.

"So, are you going to be out on a date tonight?" Peter asks playfully. This has always been his strong suit—defusing a situation with a touch of blunt humor.

"Ha, yeah, right," I say. I step out of the car and stand there at the passenger's side with the door open, facing him sitting there in the driver's seat looking pleased with himself or relieved, I can't tell. He lifts his right hand off the wheel and reaches toward me to shake. I take it and we shake hands like friends and wish each other all the best.

"Love is the revelation of the other person's freedom," wrote the Mexican poet Octavio Paz, and while I'm pretty sure he wasn't thinking of lovers parting ways when he wrote it, I do know there was love in that handshake, and it had something to do with honoring each other. I feel warmth for Peter again, and that has to be good. I feel grateful to him for starting the conversation today. I've been starved for affection of the manly kind, and since it's not going to come from Peter, at least now I'm free to accept it from another source. There could be something satisfying for me out there in my future. Something more nourishing and real than the thrill I get in the arms of other men on the dance floor.

Still, I can't picture "dating," whatever that means when you're my age and living with a husband and children. I have no desire to date. I would like to know successful real-life partnership, the kind I've been learning about on the dance floor, and yet it never occurs to me to try one last time to channel all that good energy toward Peter, who is still, after all, my husband. No, we have both left the scene, and we will choose others from now on.

DURING MY ANGUILLA assignment for *Town & Country* last fall, I came up with the idea to offer a ballroom dance program at Cap Juluca. I was having dinner with the hotel's manager, Eustace Guishard (Guish), a corpulent, well-traveled, bon vivant and Anguillian native with a taste for fine wines, five-star meals, and cigars. He'd surprised me with his reaction: "I love ballroom dancing. Waltz is my favorite dance. I'd really like to do this." It made sense: a romantic resort, couples getting away from their troubles and chores back home, having sex in paradise, enjoying each other. Dancing would fit right in.

I didn't think about it again until a month or so later when Sue, the marketing manager for Cap Juluca, called to say that Guish wanted to move forward with the program. I was taken completely by surprise, but game to talk about it. Hell, I've got plenty of free time, with children and a full-time job; why not go to paradise five times a year? She and I hammered out a five-day program and named it Dance for Joy. Then, I needed to enlist a teacher because even though I'd trained as a professional, and had a framed certificate on my wall, I had no real teaching experience yet.

So after my lesson one day, I craftily show Bill the brochure for Cap Juluca, with its stunning blue sky and sea and white buildings glistening perfectly in the tropical sun. I figure he is far too busy with teaching and judging competitions around the country to even consider flying down to the Caribbean to spend five days in castaway luxury. But I ask him anyway. "I need a teacher to go with me. Would you do it? I've been going to Anguilla since I was a little girl. It's great. You'd have a blast."

He studies the brochure, but doesn't say much. Nor does he say no. Sometimes I get carried away by my own enthusiasm, and in this case, I see I've gotten the organizers at Cap Juluca carried away too. Now I have to deliver. I know I could muddle through on my own, but I'm too chicken to try to pull it off, so I'm praying Bill agrees to go. It would be perfect; I could learn how to teach by watching him.

IN JUNE THAT summer, Dance for Joy becomes a reality. Bill and I fly to Anguilla via St. Martin and arrive at Cap Juluca at about two in the afternoon. We check into our rooms and get the lay of the land with the manager, Jeff, who has made all the arrangements for the five-day program. Our dance classes will be held in the air-conditioned library. The nightly practice sessions after dinner will be poolside on the tiled patio under the stars, by torchlight. The staff, who are mostly Anguillians, seem excited to be helping us launch the program. Though they are shy and formal around us, they seem keen to check out the talent from New York who've arrived to teach merengue and salsa, dances that originated in this part of the world, to other Americans vacationing here. It strikes me as hilarious because the Anguillians could most likely teach us a thing or two about merengue and salsa. We put a CD of merengues into the boom box to test it. Check. Then we try the jive CD. Check. Now the remote. Check. Bill shows me what he plans to start off with, a few basic movements. Then a simple social foxtrot going in a zigzag pattern around the room. The social versions of these dances are easy and casual—nothing like the strictly formatted, more athletically demanding dances of the competitive ballroom style we do back in New York. Social dancing is purely about enjoying your partner and the atmosphere. Okay, I feel relaxed. This should be easy enough.

Two women from the office in Cap Juluca uniforms are smiling as they watch us, swaying, lifting their heels as if they're ready to dance. I indicate this with my eyes to Bill, and he turns and invites them in. They're painfully shy, but it's obvious they're dying to step out on the floor. Bill walks over and extends a hand to Juniqua, who looks to be maybe twenty-five. She giggles and steps forward. They do the merengue and Bill is smiling ear to ear. This is the dance I learned on Anguilla when I came here as a little girl: all hip action, side to side, no upper-body movement. The merengue you'll learn in a dance studio in the states is nothing like this—it's a laughable version with flailing arms and overfancy turns. Next it's Lydia's turn. She's older, maybe fifty, a large woman with a confident air, and I get the impression she's about to show Bill how to dance. She moves her hips subtly but dreamily, with prowess that says she grew up moving to music and loving it.

We go to our rooms to change for our first class, which is at five, right after teatime on the terrace. I put on a short, flounced ivory skirt and a matching tank top, check the color of my legs to see how the self-tanner has developed, step into my Manolo mules, and take a moment to wonder how this came about, that on an island where I normally wear shorts, a T-shirt, and flip-flops, I am doing this— dressing up and acting like a dance teacher. My nerves kick in for an instant. I feel responsible, suddenly, for making Dance for Joy a success. I head downstairs to meet Bill. He looks so different in his tropical outfit: long white pants and beige linen shirt. We walk up the road to the main building. I'm about to find out how he teaches beginners. I only know he's terrific with high-level dancers on the competition circuit. *Uh-oh.* Now I'm worried that maybe he doesn't know how to do this because he's too good, and has no patience for beginners or for informal social dancing. *Did I make a mistake?*

We meet our group of five couples—husbands, wives, fiancés, honeymooners—at five o'clock sharp and I have them sign in. Bill asks each of them about their previous dance experience. Mostly, they've tried either group or private lessons back home in Philadelphia or Boston or Dallas, and they've been disappointed or too busy to keep it up. In all cases, the woman has dragged the man to the dance studio. Why is it men don't like to dance as much as women do?

We begin our first class. Bill has the couples stand separately at first in a line, and he leads everyone in an easy merengue action, small side steps, hips swaying. Some get the hips right; others make the common mistake of trying to move the hip of the moving leg in the same direction as that foot, when it's supposed to be the opposite: step sideways with the right foot, right hip down, and the left hip presses to the left. I help demonstrate and answer questions. The women stand behind me and try to imitate me. I glance at the palm fronds outside the window, and the sun's rays slanting through it make me squint. Suddenly, things seem to be going exactly as they should, and I feel a little wave of contentment. We wrap up with some swing and foxtrot. It has gone well and the partners seem cheerful at the end, eager for tomorrow's class. I hand each of them a schedule and tell them about our trip planned for Friday evening to Johnnos, the beach shack where a live band plays. "If you can stay awake that late, you'll love it," I say as they leave. "There's a fantastic live Caribbean band called the Mussington Brothers, which is not all boys and not all brothers. They're really good."

GUESTS WHO COME to Cap Juluca are mostly there for the privacy, sleeping late, long lazy beach days with sorbet served on the beach at four, piña coladas, boat excursions, romantic strolls, and those five-star meals that make them too sleepy to come to the nine p.m. practice under the stars. One night, we have seven couples in the air-conditioned library, cha-cha-ing to their hearts' content. For other classes, we have only two couples, so it is more like a semiprivate lesson. One time, I sit in an armchair and watch Bill give one couple a half-hour private. They start out typically enough: she saying she loves to dance and pointing a finger at her husband, saying he has no rhythm or won't take lessons. Bill looks into her eyes and says, "You know, we guys, we just want to please our woman. But we sometimes need to learn how to do that better. Let's work on that, shall we?" Well, that takes the wind right out of that woman's sails. She says nothing, and stops criticizing her poor husband, who I'm imagining is probably a terrific athlete and perfectly confident in his racquetball or tennis or football, and Bill goes on to help them do a foxtrot together without stepping on each other. I watch them struggle at first, looking down at their feet, shuffling tentatively. Bill shows the husband how not to pull the woman off her feet, and he shows her how not to push and fuss and to just enjoy the ride. Near the end of the half hour, I feel a full swell of joy for this couple who came in disillusioned, probably expecting little, and now are gazing into each other's shining eyes while they sashay easily around to Louis Armstrong, whom Bill refers to by his nickname, Satchmo.

These couples are rekindling their passion, and meanwhile, back at home, Peter and I have fizzled out. We still function okay as business partners keeping our household and our family life working as best we can, which, granted, often means bare minimum. We don't cook meals together at home; one of us makes dinner for the kids and we try to sit down with them, but as for ourselves, we each heat up leftovers, separately, to eat on our own. We do almost everything separately. He takes Alden for a bike ride, I plant flowers with Erica. He goes to Home Depot, I stay with the kids. He stays home with Erica to build a rabbit hutch; I take Alden out for sushi. He goes on a ski trip with his sister and brother-in-law; I stay with the kids. He stays with the kids, I go to Anguilla.

I am in awe of what Bill has fostered for this couple seemingly so casually. And here I was worried about his ability to handle beginners! It comes to me now that we aren't teaching these couples dance steps so much as we are teaching them partnership skills. Relationship strategies. Later that evening, at the banquet, one of the men from class, who struggled at first with foxtrot but then had a minor breakthrough, says to me, "You're not only teaching a dance class here; what you're doing is really an extension of marriage counseling." Yes, this is much better than showing them where to put their feet. Life would be so much easier if we only had to learn where to put our feet.

PETER HAS STARTED sleeping on the futon in our spare room. Though our king-size bed gave us plenty of room to be literally out of touch, sleeping, each of us, at a distant edge, it had become unpleasant to experience the intimacy of nighttime with him—accidental touching, hearing his breathing or his dream-state moans, seeing him naked in the morning. Now our huge bed is all mine, and I still sleep way over at my edge, near my nightstand gear: the alarm clock, the pens and pads, the valerian-root tincture that helps me sleep. And I'm happy not to be awakened through the night by his snoring. He can saw logs in the other room, which we call the red room because we painted its walls a deep, rich ochre color.

I notice our kids live with the ambiguity, but only up to a point. Mommy and Daddy aren't sleeping in the same room any longer. No big deal. But then, after a few months, comes a casual curiosity:

"Hey, Daddy, how come you sleep in the red room now?" Alden asks Peter one morning.

"You know, my back has been bothering me and the mattress in there is much better for it."

"Oh." And that is apparently a sufficient answer.

Do they notice, I wonder, that Mommy and Daddy play separately more and more? Never all four of us together. Maybe there is no ambiguity for them—it's all they know. Well, then, I guess it's about me living with the ambiguity.

I'm still lighting a scented candle every night at the kitchen sink to remind me of something. But what? What does the candle's light signify? I am a nomad. It could be the candlelight is showing me the way home.

12 No‑Fault Foxtrot

IT'S JANUARY OF the following year, right after New Year's, and Cap Juluca is fairly quiet. Only a few couples have signed up for the program, and I don't mind, I'm thinking as Bill and I arrive to greetings from all the Anguillian staff, who smile and welcome us back. It will be less hectic for me. Fewer people to organize and shepherd through their dance experience, which includes not just two lessons daily, but a yoga class, the after-dinner practice session, a gala dinner on the beach, and the Friday night field trip to Johnno's for dancing amid a wall-to-wall crowd of locals and tourists.

After we check in, a staffer drives us to our rooms with our luggage in one of the electric carts. "We should go back up to the library in forty-five minutes," I say to Bill before we each get settled in our rooms. "Class is in an hour. Come knock on my door?"

"Okay, see you then."

It's good to be back. I'm more relaxed this time. There are fewer unknowns to make me tense, though Bill and I are concerned about how many couples will show up. Three couples come to the first class, and a few more seem to be lingering by the door looking semi-tempted, but we don't succeed in luring them in. The men, mostly, are too shy to just give it a try. Well, anyway, not bad for this quiet time of year, and the manager keeps telling us these programs have to build slowly.

The next evening as I am dressing for dinner, my phone rings. It's Alden.

"Hi, sweetheart, what a surprise! How are you doing?"

"Mommy?" Her high, thin voice sounds unhappy or something—I can't quite tell.

"Yes, what's wrong?"

"Lucky's dead."

"What?" I'm horrified. How could that be? Our rabbit, who lived in a hutch outdoors, was fine when I left.

"He froze to death. Dad found him this morning."

"Oh, no, I'm so sorry. Oh, Alden, are you sad?" I can barely imagine. My vegetarian daughter who loves all animals and cares for them so tenderly. And our own pet froze to death in the subzero snap that I'm not experiencing because I'm enjoying the eighty-degree temperatures of the Caribbean. I feel overwhelmed with guilt. It's my fault. I should have known. I should have called and instructed Peter to bring the rabbit indoors for the night. Lucky died because I stopped managing. I want desperately to roll back the tape and start it again at the point where I was packing for Anguilla. I would listen to the weather report and think about the poor rabbit. Sure he has his fur, but being in a hutch out in the open, instead of down in a hole in the ground, he couldn't really stay warm. Why hadn't I thought about Lucky? I talk to Erica, who is sobbing; she tells me she saw his frozen carcass when Daddy was looking in the cage and she silently came behind him to see what the trouble was. He yelled at her to stay back, which scared her. But she was curious, as some kids are, to see the dead animal. I am crying when Bill comes in to get me for dinner. Poor Lucky.

When I return to New York two days later, I see his empty cage and start to cry all over again. The kids are strangely unemotional. Peter, it turns out, without me there to manage him, had imposed his system of coping with death, which is to go straight to denial. No big deal. It's over with. He wasn't a good pet, anyway.

"I'd like to have a funeral," I tell Alden and Erica. They ignore me. "Where's Lucky?" I ask Peter. He glares at me, so I keep quiet. But I know what that means.

I go outside in the dark night, around the corner to the trash bin, open up the lid and take out the trash can. I remove its cover and in the dim light from the porch I see a plastic bag full of garbage. I haul it out, put it down, and lean in to the can. At the dark bottom, I see another plastic bag, a black one. I pick it up gingerly and instantly feel the weight of a rabbit, lighter now without all his warm fluids. I feel Lucky, our frozen rabbit, his body so slight now. How could I have been dancing in the tropics while he was taking his last little breaths, falling to sleep, freezing to sleep? I lift him out of the trash and keep him safe in a Rubbermaid bin until I can figure out how to bury him.

On Saturday, I cry and cry and then I make calls. The vet can cremate Lucky, but Alden and Erica refuse to allow it. The pet cemetery will accommodate us for $1,500. No way. Our neighbor, Jimmy, a handyman, agrees to dig a hole with a pickax in our backyard.

"There's a lot of solid rock out there, but I think I got a hole big enough," he reports.

I pay him fifty bucks and carry Lucky out back to lead a service and bury him amid the bamboo, which he loved to eat. Nobody in my family joins me. This is my first solo funeral. I feel lonely. I keep apologizing to Lucky. I make sure to put him deep enough so the raccoons can't unbury him. I place his little wooden nesting box on top of the grave, and circle it with three metal, curlicue fencing pieces from my garden; I'll be able to see the site from our sunroom windows. I pray for Lucky, rename him Unlucky, and wish that just this once I hadn't gone dancing.

"WHAT COULD I BE doing to cause that?" Bill had just asked me. Come again? I can't be hearing right. Girls, there is a man standing in front of me asking what he *might have done to cause the problem*. I swear. That's exactly what he said.

My immediate response is to say nothing at all, in part because I can't believe my ears, but also because I surmise that he might answer his own question. That's right, blame himself. Just like a woman would. After living for all these years with Mr. Teflon, this seems too good to be true. Here's why Bill has asked the question: a moment ago, we got tangled up somehow in doing a Fallaway Reverse and Slip Pivot in our foxtrot, a nice, long flight of steps with a quick leftward pivot at the end, and he wound up "off his feet" as he says.

"What happened? What did I do wrong?" I asked, as I always do when something goes awry. I'm the student; it's got to be my fault.

"I don't know. I lost my balance." Bill has said this before, and at first I found it frustrating not to get a satisfyingly specific answer, but now I'm realizing this is a careful and respectful thing he does, bless him, saying only what he knows empirically, rather than presuming right away that the student screwed up.

"Let's try that again," he says. "I want to see if I'm doing something to cause you to step too far to the side on that third step." So even if it does turn out that I'm causing the problem, he's open to the possibility that it's him! I could hug this man. He knows something most of the couples I observe in the studio seem not to: that finger-pointing begets only finger-pointing, and life is short, and if you're going to take time to fix blame, defend, justify, find fault, and so on, you're not going to get much dancing in. I know because I did that with Peter for years. I've even done a lot of finger-pointing in my own direction. Bill, on the other hand, knows something about the value of neutral self-study as a substitute, a good way of producing a different (better) result in the future. Many couples stall out on the floor to argue. I see it all the time, especially among the temperamental, melodramatic Russians, who've suffered through too many long, depressing novels. And I endured it myself with Yuri. It does seem to be a waste of time, except when it's a case of the woman standing up to a man who is being a bully.

Placing blame—something couples out in the real world tend to get remarkably good at, which makes them really tedious at dinner parties when they indulge in front of a captive and uncomfortable audience—is tied up with the need to be right, or blameless. I know this because I have been right most of my life. Peter and I were the perfect dysfunctional couple stuck in our opposite corners, me being maniacally productive, he the laid-back Colorado-type hippie with a knack for simply being, which to me meant he never got anything done. I was a manager; he was Peter Pan, or maybe one of the Lost Boys, looking for Wendy to manage things. And he shunned blame as if it were a disease, while I, despite a fervent need to demonstrate my rightness and blame him, had an internal mechanism of self-blame and its switch was stuck in the on position—it's my fault; I should have; I shouldn't have; if only I'd . . . This private, insatiable appetite for blaming myself, curiously, drove the need to publicly establish my blamelessness. It was enough to cause a girl to lose her mind, such fraudulence.

I wonder how it would have worked if Peter and I had been dance partners. Both adamant in our blamelessness, one of us secretly taking all the blame regardless. The dance would likely have been a bumpy ride, an untrue dance limping along—hardly something lovely to watch. On the other hand, if Peter and I had been able to ask, "What could I have done to cause that?" I know it would have led to good things. I wouldn't have felt so defensive. Had he ever asked that question out loud in my presence, I might have been more willing to look at myself and my own failings rather than point the finger at him all the time. See? It's always his fault.

"Yes, I think that's it," Bill is saying, and his words draw me from the walkabout in my psyche back to our dancing.

"What is?"

"I was being too strong with this arm, and it was pushing you sideways. Still, I think you could resist a bit more. Let's do that Fallaway again and see if you notice a difference."

We do, and it feels so much better. Is it because of the technical adjustment alone, or because I am dancing with a man who doesn't mind being wrong?

As for Unlucky the rabbit, a few of my friends have asked me since why I blamed myself for his ugly demise. It's true, I'd wondered only what I did wrong: did the omnipotent mother really blow it this time? How could I have left home in the dead of winter without having made arrangements for Lucky in case of a subzero snap? Then a friend suggests it might have been Peter's responsibility, since he was home, and I think, oh good, I can blame Peter; what a relief. Any complaining, angry wife in her right mind would have blamed her husband. After all, she was away on business, he was home. He should have brought the rabbit in. I'm zipping along on this tack, but it stalls out once I take a second to reconsider; how could he be expected to take initiative or make executive decisions when I had taken on most of that responsibility for the entirety of our marriage? From where he sits, maybe it feels like in our home he's always done what he's been told—except when it comes to the cars, the computers, and the preset stations on the radio. But now I'm starting to realize I can't go on forever hogging the blame either—for Lucky and for everything else. It's not producing the desired results. It's wasting time. The only useful question here is a nice, neutral, What might I have done to cause this problem?

And my answer is easy: I overmanaged. There, not so hard. Unlucky is dead, nothing to be done about that, but next time, next partner, it won't happen again. And I won't harvest punishment for going to paradise.

13 PASSION IS A CONTACT SPORT

W HAT IS THE purpose of balance?" Bill asks me one day when we stop waltzing to stand in a corner and talk about how something in our dance went wrong, and what might be done to improve our connection, or my body position, or our flight.

He loves putting questions to me and I still love the opportunity they present to quit momentarily the hard task of integrating body and mind, and just to rest for a bit in my mind. Like most good teachers, I suppose, Bill has a few catchphrases he'll use with his students—or, rather, catch questions—and he has a delightful answer ready if the student doesn't come up with something on target. One of his very first questions to me was "Which member of the orchestra does the dancer correspond to?" I stood for a few minutes, thinking hard, with images flashing through my brain, and then said tentatively, "The conductor?"

"Yes!" Bill said, looking very pleased that I'd got it. Boy, did I feel like a smarty-pants. The dancer describes the music with her body in perfect timing, anticipating to make a picture of the melody just as the song is heard, much like the conductor does with his body and a baton. Another time, he asked me, "Who is your best teacher?" I couldn't imagine he wanted me to answer, "You are, Bill." And he didn't. "You are your own best teacher," he told me, and I had to believe this man who'd been teaching ballroom dance for over forty years.

At this moment, I am deep in my mind searching for the answer to his question about balance. I mutter something about staying upright, but he shows me how a dancer, or a child even, maintains balance in a beautifully cockeyed position having nothing to do with staying vertical.

"The purpose of keeping our balance is to protect the brain," Bill announces. "We human beings, we have these large heads with great big brains in them, and we must protect them. Without the mind, we don't survive." And so I come to grasp the Darwinian theory of balance. Everything I do with my hips, my knees, my feet as I move through space to romantic music is for the protection of my ample brain. Got it.

NOT LONG AFTER this, during my private lesson after our regular Monday class in the studio in New York, I am enjoying the tango music and my theatrical position, with my head way out to the left, my left elbow practically in New Jersey, and my right hip balancing all that leftwardness nicely, just like Bill said it should, and my brain is safe. We are doing pivots, one after another, so the room is spinning, and I am not panicking. No panic at all. In fact, I might be feeling a small amount of pleasure. Like a child on a swing as it swoops down toward the ground, then up, toes pointing to the sky, wind blowing through golden hair. The staccato music of fierce and insistent passion, then the legato interludes, the windows open to the warm new breeze of the spring day, my body in a position that feels just right, my left arm holding tight under Bill's right upper arm, our other hands clasped high, our movement together sharp, crisp, and fast like Thoroughbred horses. Whoom, whoom, whoom, we are carving these pivots, counteracting huge centrifugal force, and then—CRACK.

Louder than any noise I have ever heard, and so close to my ears. A ringing. Where is the floor? Loud ringing in my head, and I am dropping to the ground, slithering through Bill's arms, his belt buckle scratching my cheek, down his legs, he can't hold me up, I am a rag doll. So loud it hurts and spills out into the room, then back into my head. Where did it come from? What happened to the music? People are gathering too close. Leave me alone here on the floor. It hurts.

Someone is pressing ice to my head. I have not lost consciousness. I can see, and the light is too bright. I squint. Two men help me walk over to the benches. I lie down and hope the queasiness won't worsen. I don't want to vomit in front of all these attractive dancers. I want to rest. No, I should get up and dance again. Back on the horse. I sit up. Now I see Yelena, the other woman. She has a lump the size of a peach on her forehead, the evidence of the back of my head. She is crying, her mascara running down her cheeks. Her face is red. She looks scared. We look into each other's eyes without saying anything, but there's an apology between us in this aftermath of a horrible tango crash. Our heads collided, our skulls cracked together, mid-flight, at top speed. How is it possible we are both conscious?

Passion is a contact sport. My brain, I trusted it to Bill, who is in charge of our direction in the dance traffic. And yet, I know, because this is his teaching, that we are both responsible here. I'm not navigating, because I am for the most part flying backward. I must trust him to watch my six, as SWAT team leaders say. I am not angry; he is one of the most skilled in the business. Accidents happen. But still, I wonder, Why did this happen? I know perfectly well why, and so does everyone else in the studio. It is Richard Gere's fault. He is training in our studio for his role in *Shall We Dance* with Jennifer Lopez. He is learning to waltz and he requires a private space, which obliges the managers to curtain off one end of the rectangular main room. Our room has become a square, and this changed shape confuses other dancers. Bill knows what the new traffic rules are, but others don't. Richard owes me a dance, as far as I'm concerned, for getting me conked in the head.

I stand to dance again. Bill is not sure we should, but I insist. I am a little shaken, but okay. I imagine for an instant that my weakness now is probably good for my dancing; it makes me more pliant.

The next morning, I go to the radiologist for a CT scan and learn the obvious: I have a concussion. Not a mild one. I am told to pay attention to my headaches (no problem there) and nausea, any vomiting. I am supposed to be quiet, resting, no dancing. I take a few days off.

For months after the collision, when Bill and I dance, I try so hard to be brave, but with my head way out there, I can't let go of my fear. Without realizing it, I am dancing more upright, and I have stiffened. Often, as we fly around a corner, I flinch when I see a couple too near in my peripheral vision. This seems to annoy Bill, who is usually so solicitous and unflappable. I think he's resisting feeling bad that it happened, struggling to reconcile his belief that dancing is a joint venture with no leader and no follower and his desire to protect me, because he is the man, the . . . leader. I feel bad for him; I don't blame him in the least for what happened. He used to say to me, "You can trust me," when we were working on a pose or something else requiring me to reach or stretch way beyond what I thought was possible. He would hold me up. "Trust me. I won't let you fall." He didn't. I never bring this incident up with Bill, and after a few months I stop flinching.

During this time, I ruminate a bit about trust. My conclusion is that it's about trusting yourself, and taking responsibility for your own safety. I have so yearned to hand it over to someone else. I still do. But this is nothing more than a childhood fantasy, a fairytale foisted on me, and oh boy did I eat it up way back when. Count on other people, that's fine, but don't have everything hinge on being able to trust them; trust yourself, I say to myself, again and again. But I think I'll always want to be taken care of.

One thing I do know for sure: trust comes with no guarantees that you won't get hurt, no guarantees of success, no medals. Bad things happen to brave people. But trust does something far more valuable. It allows you the possibility of something happening—experience, and if you're lucky, the monumental experience. Trust is your ticket into the game. Risk is part of the deal. The payoff is survival. Bad things happening—in dance, in love, in anything—is not the worst thing. The worst thing is nothing happening. The worst thing is protecting ourselves from experience. The bad things happening is out of our control; all we can control is how we face them.

How do we let go of the fear of the bad things? I think of the film *Finding Nemo,* in which the frantic father fish, distraught over his missing son, who's caught up in a hapless adventure far from home, says to Dory, the charmingly loopy girl fish, "I promised I'd never let anything happen to him." And Dory says, "Hmm. That's a funny thing to promise . . . You can't never let anything happen to him. Then nothing would ever happen to him. Not much fun for little Harpo." Nothing bad, but nothing good either.

Perhaps Bill and I have become too close. I don't know if it's a natural progression for a teacher–student relationship, but in the past year or so, we've gotten closer and closer, even a bit entwined. We've come to the point of overinvestment, knowing so much about each other, caring about each other, which starts to complicate the teaching and the dancing. To be perfectly professional, which of course nobody is, we would be keeping our emotional needs out of the picture. Instead, I've just been tumbling along impulsively, as if conventional wisdom doesn't apply to me. Right from the start, I drank up Bill's attentiveness, his eagerness to communicate, and his other loving qualities, and early on I came to see him as everything wonderful that Peter, and Yuri, were not for me, forgetting that he is just my dance teacher. Not the sort of thing one can exactly say "oh well" to. I get the impression Bill has done the same. He has come to value dearly my view of him.

IT IS A pleasant Wednesday afternoon in the studio, and one of the other teachers just cranked up the volume on a rumba that has an ir-resistibly captivating rhythm, and it impels me to move my hips slightly. Latin champions, the best in the world, regularly practice or coach here, and I often glance over to them with a longing to be more like them, more overtly sexy. Bill takes a few steps toward the Latin practice area, his right arm extended behind me, hand out-stretched backward to me. My stomach flips. He wants to do International Latin with me. *I can't! I'm no good. I haven't done any real Latin since the comp with Sergei! I'm a Standard dancer now.* Too late. I follow, giving him my right hand, putting my left on his shoulder. I'm dying to somehow, miraculously, be able to writhe, to move my hips in that unctuous way the professional Latin dancers do so automatically. I can be uninhibited at home, alone, or in front of people who don't know how to dance, and I feel relaxed at Cap Juluca, where we do social dancing, which is so easy and less flamboyant. But trying International Latin here in front of Bill—one of the country's top judges—and all these accomplished pro-fessionals, I'm nervous and uptight. I want to be perfect before anyone sees me; this improvisation isn't supposed to happen. My body is a foreign thing I can't control. I'm dancing high, not down into the floor, skimming, wooden when I want to be gorgeous. At twenty-something I could do this, but it's been so long. *Oh, please, let this music stop!* The song is still playing, but Bill stops after an underarm turn when I end facing him. We drop our hold, and I ex-hale in relief.

"Oh, I see," he says to me, looking very judgelike with his chin tucked slightly, "you don't really *dance,* you just do the steps." Yup, I'm no Marilyn Monroe. And I want to shrivel up and disappear.

PETER AND I KEEP up our nutty pattern—separate lives, separate bedrooms—for months, hunkering down in our corners, then coming out with our dukes up, back and forth, until the moment comes when we decide, really come to a decision, to call it quits. It is after my trip to Machu Picchu, a plum assignment for *Town & Country* entailing a five-day hike at astronomical altitudes to Peru's mystical ruins, with time in Cuzco and Lima. I'm thrilled to have survived four nights in a tent, not to mention eighteen thousand steps up Andes mountainsides along the Inca Trail and another eighteen thousand steps down—for which, if you'll permit a brief interlude for boasting, I'd trained by climbing forty flights of stairs in my office building three times a week. But the personal trainer I consulted attributed my fitness for the mountain to ballroom dancing—she said it was terrific interval training.

I had a fabulous time in Peru, but I've missed the girls a lot; I've never been away from Alden and Erica for so long—nearly two weeks—since they were born. So naturally, I am incredibly excited to be coming home. I arrive at the front door, having noticed there is no car in the driveway, and find the house quiet. I kind of expect Peter and the girls to be waiting for me, maybe with a welcome home sign, even. No such luck. No one home. They must be out doing something. But, gee, I bet Alden and Erica are really excited to see me. Why does Peter not have them here? He knows what time I'm due home . . .

I walk into the kitchen to look for a note from him. No note. I see only dirty dishes on the counters, not just in the sink, but everywhere, and the peanut butter jar left open, the bread, the bag of pistachios. My spirits, so elevated in Peru, sink to a new low as I stare at the garbage disposal switch. I thought I might have an epiphany at the magical Inca ruins under the full moon that lit the night of our arrival there. Instead, I have one here in my filthy kitchen where love and thoughtfulness are absent. *Screw the compassion. What's broken here can't be fixed. Accept it.* And that is that.

"I'M GOING TO look for an apartment, but I can't afford much." Peter surprises me with his announcement. I haven't asked him to move out, haven't assumed he'd be the one to leave. I would move out—but I'm pretty sure he doesn't want to be primary custodial parent and I'm sure that I do want to be. I've heard of a new arrangement by which the kids stay in one house and the parents rotate in and out. This makes divorce a little easier on the kids. I read about this in the *Wall Street Journal* and mention to Peter that I think it could work. But then I imagine some other woman in my house, sleeping in my bed, using my china. Never mind.

First comes the difficult task of telling Alden and Erica. We learned what to say in a session with our mediator. I am the designated conversation starter—Peter and I both knew I'd have to be, mainly because I'm braver in such circumstances. We have waited until after Halloween, so as not to wreck this most important holiday. Friday evening, when Peter and I get home from work, we decide to get it over with right away.

"Alden, Erica, come on over and sit here with me and Daddy. It's time for a family meeting," I say. We never have family meetings, so this immediately catches their attention and they stop horsing around and look at me in a state of alert. Peter is sitting in his black leather chair looking stunned.

"Daddy and I have decided to get divorced," I begin. I use all the right language our mediator gave us about how we did love each other once, and tried to work it out. I say what you're supposed to say about who's living where, to reassure the kids that nobody's going to be out in the cold. As I speak, Alden, the one I thought would be stoic and suppress her feelings, instead collapses in tears on the floor and lies on the dog moaning. She starts to tremble and hyperventilate. Erica, meanwhile, doesn't believe a word of it. She looks at me for confirmation that this is a gag. Peter and I insist it's true. Then she joins Alden for a bit on the floor, her face streaming with tears. Next come the questions: Why does Daddy have to be the one to move out? Where will we be? And where will *we* be? Here? There? Where? While Alden sticks like a tick to Cookie, Erica gets the phone and calls her best friend, Katrina, to tell her the news. Twenty minutes later, things are calming down. Only the familiar buzz of my own adrenaline keeps me from collapsing in a heap of grief at causing my children pain. I go upstairs for a few moments with Alden because she wants to splash her face with cold water and find comfort in her own bedroom. When I come down, Erica is at the computer with Peter making a Power Point presentation, their favorite pastime.

"How do you feel now, Erica?" I ask.

"Well, if you'd told me, like, a few weeks ago that you were going to get divorced, I would have said, 'No, you can't, no way.' But now that I know you're not happy together, I'm okay with it."

Tears well in my eyes as I take in the strength of my nine-year-old child who sounds like a wise adult. She is the age I was when my parents divorced.

A few weeks later, I tell Pamela, my boss. We are in her office, door closed. Unexpectedly, I feel like I am admitting an awful failure.

"I'm sorry," she says, and I know she doesn't need to hear much detail as to why. "You know you're supported and loved here," she adds as she comes round her desk to give me a hug.

As the weeks go on, not on any particular schedule, I tell my inner circle of colleagues and friends. I wonder what the etiquette is. You're having lunch. The business acquaintance across the table asks, "How've you been?" And you say: "Oh, fine. I'm getting divorced." Or not. Sometimes I'd just say the "Oh, fine" part. There is always the need to help the other person hear the news.

"I'm so sorry" is one typical response. But another is: "Congratulations." Some women just know it's for the best, and that's the right thing to say. But I always steer them, both with my facial expression (cheerful) and my words ("It's good news," I say, to get over the awkward hump). I find young, newly married women friends take it the hardest. Heather, a thirty-something editor at *Town & Country* with a wonderful husband and an infant at home, looks like she's going to burst into tears when I tell her.

Often, people ask *why* Peter and I are getting divorced. Depending on my mood, I say something reassuring about us being too different, or if I am being really small and mean, I'll hint at how Peter fell short somehow, but now and then I say what I really believe: "We're getting divorced over the dishes."

And as flip as that may seem, I am dead serious. It's a joke. It's not a joke. All couples fight, and most fight over housekeeping issues. No one would actually let the dishes lead to divorce, would they? But now I know it's not just about the dishes really, and never has been. The dishes stand for something larger: the anger of disappointment overflowing like lava. The competitiveness. The erosion of the bedrock caring that sustains a marriage. If the dishes *are* a test, we both have flunked miserably.

ON GOOD DAYS, I manage to look at our success. We made children together! And they'd blossomed into two lovely young girls by the time we fell apart. We had something good for much of our marriage—love, fun, a home, our private jokes and cherished rituals, and little knowings of each other. We were a team, first two, then four. And one day, we were not. Four days after Christmas that year, Peter moved to an apartment a town away. No fanfare. Just . . . gone. He did tell the girls he'd show them his apartment that weekend.

It was hard to tell our unsuspecting children on that Friday after

Halloween. Nothing could have prepared me for the agony of breaking their home and breaking their hearts. But a couple of months have passed now. I watch them; I listen. I try not to push too many heavy conversations—just enough to keep emotional tabs. They seem to be doing all right, and I am relieved.

I get busy learning how to be a single working mother, which takes more courage and persistence than I could ever have imagined mustering. Over the next six months, everything that can go wrong does; major appliances break down conspiratorially—the car, the computer, the washing machine. I decide to look at it as a crash course in competence, and I'm learning all kinds of essential stuff I didn't pay attention to before. One day, for example, the upstairs toilet—a big old porcelain thing with its tank attached to the tile wall—falls away from the wall. *Oh dear,* I say as I walk into the bathroom first thing in the morning and see the tank leaning forward at an ominous angle, and some tiles unglued and about ready to fall off. *Was that always like that?* I peer at the thing, trying to recall. I look down to check for pipes and any telltale leakage, but I see nothing. Any other adult person on the planet would probably know to go shut off the water in the basement, but not me. No, I go to work and then call the plumber. But on the upside, I am lucky. The toilet doesn't crash to the floor before the plumber gets there. My plumber, Jim, is special; he tolerates all my questions, and he answers them all as though it's enjoyable to him, training me. So now I'm conversant with toilets.

I evade grief over the loss of my marriage by escaping cleverly into my necessary competence and productivity—until it comes time to clean out Peter's walk-in closet in our bedroom. No handyman can help me with this one. The door has remained closed since he moved out, as if someone died, and Peter has neglected to come and collect the contents. Inside are his clothes, shoes, travel gear, photography portfolios, stashes of paraphernalia, drawers full of socks, with memorabilia tucked in the back. Secrets. Treasures. The day I pack it all up and stow black plastic garbage bagsful in the shed is when a shock of sadness hits me. With each drawer I empty, I am an invader, and yet it is obviously time for his things to be gone. Why did he leave everything behind? I suspect it's got something to do with the fact that he has already set his sights on a new life, and acquired a live-in girlfriend twenty years my junior, and they have a new house together. Shiny brand-new everything.

It is a most intimate experience, being in his private space, and I realize that this is the closest I've ever been to him, here in his walk-in. I was never so in-his-space while we lived together, never shared these secrets. There is a gigantic metaphor here and I get it; tears spill to the floor as I find pictures of people I don't recognize, the EMT stethoscope he used to love to show me from his ski patrol days, and the ski instructor ID cards from before we met. Perhaps I should have asked him to tell me more stories about himself. Too late. His closet contains only ghosts and dust now. It suddenly looms—the opportunity lost, and I mourn a part of myself (the best, most generous part?) that was absent in our marriage.

Still, I know this marriage was not to be fixed. I can grieve for it without wanting it back, simply feel sorrow at the loss of a dream. And yet there is something I do want back. One Saturday afternoon not long after this solitary housecleaning, as winter recedes, I am outside raking the front yard when Peter pulls up and parks his car curbside to pick up our daughters for soccer practice. It's one of those brilliant spring days with a clear blue sky, sunlight sparkling off the sidewalk and warming my arms, and the gleeful shoots of my perennials shoving up out of the earth. I stand, rake in hand, watching as both girls climb into his car with a quick "Bye, Mom." I watch as the car drives down the street to turn a corner, disappear, bearing a family off to their Saturday adventure together. *Why am I alone and doing chores on this beautiful day?* But it isn't the work I mind. I stay still there for a few moments in the fragile sunlight to take in the delicate approach of spring and love turning a corner.

You're Not
the Boss of Me

ONTROL IS A beautiful thing in ballroom dance, any kind of dance, because with it you can master technique, and that frees you to be the artist creating something spontaneously divine and wonderful, something others enjoy watching. So how come control has a bad rap in real life, in relationships, and around the house, not to mention in the habitat of the psyche (as in "she has control issues")?

I've lived in my home for fifteen years, most of that time with a husband, thirteen of those years with children. I have maintained the house more or less successfully. Okay, it's been extremely messy for a long time, the kind of messy that means you can't invite people over or let the Con Ed man in without apologizing as he trips over stuff in the cellar, or find anything you need without putting out an APB. It got this way not only as our family grew, but also as Peter and I became more careless with each other and stopped being the happy couple puttering lovingly about the house. The decor is a mix of frayed flea market, Ikea, and Toys "R" Us. I pick up incessantly, and I sigh a lot. That's life with kids and two working parents (and then one) and lately no budget for a cleaning person. But these days I am developing my systems, routines, and juggling methods that seem to work well enough, judging by the health and happiness of my kids—though not yet by their habits of housekeeping, but we're gradually getting to that in between doing the homework, practicing the flute, walking the dogs, and sitting on the couch all three in a cozy row watching TV. That's quality time for me, and so is bedtime, which can take a full hour because both girls will start talking; they'll tell me what's going on in their lives, fill me in on their frustrations, hopes, and wardrobe problems. There's not a chance I'd trade this for tidiness.

I'm thoroughly absorbed in being the best mother I can be, and in keeping my current life together as I dissolve the previous one, but every now and then I find myself yearning for alone time. I need to refuel. Am I nuts that I'd rather be alone than have a social life? Since Peter left, I've had a few dates, and they're actually not as bad as I'd feared. I even ventured into one short-lived relationship. At first, I assumed my antisocial tendency was a shortcoming. But now my attitude has shifted to: *It makes perfect sense, thank you very much*. I get up at five forty-five a.m. and power through the day on adrenaline, stealing an hour to dance at lunchtime, and I come home at seven to throw together some dinner, do homework with my daughters, listen to their accounts of the day, sign permission slips, pick up a zillion little things that have landed on the floor since this morning, avoid returning phone calls, finish the laundry, do the bedtime thing with my sweet girls, take a quick bath to punctuate the day, and fall asleep in the tub.

When I get to be alone every other Friday evening into Saturday morning, it's just me and the dogs: Cookie, the muscular, dainty, and neurotic pit bull mix with soulful eyes, and Rizzo, the imperturbable rottweiler. I can be with them and still feel the benefits of being alone. Why is that? What is it about dogs? Is it merely that they don't speak? During this time, I wander about the house tidying and I turn on the television to watch or listen to CNN as I defrost a salmon fillet and make some salad. I think, I stare out the window, I write, I ride my exercise bike, I stretch my hamstrings, I pull everything out of a drawer or closet and sort and toss and reorganize. I talk on the phone with Julia, who also wanders around her house picking up while we talk. It's all very desultory. I love it. I doubt I'll ever be able to learn to meditate, but my Friday nights may do the trick.

It has now been almost a year since Peter moved out, and in this year I have enjoyed slowly, in baby steps, reclaiming the house. No more do I have to discover a paring knife jabbed into an apple core left on the sofa at midnight for the kids to sit on in the morning, or tolerate a giant heap of photo equipment gathering dust for months in the foyer and blocking passage. A nice contrast to the occasional sadness I feel is the sudden elation that overtakes me at the realization that comes in this corner of the house: I can redecorate! So I've been restoring more of a sense of order here at home. It's very slow going, because now I'm in charge of 100 percent of the household maintenance (guess I shot myself in the foot there, and I very reluctantly will admit that Peter did more than I claimed he did). But the cleaning and ordering do give me a nice false sense that my life is more in control. I'm trying to tap into the old Zen aesthetic I used to cling to as a young, single woman—empty fridge, shoes and Champagne stowed in the unused dishwasher, one toothbrush in the holder, not a thing out of place, not many things in the apartment to begin with, just a sofa, a coffee table, and a bed, and hardly any mementos. Kids and a Zen aesthetic are, of course, antithetical, so that degree of neatness is a distant fantasy now. Sometimes I tell myself it's better to appreciate the glorious messiness of a full life—but don't stop picking up, whatever you do, just in case the doorbell rings.

IN BALLROOM DANCE, two people dancing can be like two people having a conversation, but often enough, dancing is a one-man show—the man pulling and pushing his partner around. This is like when one person dominates the conversation, which then becomes a monologue. Although I didn't know it at the time, Yuri, my Russian with control issues, was one-person-dancing, and I was along for the ride. He was in control. Period. That's one reason I didn't stand a chance of being a good student, let alone a good dancer with him. With Bill, it's always two-people-dancing, or so he has said. It was clear to me from the get-go that I have a job to do in our partnership. I like this idea of dancing in which the woman is not simply following, and the man is not dominating. Ballroom dancing is less old fashioned than most people think.

The trick of good partnership dancing in my opinion is to walk a fine line of control. You need to be in control of yourself, your body and your emotions, without succumbing to the temptation to try to control your partner, or to be in charge of the "us" as it moves. I often see professional partners in the studio standing and facing each other, not dancing, because they've stopped to argue about who's doing what wrong. There's friction. He thinks he's right, she wants to get her way—or vice versa.

And yet, even if you stick to self-control, there are pitfalls. I found them in myself. There's functional control, the kind that allows you to master the fancy footwork and to stay balanced in an outrageous pose, and then there's dysfunctional control, which I can personally assure you is nothing more than clear and embarrassing evidence of your own complex psychological defense systems. This control is a sleight of mind by which you delude yourself, the illusion being that you are master of your universe and your future. This kind of control, fed by past traumas, is used as a pain avoidance maneuver.

Take the waltz, for example, a lovely, lilting dance everyone recognizes: one two three, one two three, swooping romantically to wistful music. In order to have the lilting quality, you have to use your knees and your feet to propel yourself up and down while traveling round the room. It was a big day for me when, in trying to learn this, or rather, in being frustrated by consistently failing to get it, I discovered that I'm not in charge of gravity. Seriously. I had never before accepted that I was in any way a control freak until Bill urged me repeatedly to let my weight go in the waltz. I tend to hold on to my mass for dear life, tensing my quads and torso in an ancient fear that letting go means total collapse—death! That day when I finally confronted the paradoxical command to let go but survive, I released my weight in reckless abandon during a downward whoosh—one two THREE—and I felt an extraordinary ease traveling through space. Wow! I realized right then that I'd been expending tremendous energy both to keep myself off the ground and to bring myself down to earth. How inefficient; gravity can do that for me, and isn't it perfect that a micromanaging working mother would think she controls even the forces of nature?

One of the great things about learning a big lesson like this through my physical body is that I can't ignore it. There it is: I can give up that silly control, let go and survive. The proof is there, right out in the open, on the floor—me, my skin, my bones, and my muscles showing me everything is going to be okay. And I can do it again and again. A useful side effect of such a lesson is that I can make fun of myself. Oh, the baggage I've brought onto the floor—suitcases full of wariness to make my dancing heavy.

No surprise that, when I came back to dance in my forties, I got busy managing my various body parts, heel here, shoulder blades there, tummy muscles engaged, etcetera, and I assumed I had to take care of everything myself. Did I even realize there was a man right there in front of me dying to help out?

There's a step called Hover Cross, in which the woman ideally acts a bit like a slingshot—if she can trust her partner and surrender. For a long time, I couldn't give in. Instead, I naively tried to manufacture the look of the figure using my own muscles and willpower. Bill kept stopping after the check to say, "Hmm, do you think we could try that again?" He said I felt like a lead weight; his biceps were killing him. I wanted so badly to rise to the challenge.

"I just need warning when you're going to do this step," I said. "Or more training."

"Ah, the trainer asking for training" is all Bill would say.

Let's try again. And again. Once more. Eventually, after many attempts, and after noticing that Bill's arms cradled me no matter what, I found the courage or lunacy to give in ever so slightly. Then a little bit more. Finally, I was a veritable rubber band, my spine amazingly willing. I was overcome with exhilaration. I'd had no idea how good it could feel to give in to my elasticity, get fairly horizontal, and let my partner support me through the danger. I'm supposed to support him in other figures, don't worry, so it works both ways.

I've often slipped back into old habits, being in charge, but there are times when I can enjoy being cared for—it feels womanly! Plus, I see that it gives the man a kick to do his job. Two points for my inner tango goddess.

Trust is hard, though. The surrender it demands was (still is) counterintuitive for me. Physically, for example, it means dropping defenses, thinking of my skin not as a protective barrier but as an organ of communication with my partner. No dance offers more of the heady pleasures of surrender, trust, and faith than the quickstep. In this spirited, zany dance, the woman runs incredibly fast backward without looking while the man steers. I'm a rational person; I was sure this wasn't smart when I first tried it with Bill. His eyes would light up at the opening bars of speedy music, and I was like a horse being backed into a trailer. But after a time, racing around the room backward grew less scary. Practice again softened my stiff resistance, and I've come to feel safe while surrendering my safety—my tight mind more willing to try new things. Not bad for an old broad! I'm prouder of that than I am of my muscle tone. To me, this is the big payoff of dance: giving up control in order to get, ultimately, exactly what you want, or at least something you want more than a false sense of security. Sometimes now, I run fast backward without knowing where I'm going and find it kind of thrilling.

Through the cheerful quickstep, I'm learning that if I saddle myself with the need to know the outcome before I set out, I'll be chasing a mirage and spoiling my own fun.

ANOTHER LUNCH HOUR, another dance lesson. Bill and I have been working on our waltz group for a good half hour without pursuing much if any conversation. I like the dry technique work in particular. For a good ten minutes, we dance without stopping for instruction or adjustment. It's good to blow out the pipes. Next, he has me put my hands on his ribs and dance without benefit of holding on to him. It is insanely difficult. When we stop, I can tell he's over the moon.

"That was excellent. The best you've ever done. Wasn't it?"

"I don't know—I can't tell."

"You're getting so good, I only have to think it and you do it."

I don't know how to take in such a large compliment. "That's great," I say. "So we can dance even when you're in D.C. and I'm in New York."

When we stop for good we're both breathing heavily. Bill asks me, "Did you do sprinting in school?"

"No. I did gymnastics, though."

"Oh?"

"Uh-huh. I did the unevens, and floor ex. You know, like tumbling and dancing combined." As I'm saying this, I take a step sideways and do a flourish with my arms, a balletic blossoming.

"What was that?" He is suddenly excited. "Where'd that come from? Can we see that again? It's as if you just lit up from the inside."

But I freeze—can't do it again, won't even try.

"Okay, let's work some more on your curve. Can you just let your arms hang? Don't hold tension in them. Don't pull your elbows back. When you use the arms like that, it takes away the power from the legs and the body. Let's go."

We're moving along and for a brief instant I can let my arms hang, but like the last time, it's almost painful to allow them to do nothing, to be like ice cream melting.

In a few minutes, Bill has us dancing a quickstep. When the song ends, he steps back and says, "Okay, now I want you to go around the whole room by yourself, with your arms up in solo dance position, doing the eighteen basic steps of foxtrot, just keep repeating them as you go around."

"No." I say it flatly, partly to be funny, but also because I can't bear dancing by myself out there in the open. That's tantamount to declaring, "Look at me; I'm a dancer," which I'm not prepared to do. Yes, I've accomplished a lot as a *student* of dance, but I'm still diffident, still unwilling to say, This is who I am; I'm one of you—and I can really do this. No, *really* I'm a magazine editor. But here, right now, I'm revealing to Bill my discomfort with standing out there alone, lifting my arms to dance position and commanding my audience to believe I'm a thing to behold. My coach is calling my bluff.

"Yes," he says. "Go on."

"No," I say again, looking around the room picturing the absurdity of doing what he's telling me to do. I'm not perfect yet. I don't want anyone to find out. I'm freaking here at the prospect of performing without benefit of a partner to hide behind.

"It's time."

I see I have no choice. He's not relenting, so, finally, I do. I stand in the corner and take what feels like three hours to gather my courage. I propel myself backward in a Feather step, four steps backward on a diagonal line toward the center of the room. I'm weak in the knees, but I carry on into the leftward Reverse Turn, which takes me toward the wall, now forgetting where I am in the sequence, now starting again. I'm sure I look ridiculous and I'm hoping nobody's watching. But Bill is. I look toward him anxiously. He is examining me closely, judging me.

After about fifteen minutes of this, we dance together again and

I'm back in my comfort zone. At one point, he pulls away, saying, "I can't feel you in my hand." I try again, but again it's not right. He stretches his left arm across my chest, moves it up, and forcefully presses my neck and head out with his forearm, keeping me out as we move. It is beginning to hurt my neck, especially with the weight of my head pulling on it. Like a dope, I say nothing.

We continue with a slow waltz. I am dancing less stiffly, but going into a corner, in promenade, out of the blue, my feet tangle—tangle!—around his feet somehow, I don't understand, and I go down, right to the floor, landing with a thud on my ass. Luckily, he doesn't fall on top of me, but stumbles off to the side instead, reaching to rescue me, but it is too late.

He helps me to my feet and I brush off my skirt. We start again, though I wish we didn't have to, because I'm about ready to quit. "Shit," Bill says almost immediately. Again, he says I'm not in his hand. I wish I knew what he means, but I don't get it at all. I know everything would be okay if I could just get centered and find my backbone. But he seems to be on a mission to find that himself; with his left hand, he now presses my clavicle back and to the side. As we dance, he uses the edge of his right hand against my back to induce more upper-body curve. What am I, a doll?

IT'S A FEW days later, a Monday, and a fresh new week in the dance studio, which means I can, thankfully, forget about last week. We've just finished the morning's group class. Ariel and I are taking a moment to examine what it is exactly that Bill does with his hands. She's been dancing with him for decades, on and off, and is thoroughly loyal to him as a teacher. We're both members of the Bill Davies fan club.

"You don't even know he's doing it," she says, standing there with a toothy smile, looking at Bill, who's taking it in. "But then with a little flick of his big wrist, poom, you're turning in the opposite direction. It's very sly." I look at his hands dangling now at the ends of his arms, and I see how massive they are. Like meat hooks. I look back at his face, which has an expression that says, "Why, I'm sure I don't know what you're talking about."

And suddenly, one small perception changes everything, just like that. What a fine line there is between assumption and reality when such a thing occurs in the mind. Is it possible Bill talks about two dancers in dialogue, both leading, both following, but all the while he's controlling his partner with small, almost imperceptible movements of his hands?

"Here, do a Weave or something with arms down in practice position," Ariel suggests. Bill steps over to me looking as if he enjoys being scrutinized. We do a few steps and I am paying close attention to what he does with his hands. Focus, focus, just the hands. His are firmly in control of my forearms now, gripping, just shy of tight. *There, he did it. He bent his right wrist in, his left out and look where I am, all the way over here. Wow, this is big. I never really absorbed this before, how in charge he is of me! And it's not because of his height or his weight or his strong legs or anything else—it's his hands! He's in charge by stealth. Maybe it's not really two-people-dancing after all. He just says that.*

There's something vaguely *Pygmalion* going on here, very possibly. I think of the word *manipulate*: "mani-"surely comes from the French word for hand, *main*. Handle, manhandle. And all this time, I assumed these hands were just cradling me. Now I see with what impressive mastery and sleight of hand he controls my every move. He probably even gets a kick out of it, the crafty sonofabitch. I wonder if he's aware of what he's doing (which would be sinister) or not (which would be maddeningly, old-fashionedly sexist of him). At last I'm beginning to see Bill as a complete, multifaceted person, warts and all. He couldn't be merely human in my eyes—until now.

15 I Can Take Care of Myself, but I'll Get Over It

I 've started to do a little Latin up in Westchester," I say to Bill one day when we're on the phone talking about scheduling some time to dance now that I've recovered from a nasty bout of pneumonia that's prevented me from dancing for weeks. But it was a profitable time, being sick in bed starting in January; it imposed a kind of Buddhist practice—hours on end of no productivity, just being (which I'd never tolerate otherwise) and an allowing of reflection. For a full week at home, I could do nothing but drink plenty of fluids and take stock. As I reviewed the Big Picture, I saw this as a time to make a fresh start. I'm nearly sure I have become "Bill's girl" in the eyes of everyone at the studio. Many students dance with more than one teacher if they can afford it because it can be useful to get a variety of perspectives. Not me; I'm a disciple devoted to one at a time.

Another revelation I've had in bed is that all this time I've been hiding my sense of deficiency in Latin dance, I was really yearning to return to it and become an expert in sultry. After Bill made me do rumba with him that day, I decided it would be good to take up

Latin again and get over my phobia. But not at Dance New York, not in front of him and all these Latin pros. I need a place where I can admit my awkwardness to a teacher and ask him to help me get over it. There are smaller studios with just a couple of teachers, studios where amateurs take lessons but pros don't practice and certainly the most dazzling champions are not getting in the way. Nice, quiet studios.

"WHO'S THE LATIN GUY?" Bill asks.

"Oh, you've seen him do coaching lessons every now and then at Dance New York. His name is Dmitri Ostashkin. His partner is Svetlana." Of course, every other woman on the ballroom floor is named Svetlana, but Bill knows who I mean. He's probably judged them in competitions.

"Hmm." He may have grumbled slightly, but I don't mind. I've been a loyal, regular student for Bill these past four years. I needed a mentor when I first came to him. My mistake was in gradually, imperceptibly, putting him in charge of Dancing Janet. He gladly took it on because he likes that role of maestro shaping the young ingenues and turning them into champions. Maybe I'm not young, but I was still a ballroom ingenue when I first stepped into Dance New York. And I'm not a champion, but I am a much better Standard dancer because of Bill.

Since my return to dance, I have come to know teacher-love, a kind of misguided devotion in which the student confuses love of the craft or practice with love for the teacher. It's pretty understandable. Women who've given birth sometimes have such misdirected feelings—often dismissed as a matter of hormones—for their obgyn. In the ballroom, there are these extraordinarily beautiful lessons coming from the dance itself. The teacher conveys them—but you don't at first see that the teacher is merely the vessel, the artery; you attach to the teacher as though to the lesson itself, identifying the messenger and the message, and possibly, if you're as hopeless as I've been, investing the teacher with a sort of divinity. One of the several dangers in teacher-love is that you lose sight of your own considerable contribution to the beauty of your dance. Another is that you view your teacher as infallible and believe whatever he says. The worst is to give over your dancing—to make the teacher the superintendent of it, as I have done. Now, I will reclaim my dancing for myself. At the end of the day, it's mine, isn't it? I'll have to take responsibility for myself as an artist if I want to be any kind of artist at all.

DMITRI, A RUSSIAN of about thirty, is married to the diminutive and adorable bleached blonde Svetlana. They own a studio five minutes from my house above the Beverage Center in Ardsley. Compared with the last time I made my way bravely into a studio to seek out a new teacher, this time was easier. I called, I deciphered the heavily Russian-accented English, I showed up and said, "Make me a Latin goddess," and voilà. We're deep into our third lesson or so. I don't have to reconcile anything—Dmitri and I dance in Westchester; Bill and I do Standard in New York.

Perhaps I'm not being totally honest about how easy it was to start working with a new teacher. By now, it's clear that I have a tendency to attach rather like a barnacle to my teachers. Detaching is a challenge. But once I saw that my devotion had a childlike, unquestioning quality, I could start growing up, or away. For me as a child, discovering my parents to be merely human was a very sad moment. With Bill it is different. As the weeks pass, I am delighted to find it's a huge relief that I no longer have to hold him up for such unreasonable devotion. And lucky for unsuspecting him, he doesn't even know what he's had to live up to in my imagination. He can be just Bill, a combination of qualities and attitudes, some of them admirable, some of them a pain in the butt. I'm not the student bowing down anymore. Bill actually helped me get over that. And so I'm doing rumba with Dmitri now.

DESPITE HIS YOUNG years, his babe-in-the-woods aura, he is on to me. For as long as I can remember, I've worked very hard to manage people's impressions so that they'll think highly of me, but it's not working with Dmitri. Thank god. I think this will do me good.

"Will you please use me?" he asks. He says it as if it's a no-brainer, but I really don't get how to do what he wants. In this step called the Continuous Hip Twist, the man stands still, feet apart, and with his arms directs the woman in swiveling her hips practically 180 degrees one way, then the other, then back again (you can picture her skirt flying, wrapping alluringly around her thighs).

"How?" I ask.

"Here, after you break back on your right, you have to get all the way over here very fast. But I think you are trying to do it by yourself, without me."

"Yes, I am." Hey, I expect praise for my self-sufficiency. "Is that bad?"

"Yes, it is. I will show you why. First, though, Janet, tell me, what would you do to use me?"

"Oh. Um . . ." I have to think hard. I know he has told me this before. "Oh, I know, with my hands, I could hold on to you to get myself around."

"Yes, could you please?"

And so I try it, my left hand behind his right shoulder and my right hand in his left applying pressure.

"Well, I feel you pressing me, but it's as if you hold on to it too long. Do it, then forget about it. Do it, forget about it. Like when you turn on a light, you flick the switch." He actually goes to the wall to demonstrate turning on a light. "But you don't stand there and hold the switch in the up position in order for the lights to stay on." The way he teases me cracks me up. He gets me. "You walk away, and the lights stay on. You don't have to keep working. Here, in the Hip Twist, you use me, quick, then forget about it. Okay? Try that."

I have to laugh at myself for my long-standing habit of self-reliance. Being an American, I of course never questioned that the trait is anything other than an absolute good. I read Ralph Waldo Emerson in high school. But now I see the comic aspect of going about things earnestly and with great effort, holding the light switch on, head down, shoulder to the grindstone, while a perfectly capable, strong, and willing person stands by, ready but helpless, superfluous in the face of my one-man-band competence. Until dancing started revealing my foibles to me, I didn't see that self-reliance should be a tool, used as needed, rather than a way of life. I've mostly expected to do things myself. Carry my own suitcase, so to speak.

I grew up during the 1960s and '70s, the time of women's lib. That experience, combined with the long aftermath of my parents' divorce, taught me about self-reliance. By the time I wound up on the dance floor, I was good at taking care of myself—and utterly inept at accepting support graciously. It seems to me that something backfired in the way women were liberated back then, and I was a prime example of it—self-sufficient, but isolated and, as a result, less successful than I probably could be.

On the floor, it would never occur to me not to use my strength to get myself around in the Hip Twist or to ask anyone for help, certainly not a man. But the step is supposed to be gorgeous, and for all my praiseworthy self-reliance, I'm probably making it look effortful and strained. I think it must be an art, knowing when and how to rely on another person.

Next, Dmitri has me practicing a back bend with my left leg up to the side and bent so my left foot is tucked behind my right knee.

My arms are overhead, reaching to the ceiling. He is sideways to me, holding my waist. Back I go. In my twenties, I was as flexible as a wet noodle, but not now; the bend is hard and uncomfortable. I feel pretty stiff. This can't be good.

"You didn't use me," he says and he looks puzzled, as if my aging tendons have nothing to do with it. He's obviously used to dancing with Svetlana, who is skilled at using him in their dancing. He gestures to my inner left thigh and knee. "Press this against my leg. Use me to hold yourself up, so not all your weight is on your right leg. It will feel much better, and there will be the illusion of a very deep back bend."

Sure enough, he's right; it's easier and much more fluid. I'm getting what feels like my very first taste of relying on my partner in Latin.

"Hey, I like that. I never felt that before," I tell Dmitri.

"It's better, yes? But why is it so strange? I'm your partner. It's my job."

Well, Dmitri, do you have a couple of hours? I'll tell you the story of my life. But I spare him the deep background: apart from discovering, while growing up, that I had to rescue myself, I learned how not to impose myself. Not to make demands on other people. I've expected maybe too little from my partner.

I'll never forget the most bitter thing my husband ever said about our relationship. It was in one of our sessions of unsuccessful marriage counseling. That morning, we were discussing our household conflicts as usual, and it was suggested by brainy Dr. K. that Peter might try helping me out more—I forget the details. Peter scoffed and blurted out with a sarcasm that startled us all: "Huh! No one takes care of Janet. Janet takes care of Janet." It was an arresting and poignant moment that, in retrospect, we could have pounced on. Alas, we didn't. I wonder if I felt proud to be described thus. *See? I don't need anybody. I can do it all myself.* As if that were a good thing. It pains me now to look back and see that I didn't let Peter "do his job," as Dmitri would say. Peter might have been saying, "Use me," but I couldn't fathom what he meant. Nobody takes care of Janet. The words echo through the sad hallways of my memory.

That's not true. That's so not true, I might have told him then, but I wasn't able. *I can't tell you how badly I want to be taken care of. Why don't you see that? Why do you give up so easily?* And so the unanswerable questions of failed partnership pile up like cars in a wreck on a highway.

NOW THAT I'VE been attempting it on the dance floor, I think how funny it is that we use the phrase "I bent over backwards" to imply we did something difficult and strenuous and the other person should be grateful. "Hey, you owe me. I bent over backwards." Here's my teacher *correcting* me now for bending over backwards alone. "You have been trying very hard to do it wrong," he says, as if it's obviously nuts to do such things without support. All I can say is I envy him his marriage.

Dmitri also says I'm hogging all the work. He's impugning the stout-hearted, brave soldier who gets it done. I assumed the good soldier was exempt from all criticism.

"I think you are trying to do too many jobs. All you should be doing is your job. Do your action, get your weight one hundred percent over your foot, then let the next thing happen. If you try to control every action, you take away my job, which in this case is to turn you. But also, some things should just be allowed to happen. You don't have to make it all happen. Like with the Whisk in samba: after you place your foot behind the other one, just fall to the side. Don't move to the side, just fall. The other way, it looks stiff and uninteresting." Allow gravity to do its job. Echoes of the waltz. Dmitri wants to lead me, but I'm going it alone, so he can't; and there's no connection between us as a result.

I KEEP SEEING the parallels to my marriage. I didn't let Peter do his job, and I'm not talking about taking out the trash. I mean his *job*: to be a partner with me in nurturing our relationship, running our house, parenting our children. He held his own in some things, like parenting decisions, but I took all the rest of it on, as a well-intentioned manager does, and eventually he forgot or ignored his tasks because, I imagine, he felt like a lackey, not a partner. I didn't use him well. And if we look at the shoe on the other foot, and ask if Peter prevented me from doing something I was supposed to, what was it? Perhaps it's that he didn't inspire me to be a loving partner, and to support him the way my ballroom partners support me in dance. As it ended up, I enabled him perfectly well, but I couldn't support him.

It's such a challenge, walking the tightrope of togetherness. In partner dancing, how do you touch the guy but not lean on him, and then move in the world like that? How do you merge but still stand on your own two feet? I have watched some of the world's top professionals fly around the room doing this. The beauty of their movement is breathtaking, and it is proof that the paradox has a resolution to inspire us all. Behold, they are one, and yet they are standing on their own.

WHEN WE WERE teenagers, my sisters and my brother and I all took tennis lessons from an extraordinary man named Jerry Alleyne. Jerry was then probably about forty, and he was one of the first black men to play in the U.S. Open, in 1959. He opened a tennis club in Hastings in an old riverfront factory. He was a thoughtful, fiercely intelligent man, and we described him as the philosopher-king tennis teacher. "You are born alone and you die alone," Jerry once generously pointed out to me during one of our post-lesson discussions of my teenage angst. I nodded, and understood that he meant that in between, we must take responsibility for ourselves. I thought of Jerry as I filled out my college applications by myself, paid for college by taking out loans from New York State and Yale, got a full-time job after college, earning $9,000 a year in 1976, found an apartment and a roommate in New York, and paid off my loans. And I remember, when I had dinner with my father in the city after work once a month, before we kissed goodnight, standing on the corner of Madison Avenue and Sixty-eighth Street outside the Right Bank, a cozy French restaurant where we always ate filet of sole meunière, he would hand me a five-dollar bill to pay the taxi and I was so grateful. I even felt happy to be able to keep the $1.25 surplus, knowing he wouldn't mind.

I may bitch at times about my single-head-of-household working parent insanity, but at the same time, I am proud of what I have accomplished by my dogged self over the past thirty years, and especially lately. I can edit or write any magazine story, get to work on time dressed nicely enough, get back to Hastings for the teacher conference, and in between delegate errands to the babysitter, fix a broken appliance, and plan a birthday party before helping with homework and making dinner. If you're going to be self-sufficient you also must be indefatigable. I can drive six hours to Vermont for parents' visiting day at camp on a hot July Saturday with no air-conditioning in my broken-down old Buick, wearing earplugs to muffle Cookie's anxious wailing from the backseat, and deliver solace and avocado sushi to my homesick daughter. I can buy a new car at auction for a good price. I can survive the gut-wrenching feeling of overdrawing my bank account every other week before my payroll direct deposit registers. And I can play the helpless female at the gas station or at CompUSA when necessary.

Mostly, though, I get a big charge out of being in the I-am-woman-hear-me-roar mode. A few months ago, I researched and purchased a starter PC for Erica, who was begging for one because we're a Mac household but she wanted to play a specific game that's only for PCs. I bit that bullet and got a decent deal. Driving home from CompUSA in White Plains, I called Erica to say proudly, "Hi Erica, it's me. I got it and I'm on my way home." She said, "Oh good. Mom, can you call a man to come over and help set it up today?" My own daughter! I couldn't believe my ears.

"No way!" I shouted into my cell phone. And clueless as I was about technology, when I got home I set that sucker up myself, without any instruction booklet even, because that was, of course, missing from the box. At first, the Internet connection didn't work. Defeat. Guess we'll call Julia's husband, Chris, or, as a last resort, Peter. But instead I kept at it, and clicked "continue" even when I didn't really understand until, to my utter amazement, up popped the Google home page, and I shrieked, and Erica shrieked—full-blown girl shrieks like a fire alarm—and we slapped high fives at the triumph that required no testosterone.

Who needs a husband? Anyway, I'm not going to remarry for money or handyman skills. I'll make my own money, thank you very much, and I'll hire the household help I need. Any future partner has to be for something else. Something beautiful and enlivening, like dancing.

DMITRI'S PERPLEXITY OVER my self-sufficiency has reminded me of one day a few years back, during a lesson, when Bill asked me what I was so afraid of when it comes to letting go in dance.

"Death."

He looked shocked and sorry for me at the same time. Like maybe he was expecting me to have answered, "I'm afraid of the Hover Cross," or "falling," or "looking silly," or something a little less dire. But I've thought a great deal about my fears, and they are all about the endpoint.

I told him I've always, as long as I can remember, awakened to a general fear of the day, fear of what might happen, fear of failure, fear of not getting everything done.

"Where did that come from? Why do you think you feel that way?"

"I don't know, it's from my childhood. From my teens, I think." I told Bill that as a young girl, I often felt I had to hold on to the edges of the rowboat as it tossed in heavy seas. I didn't mean to sound melodramatic; that's honestly how I felt.

"But you can swim," he said. Funny, I never thought of that. I'd accepted the rowboat as necessary to my survival, the seas as certain peril, and here was my instructor suggesting something reassuring and so sensible: if the rowboat capsized or spilled us out, well, so what, I could swim—the ultimate self-reliance. I guess I still had a thing or two to learn.

"DO YOU HAVE a support network now?" my friend Tony asks me as we take the escalator from the bowels of Grand Central Station up to Madison Avenue one morning. Tony is a fellow commuter, a Hastings neighbor, and an art director for a big ad agency, not to mention a really good guy. He is happily married to Madeleine, a photographer, so I feel free to be friends with him. On the escalator, he shows me some unexpected sympathy for getting divorced.

"Yeah, I have a network and it starts with the handyman," I answer. He laughs. That clearly isn't what he had in mind. He means a network of women friends who've been through this and could offer support and advice.

It was easy to overlook this in the first year that I handled life without a partner: support can come from many sources, if I allow it. From the handyman, the plumber (I call him my sewer troll), who rushes right over when something springs a leak and my basement is flooding, from the car mechanic who reminds me when it's time to change the oil. There are also my siblings, who have been my best friends all my life, and my dad—he checks the air in my tires whenever we get together. Mom reminds me that there was a time in my life, way, way back, when I was, quite simply, happy—not this . . . complicated; and there's Rita, our new sixty-four-year-old babysitter who raised eight kids of her own and does stuff like sit with me at the emergency room long after her quitting time just to make sure Alden's okay after being thrown from her horse and then says at nine p.m., "I'll go to your house and feed the dogs," which of course I'd totally forgotten about. My friend Julia is my central support, emotionally speaking; then, I have the women at work, my sorority in Manolos; and even the handsome stranger on the subway who makes eye contact after the sudden, unexplained explosion under the car, and answers my "What was that?" with "I don't know, but if it's what we were both thinking, we wouldn't be here talking about it." For a brief time, we have a profound bond.

My appreciation of network and community is new, triggered by my new life without a copilot. Until now, I've been maybe too content to be a loner. In the face of adversity lately, my heart is warming up bit by bit and counting more on company. To be perfectly honest, I even want protection. One night, during a terrible storm with high winds, when I'm home alone and worrying that one of my giant oak trees might fall on my house, I feel a powerful need for a man around the house, a man to hold me.

There must be a reason the lone soldier found her way back to ballroom dance. I say the soldier character because, frankly, when I chose to throw myself into it, I hadn't met any of the others yet, except the good girl, and she was busy with other things at the time. So let's say it was the soldier: she didn't choose ballet, or some other more solitary pursuit. Why? Was it a mission to temper self-reliance by balancing it with partnership? A reaching out for connection?

16 PERFECT TIMING

I F TIME DIDN'T exist, everything would happen all at once." I heard that on the radio the other day and it made me laugh out loud. I love that notion. If everything happened all at once, what an unintelligible mess life would be. Pointless. And pretty short. Like when a printer or a typewriter from the olden days gets jammed and the words get printed one on top of the other. It's all there, but it's illegible.

I said that to my sister Alison just now, when we spoke on the phone and she was complaining about her inability to know whether such and such is the right choice for her life, or would she do better to make the opposite choice, and how come she can't tell, and what if she should have—then she'll know in retrospect that she was an idiot, or that she was stuck. I go through the same circuitous self-analysis in my own head a lot, so I am sympathetic. The other day I got a big laugh when I was talking to Julia and used a phrase to describe myself in a state of intensity and paralysis about something—I said I'd gotten "wrapped around the axle"—and she said, so amazingly lovingly: "One of your best qualities is your stick-to-it-ive-ness. That's why you get wrapped *around* the axle as opposed to just flopping down on the road underneath it."

"Ali," I started, confident that she thought I was about to give her my opinion, choice A or choice B, but no, I was about to hit her with a more helpful little bit of pontificating as her older sister by eighteen months. "You say 'and yet' as if the two opposing things shouldn't coexist and you should be able to have a resolution right now, on your timetable. But I don't think that's how life works. The river has to flow. Time has to pass, and eventually you'll know. But you can't know right now. And the hardest thing you have to do now is to live with the ambiguity, to let the two opposites coexist for you, despite your need for a 'right answer.'"

She said she liked that image, the river flowing. I do, too. It reminds me of the *Desiderata,* which my mother loved; when we were young, she framed it and hung it on our bathroom wall, and she reprinted it to hand out to people—passersby, dinner guests. I memorized it. "And whether or not it is clear to you, the universe is unfolding as it should," it says. Unfolding, as in something happening over time, strikes me as such a beautiful word. Music is beauty unfolding over a defined amount of time—a measure. If not for time, all the notes would happen at once, a horrible cacophony. Bill says that if we didn't have the concept of rhythm, the singer wouldn't know to change notes; he'd just keep singing that one note . . . forever. When I think of musicality, I think of Luciano Pavarotti's voice filling in the measure exquisitely. His voice using the time absolutely perfectly; the quality of the sound, what it looks like, how it plays with the measure to break your heart with rapture.

A dancer can provoke rapture with the same musicality, expressed through the body in motion. It's more challenging when two people attempt to do this as one. Picture the man choosing the figures and the direction and the woman responding. Her skillful anticipation is critical. In a split second, she commits to what she *thinks* is coming next, let's say a Chassée after a Whisk, but if the man intends a Wing or a Weave instead, she has anticipated wrong, and they get entangled in a footwork mess. What a microscopically fine line it is between too early and too late. Finding that line is the magic of the merging.

I myself, at first, could respect the importance of time passing in some senses but not in others. Back when I was first getting reexcited about dancing, I remember telling Julia about how I wanted to get "it" faster: the figure, the routine, the technique Yuri was teaching me. I was impatient with myself for being plodding, taking so long to master something. Julia said "That may be where your work is, in getting the ego out of the way of your practice." Yes, I can be a greedy student, wanting to have it all now rather than work toward it. I reluctantly applied myself to accepting humbly that I would improve over time—not only by being dedicated to the learning, but also by merely existing. Because, as Yuri had told me, I am like a fine bottle of wine. A red wine. Better with age. But, on the other hand, there does need to be a time when you decide to drink the damn wine. It would be such a shame to kick the bucket and leave all that wine in the cellar undrunk.

Haste has its place, certainly. Speed is indispensable in the big picture. I love a good tennis stroke: watch the approaching ball hit the ground, prepare, WHAM! Without the requisite speed in the arm (generated by the whole body) to send the ball back over the net, the stroke is unsuccessful. There is either no contact with the ball due to poor timing, or there's flubbed contact that sends the ball out of bounds, or the shot has no power in it and the other player gets to put it away. But with the right speed, the sweet spot of the racquet head bangs that sucker and it zooms across the net, low and fast, making your opponent scurry and swipe off balance. That feels good. Sometimes you can make up for miscalculating your ideal body position as the ball is coming at you by adding speed at the last minute. Oops, that's coming faster than I thought, BOOM!

I'm generally ambivalent about speed though. I drive fast—but athletically and safely. I'm a graceful skier, and that's as far as it goes. Speed on the slopes feels out-of-control dangerous; I fear death by tree or warming hut. I'm more often a slow-and-steady-wins-the-race kind of girl. Naturally, this is an impediment to excellent dancing, because slow and steady violates the music, for one thing, and it's completely boring to look at, for another. I didn't appreciate this until Dmitri threw me without my consent into the Fan, a step in which we stand at a ninety-degree angle to each other, at arm's length. Easy enough, but getting into the Fan involves some fancy foot- and bodywork. *Ohhh no! What's happening here? This is out of control. Recover, recover! Whew. Okay, that's better, here I am at a full stop, weight on my left foot, left arm out, right hand in his. I recognize where I am now. Everything's going to be okay.*

We just started practicing our rumba routine for a show Dmitri thinks he's talked me into doing next month. Clearly, he's just demonstrated to me how much better it is to play with speed in dance. He's talked about it before. "If you do everything at the same pace, it's *borink.* Better to do something really fast, catch people's attention with your cleverness and then slow it down." In his show-and-tell, he moves his feet and his hips quick as lightning, then becomes languid, and his arms, hands, fingertips finish with a slow flourish. It's every bit as compelling as he has promised. Then he makes fun of me perfectly. Take the place we just were, before the Fan, me close to him, sideways, with my left side next to him in what's called the Opening Out. My left arm is straight up in the air above my head, my right wrapped around my own torso, and my right hand in his left, close to my waist. I am proceeding forward from here into open space, my back to him, and he will give a nice tug on my right hand, which will whip me around to the left so that I am facing him again, and standing at that ninety-degree angle in the Fan pose.

Here is the way he makes fun of me. Method one of doing that: tah, tah, tah. That is, plod, plod, turn—a good student hitting the beat with each step. (That was me.) Method two: t-t-POW. First it's faster than a speeding bullet, then vacation tempo, stretching like a cat, look-at-me poised, luxuriating. The first two steps are accelerated so that the third can borrow some time from them in order to be slower, and the dancer has time to gyrate seductively like a pole dancer in a strip joint. This will be followed by more speed. And so the onlooker's eye and sense of rhythm are both engaged.

THERE IS A push-pull of timing; allowing the river to flow is just as necessary as seizing the day and the trick is to know which attitude suits the moment.

It may be time for me to answer the question that has been on my mind for two and a half decades. The big question that keeps coming up, nagging me: Why did I stop dancing twenty-six years ago? Talk about time passing. I was good then; I had the talent (I dare say) and the coaching to become a top partner, maybe even U.S. champion, maybe to make a decent go of it in the hallowed competition at Blackpool, England. I didn't find out, and I never will. I walked away from dance at the crucial moment, when I was poised for flight. David Nyemchek and I were winning all the amateur comps in the East. People cheered for us; young kids asked for our autographs. We were about to turn pro. Granted, the standard of competitive ballroom dancing was nowhere near as high as it is today thanks to Bill, Joe Jenkins, and the others in their gang who went to England for training in the 1960s and brought back the best of the British technique, and also thanks to the superbly trained Russians who started coming in the nineties. But for what it's worth, I had a shot. I've had my Marlon Brando "I could have been a contender" moments. And today, I live with the fact that I will never know how good I might have been.

It wasn't exactly easy to stop dancing in 1980. I said then that I had to stop because I couldn't manage to do both my dancing—five nights a week and on weekends—and my job, as an editorial assistant at *Town & Country* (this was my first stint there, before I moved on to other magazines, only to return years later). I was turning down press trips to Italy, Mexico, and Paris because of dance competitions. I thought it was odd that I spent most of my time with dancers who didn't know who Margaret Mead was (my mother worked with her at the time). To be honest, I think I couldn't imagine myself being a success as a dancer in the way I'd been brought up to be a success. Because I cared so much what other people thought of me, choosing the dance world would have appeared a sort of failure, a colossal underachievement. That is part of why I chose my magazine career. It has been a fine ride, and I would be an idiot to have regrets about my choice, because I would not otherwise have my beautiful daughters. I would have children, but not these children, and these are the children I love. I would live in some fifth-floor walkup in the not-great part of Brooklyn and be teaching, evenings mostly, and traveling all the time for shows. I would not have been to Italy, France, Portugal, Austria, Peru, Monte Carlo, Rio, except to dance in their hotel ballrooms, would not have learned what I have learned, written what I have written. And at the age of forty-something, I certainly would not have been able to take off my dance shoes, put on a pair of pumps, and walk into an editor's office in New York City to ask for a job in magazines. But I could and did, at that age, walk back into the ballroom. And there it was, waiting for me.

Bill once told me the best dancing comes from emotional clarity, and I surely didn't have that the first time around. It has been hard to come by the second time, and even now, I hold on to it just barely, just for moments—the clarity is an evanescent blessing, like a bubble that bursts . . . because bubbles burst inevitably.

And now for the deep-down emotional truth about why I stopped dancing twenty-six years ago: I was not ready to step up to the plate. I think that is the real reason, and it took me over two decades to see it: I was not prepared for the butter, for surrendering, or even for excellence—it would have meant embracing the pain of myself, the fourteen-year-old girl, the bitch nag, the geisha, the good soldier, the goddess, all of me. It would have meant moving past my controlled competence to the whole heaping plateful—giving myself entirely to the art, to myself, to the audience, and to my partner.

"YOU AND I danced once before, a long time ago," I told Bill after he'd been teaching me for some time.

"We did?"

"Yes. I'm not surprised you don't remember—it was in the late seventies at Cherry Hill, during the Saturday night banquet. You came up to me at my table. I was terrified. It was a waltz. I've remembered it ever since. I'll never forget it. It was one of those experiences of a lifetime, the kind that makes an indelible imprint."

"Really? I'm sorry I don't recall it. I'm sure you were divine even then."

"It was the first time I felt what dancing could, or should, be like. No anxiety, no difficulty or pressure. You did a Spin Turn and it changed my experience of dance forever. It was butter."

"Butter?"

"Mm-hmm. Maybe that's why I stopped dancing then. It was too good, and I wasn't ready for it. So maybe it's your fault I quit."

"My fault that you discovered excellence in dancing?" He gives me a blank look.

"Yes. Too bad I was too young to know about all this then. Or too afraid."

"Do you know what you were afraid of then?"

"You. That Spin Turn you did with me was a dance orgasm. You know, the French phrase for orgasm is 'little death,' *petit mort*. And I'm afraid of death. Actually, now I'm thinking maybe I've been afraid of life. But, really, I guess I was afraid of finding out what my limits are. It was better to walk away than to find out, and have to face imperfection, live with being less than the best. I was brave in some ways, but not brave enough for that."

"So you thought you had to be perfect."

"Yes."

"Do you still?"

"No, at least not all the time."

"Oh. That's good. Now, do you realize, you are perfect?"

"I'm starting to. Yes, I guess so."

"Good. There is no excellence without a willingness to fail completely. Let's do some foxtrot before Satchmo finishes. I love Satchmo."

And there is no time for regret in dance. You have only now, this moment, for your performance, your glorious movement. Whatever you're going to do, do it now, quick, before the music stops.

BACK TO THE PRESENT

D MITRI IS TEACHING me to stay. I am always rushing forward to the next figure, going, going, going (gone), so that, if the dance were a series of snapshots, my partner would be there, fully in each frame, and I would be only partially visible, a few limbs and a bit of torso, the rest of me in the frame ahead.

He has just led me in some basic rumba steps. He stops to announce, "I like what you are doing, but I'm not happy with how you don't stay in the back break long enough. You rush out like a good student showing me you know what comes next." Hey, how did he peg me after only a handful of lessons? This is unnerving; I may be losing my knack for manipulation. I can't tell for sure, but I may also be the tiniest bit excited to be figured out and exposed. He says, "Stay there, enjoy that moment and show me you are loving it. In the event that you are late coming out, it is my problem, because it means I didn't lead you out of it soon enough."

Dmitri has no idea how profound this advice is for me—or maybe he does, who am I to say? I only know it is profound for me.

It feels in this moment—I am grinning at what he just said—that I have come a long way during these last five years, and now, at last, I am ready to stay. I want to stay. Not that I have a tendency to leave. It's not about space; it's about the time dimension: I don't know how to be present in the moment. That's something I've heard yogis and Buddhists describe; I've read the books, but the skill has eluded me. As long as I can remember, I've been addicted to the adrenaline, the hormone that propels you headlong into your future, and I've known that this is nothing but a big, fat excuse not to find meaning in your life in each instant, in the minutiae, the mowing of the lawn, the brushing of your daughter's hair, the chewing and swallowing of a bite of tuna sandwich.

I've been mesmerized occasionally by the notion of living in the moment, recognized its importance, and I do see how living my life in the future, with a to-do list in my hand and worry in my heart, means—and here comes the existential panic—that I'm not really living. Someday the joke will be on me because I'll get to the point at which I'm rushing to the last of my future moments: my death. "Oh darn; I forgot to live in the moment, and now my life is over." The show's over and there's no TiVo in the afterlife. That scares me. And if it weren't enough, just being scared, there's logic to inspire me to change. But in fifty-one years, I haven't managed to make it happen, haven't gone on any retreats, haven't learned meditation, haven't, in sum, been the good student of life.

I've been on that hamster wheel, racing nowhere fast, managing, planning, preparing, anticipating. Spending my time as if I were infinitely rich in moments. And now, my Russian innocent seems to have snapped me out of it, like a dog trainer, with one command: "Stay," Dmitri says at each point in our rumba when his hands, his arms, his eyes can feel me wanting to bolt. Yes, I can hear the music, which defines the length of time you give to a movement, but I'm not listening and luxuriating, not giving the music what it's asking for; I'm already busy with the next thing. Perhaps staying is musicality:

Filling up a measure of time (a moment) with movement (in dance), with consciousness (in life).

"Stay!" he barks. The command is nice and loud, and so I stay in the back break. This is often the woman's opening figure in a rumba routine, when she and her partner start by standing a few feet apart, connected with eye contact and his left hand to her right. The man steps forward on the slow four-one count and the woman allows him to get close. Despite this force coming at her, she stays! She merely places her left leg back, pointing her toe, not budging her body one millimeter; it is a quiet, teasing response to his charge, as if in stealthy preparation for what the intruder, the opponent, the hunk may try next.

And it feels, by the way, something like a sexual dare for the woman to stay: "Come at me and see if I care, see if I'm intimidated, see if I turn and run—no, I don't, see? I can take your approach, I want you close . . . But can *you* take it?" All this during only one beat of music, and then on the count of two, she swiftly shoots herself back on her right foot, pushing her hand against his to immediately straighten her arm, simultaneously snapping her right hip back and around, her left hand now alluringly brushing her left hip before the arm moves up and out to the side, showing confidence, saying "Look at me, take me."

And that's all there is. Nothing more. Nothing, that is, in this moment. Here is where I am meant to stay and luxuriate. Enjoy myself, allow my pose to convey that I have not a care in the world, that I feel good, and—well, let's just say that, up until now, I've tended to skip the "take me" part. My left arm, and probably my whole dancing being, would instead say, "I am fretting about what comes next." But I know the jig is up with Dmitri. In an instant of insanity I figure, what the heck, and I stay, milking every last ounce out of that moment, selling it, feeling my extended limbs come to life, my hip rotate fully. To my immense pleasure, Dmitri practically croons, "Bee-utifool!" And I am so surprised I stop in my tracks.

"Why did you stop?" he asks, with his own surprise on his face. I can't begin to explain.

A lovely anachronistic misconception in ballroom dance is that the woman's carefree expression in the moment of a pose is possible because she isn't supposed to worry her pretty little head about what comes next; that's the man's job. He is supposed to give the next indication—"Okay, we're going now"—with a little nudge in the hand or whatever. But in effect, with high-level dancers, both the man and the woman are in charge, both know what's coming next. And both can be carefree, confident, and captivating because they are enjoying being in each moment as it happens.

I'm moving forward toward Dmitri in this elastic dance of stretching out and releasing back, as the music suggests. My breath touches Dmitri's cheek; with a snap of his wrist he turns me, my hips and shoulders turning out to the right. I stay again, on the four-one, despite my impulse to keep going, not to loiter so close to him for so long. Then, feeling the signal through his fingers, I take two walks forward away from him at a ninety-degree angle and he turns me again, this time leftward, and I step to the side on my left foot, my right leg pointing forward toward him. I want desperately to close my right foot to my left, that's next, but he has barked again, "Stay!" So again I stay. I notice the music gives me plenty of time to hang out and listen and even look sexy. What's the rush? Without rush, there is the beautiful melody, and for the length of time that one dance figure lasts, I cease being a moth to the flame of my future.

It's not as if the whole dance is about staying, though. The staying, the languidness makes way for the speediness of the steps to follow. Quick, go! Then recover. It's the intertwining of legato and staccato, fast and slow, that makes the Latin dance dynamic, exciting, and erotic. And to think I was stuck on fast-forward like a DVD player, *borink,* frantic, and probably exhausting my audience. It does make me wonder why I dance. Surely it's not to bore and exhaust my audience. Then what?

OUR LESSON IS over and I am excited to put into practice this new skill, being present, but I do have to get going to pick up my daughters at school. They hate it when I keep them waiting at the corner for all their fellow students to see. Somehow, they're convinced that's "totally embarrassing." So whatever I'm doing on Mondays, I try to arrive at the corner of Mt. Hope Boulevard and School Street by 2:48 p.m. Today, I get to my spot with a few minutes to spare for daydreaming.

I think about how, in some ways, having children has kept me in the moment, more or less by force. I remember changing a diaper, dressing my infant girl in a pretty little outfit to get out the door on time for something, and then the thoughtless child pooped in the new diaper and it blasted through to the pretty outfit. For that, you stay. You change the diaper and the outfit. The tiny little being willfully delays your future. Children know nothing else in the early years but "feed me," "play with me." You do both constantly until they decide they'd rather take lunch money, and they'd rather play with their friends.

I had trouble focusing on the playing as a new mom. My attention was always split. I had one eye on the game, one eye on the task I needed to complete. Usually, I'd play in a distracted way, and sort a pile of papers at the same time, or jump up between turns to tidy the room. Multitasking was my nonnegotiable survival technique. Now and then, I tried just to play, but the games seemed so dumbed down and tedious. And pretty soon, my children got wise to my ways.

"Mom, your turn," Erica would say, to reclaim my attention.

"Mom, come back," Alden would call. Even her body language

would say it: I'd sit cross-legged on the floor around the Cinderella board game and she would hold my foot. If I tried to move or get up, she'd hold tighter. Remarkably tight. It was nice to be wanted, but my to-do list beckoned. In fact, that list ruled everything else. Thinking back, I cringe at all the wasted moments with my kids.

Way before dance started teaching me to stay, there was my therapist, Ruth, whom I'd started to see when Peter and I were splitting up. She bugged me about my so-called fear of intimacy. Honestly, I didn't think I had any such fear, but she had a habit of surprising me when I thought I was being clever and right.

"You certainly do have a lot on your plate," she observed one day after I'd enumerated the tasks I was facing, which accounted for the resentment I brought to our session.

"Yeah, that's my to-do list, and it's always that way."

"Couldn't you ask Peter to take half of the things on the list so you could enjoy doing something with your girls instead?"

"I've tried. He's so resistant. Anyway, he doesn't know who the kids' doctors are, or what their after-school schedule is, so I handle that. I write the checks to pay the bills. He thinks because he pays bills for his business that he shouldn't have to help with this task at home."

Then Ruth shifted the discussion.

"What do you do for fun?"

"Well, I guess dance," I replied. "Though dance has now officially become my practice, which implies work, and dedication, not fun. And just recently I studied so hard for that professional class, you know, that licensing exam I took—that really wasn't fun, though it was very fulfilling, and I feel like I accomplished—"

"Picnics? Walk in the woods?" she prompted.

"Peter does that with the girls. We wake up on a Saturday and face how different we are. He looks up at the blue sky and says, 'Let's go for a bike ride.' I look at the list of chores and say, 'No, first let's do this. Then we can play.' "

"I wonder if your to-do list is a barrier—a paper barrier. It could be that you keep it between you and your children. It may be protecting you from a greater degree of intimacy with them."

No way, I thought, I'm a good mother. We make Swedish cookies at Christmastime from my grandmother's recipes that she taught me when I was thirteen. I put a bedsheet on the kitchen floor so we can get down and messy and we make Ring-a-rounds and thumbprints. We dance at home too. We plant flowers together. I spend an hour with the girls at bedtime. Peter actually tells me it's too long. I'm a good mother!

Some time after Peter moved out, I attended a seminar at our middle school about parenting. Because the middle-school years are a difficult phase for children, a time when they tend to feel the effects of peer pressure and possibly try drugs, or at the very least drift off into a period of shaky self-esteem, the school held a presentation about communicating with teens during which Scott, a very nice counselor, advised us to "Be with your kids and I mean be there with them. One key thing you can do to keep in touch is to watch the TV shows they're watching."

Hmm. To me, that had always been the time for me to clean the house, return phone calls, unpack my office tote—because they're glued to the tube, the opiate of the American people. But I didn't want to lose my girls to drugs, and I didn't want to lose them to the self-esteem boogeyman, and I kept hearing Ruth's annoying suggestion that I'd placed a barrier between us, so that night I went home and watched TV with Alden and Erica. I sat on that sticky old brown leather couch, the same one my husband used to stretch out on, and I stayed there between them with my glass of wine while we watched American Idol. I vaguely recall the girls looked at me expectantly, as if something were wrong, because I was sitting down and not doing anything. I did not get up to do the dishes. I did not even pick up that plastic cup lying sideways at the base of the coffee table threatening to dribble juice. And since that night, we have watched *American Idol* together every Tuesday night without fail. It's funny to think I will skip a work event or an invitation to dinner with friends because I can't miss *Idol*. I love that show. Sadly, though, the word among teens now is it's uncool, so I'm not allowed to mention it when Alden's friends are over.

IT'S 2:47, daydreaming over, and I am about to see Alden and Erica emerge from school. I love to watch the girls' faces as they walk toward the car on the one day each week I get to pick them up. The second they see me waiting for them, they break into big smiles. Maybe not Alden so much. There she comes now. Her smile is demure, a little self-conscious. Here comes Erica. She's more effusive. Her smile comes with generous dimples and missing canines; it's just irresistible. My eyes become shiny with tears that won't spill; I am conscious of my love as they open doors and climb in.

"Hi, Mom. Come on, let's go," Erica says. "Oh, you forgot to sign my permission slip. Ms. Fischman says I can't go on the trip if she doesn't get it tomorrow."

"Okay."

"Hey, where's Cookie and Rizzo?" Alden asks.

"They're home. I came from dance."

THE NEXT MORNING, at six-forty a.m., I wake Alden up. I am her alarm clock. As usual, I enter silently and sit on her bed, stroke her hair to wake her gently, bring her back to our world. Her room smells of rank dog. Our lovable rottweiler is incredibly stinky, like a stagnant, algae-covered pond, plus he's a farter, so her room gets this rich aroma overnight. He raises his big, black head in lazy acknowledgment of my arrival, making eye contact like King Kong, then lays his head back down. I begin to rub Alden's shoulders, my empathy (I love being massaged) telling me where to touch. Then she pulls an arm out from under the covers to offer her hand. She likes me to massage her hands. I do this. I press the pads at the base of each finger; I rub the palm with both of my thumbs; I gently pull each finger.

And now comes the urge to get up to leave to get back to my morning routine, all the many things I must do before we leave the house: the breakfast, the notes to the babysitter, the lists for my own day, the feeding of dogs. Here is the moment when I'd hear Alden's voice, muffled by her thick hair and piles of blankets she buries herself in, say, "Mom, stay." But this morning I hear nothing except her breathing. And Rizzo's snuffle-snort inhale. *To hell with the recycling; forget makeup today.* I look out the window at the first sunlight yellowing the leaves on the distant maple trees. It is so beautiful, the life in here.

Today feels like a beginning. She doesn't need to grab my foot. I wonder if that feels good to her. I stay for her, but it turns out to be for me. For the first time, I see that changing my behavior as a mother can be as small and simple a thing as grasping one single dance maneuver. But as with dance, mastery will take endless practice. Anyway, I've been mothering this girl for fourteen years, and *now* I get a chance to *be* with her. For so long, I was convinced I'm a good mother because of everything I *do* for my kids. Has this girl lain quietly all the while, hoping for me to just be with her? Have I tortured her with my busyness, so that she has been obliged to beg, "Mom, don't go?" Cling to the coziness with me.

I'm here, baby. I'm here.

18   Good Fences Make Good Dancers

We are staying at the Ritz-Carlton Hotel on Grand Cayman in the Cayman Islands. I'm on an assignment from *Town & Country* to check out the new spa here. I was invited to bring a guest, and there she is lying on her back on our king-size bed, making the inordinately fluffy duvet cover damp with her wet bathing suit, kicking her legs in the air absentmindedly, making her nonnegotiable demands as usual.

"No, Mom, I want *Charlie's Angels* tonight. You have to call them again. Did you call yet?" Erica, as this most annoying age of almost eleven, is insisting on getting the DVD she's had on her mind since this morning.

"Why not, Mom?" Big, long whine.

"Because I called last night and they said the hotel is full and the DVDs won't be returned for two days, but the concierge said she would keep an eye out . . ."

"But MOM!" Her voice booms now. "This hotel sucks, I want to see *Charlie's Angels*. You promised!" All right, so she sounds spoiled. But that's not really it. I see her as strong-willed and intensely focused, with no ability to delay gratification. (Like you were thinking, spoiled.) I need to teach her some skills for dealing with her own impatience. I often wish I had the temperament of a nursery school teacher, but most of the time, I end up blowing my stack and yelling at her, especially in the evenings when I'm at the end of my rope. Then I regret having indulged my anger, and I spend some time in deep self-critical contemplation, after which I call a girlfriend looking for sympathy.

Here on Grand Cayman, I am determined to do what I can to make this a special mother-daughter vacation, even though I'm here on business. I want this to be a time for us to be close, to have an adventure or two and lots of fun, for me to show Erica how much I love her and how much I appreciate what a cool kid she is. I have worried that she's already decided she's a bad girl because of all the reprimands she gets. Usually, I get pissed off at her after only three or four back-and-forths. But right now, I seem not to be getting mad at her yet. I am remaining calm despite her behavior, which has gone beyond normal childish nagging into the realm of Chinese water torture. Something here is slightly different; like objects in a car mirror, things always appear different in paradise.

The next night takes care of my equanimity. It starts again just before dinner, after a nice full day of swimming, manicure-pedicures, and a boat excursion during which we got to swim with stingrays. Little tropical storm Erica, making landfall just after our showers, directs her gale-force winds at me. Finally, when her incessant complaining starts to seem incredibly selfish, I yell at her, give her what she's waiting for, a blast of my ire. She pouts. And then the concierge, coincidentally named Janet, calls our room to inform us that she has, unbidden, sent somebody named Leroy to her house halfway across the island, because she owns the *Charlie's Angels* DVD, and Leroy is now bringing said DVD to our room. I provide a generous tip to both the staff person delivering the movie and to Janet, my alter ego who clearly wanted to enable my enabling of my daughter. So Erica and I get cozy, order room service, and watch *Charlie's Angels* in bed together eating french fries, strip steak, and key lime pie.

A day or so later we are on the plane home. Erica has her usual window seat, so I get squished in the middle. I am reflecting on my daughter's temperament and how lousy my tennis game has gotten. The two seem linked somehow and I mull this over. Erica and I played tennis yesterday in the stultifying, windless heat. She'd had a tennis lesson our first day while I did my spa tour. She wanted to play with me the next day, and I was eager to play too. So off we went. We were banging the balls around, she hitting very few in my actual direction, so I'd run this way and that to show her how game I can be, what a fun mother I am, despite how running on the court hurt my ancient, pre-arthritic knees. It was so hot it was hard to breathe. I served to her. I stood patiently while she tried to serve to me. This is what parents do. It can be tedious, unless you really concentrate on the child's activity. Was I having fun? Kind of. But mostly, I was making it fun for Erica. I was doing what I could to please Erica. Aha! That's when it hit me—not the tennis ball but the realization. It is impossible to please Erica! Each new moment presents in her a new desire, a new and urgent need. And I am a people-pleasing mommy. It is my job, or so I thought, to please Erica.

Our tennis game was a laughable demonstration of the dynamic: she standing there thoroughly self-involved, enjoying hitting balls here and there, and me running after them. Fetching balls for her, serving balls right to her so she needn't run too much. So she wouldn't get frustrated. Me trying my level best to please her and feeling anxious if I didn't. Getting that damned DVD after all. I go around with strategies in my head for pleasing Erica in the near future, tension in my jaw about not having pleased her yet, pressure to keep looking for another, better way. And all this is futile, because it is *impossible* to please Erica. She's on to the next thing already, looking for more satisfaction. I'm doomed to fall behind, to fail. No sooner do I feel some small success at having accomplished one thing that makes her smile or feel successful than the next desire for immediate gratification is upon her, the next disappointment. And thus I meet my next failure. An endless cycle.

The name Erica is Scandinavian and it means "bold ruler." It appears we chose wisely. But it is not about Erica. She is just doing her job, being a kid. It is me. In seat 22B, as I look at her looking out the window of 22A, I decide to try from now on to let her experience the full weight of her disappointments in life, rather than keep trying to prevent them or protect her from them. They are *her* disappointments; she has a right to them. I have to practice allowing for this positive space between us, and letting her wear herself out with her ranting and raving over whatever she wants, as long as it doesn't disturb the neighbors.

MY PROBLEM IS I don't know how to say no. It's part of the good-girl people-pleasing complex. Take my job, for example: I get tons of invitations to business functions every week, plus dozens of requests for deskside appointments, and I turn down 90 percent of them. You'd think I'd be pretty good at it by now. But where one word would suffice ("No") or two ("No thanks"), or even four ("No thanks, I'm busy"), I have a habit of using twenty-five or thirty ("Well, I would, but tonight my husband, actually my soon to be ex-husband, is traveling and so I have the kids and my babysitter can't stay late because it's her darts night . . ."). Cut! I frustrate my own self with my long-windedness. What's with that nonsense? Nobody on this planet wants to hear that much of a reason. Either come or don't come, the poor person on the other end of the phone must be thinking, but don't tell me your whole life story. What am I doing, asking permission from the host to decline?

Because standing up often provides dubious reward and comes at a cost, I do so rarely. Mostly, I find it easier to toe the line. It took me years, for example, to recognize that during my childhood my mom was something of an interior designer, and that there were no locks on the door to my psyche. She'd come in because the door was open and make herself comfortable, rearrange the furniture. Not with any malice aforethought—it's just the way she was, kind of loose with the boundaries. This is what to think and how to think it. "It's not my opinion; it's a universal truth." If you don't comply, you're a bad girl, is what I took from it; not that she said that, but kids take stuff very seriously when you least expect it. I know that because I'm a mom now—and it's disturbing to think how I've trespassed my own children's boundaries.

The open-house nature of my psyche has left me rather prickly about intimacy because I never learned the difference between someone waltzing right in and me inviting them in. Take my fledgling attempts at dating recently: I've noticed I can be smack in the middle of making out with a man, and we're in this glorious, full-blown kiss when suddenly, without warning or explanation, I panic, terrified by the invasion of his tongue inside my mouth. A kiss that I started out participating in joyfully and lustfully has turned inexplicably into something horribly unpleasant.

Today, as it becomes clearer to me that I do have a choice—it's my door and I can close it or leave it open—I see the fourteen-year-old girl in the dark room in a new light. She hasn't been banished or locked in. No siree. She's in there seeking privacy. She turned out the lights, hoping she wouldn't be found, and yet never giving up hope for rescue.

I understand it now: in my fantasy of finding a perfect connection with a man, I have always longed for rescue. And it took me half my life, but I'm starting to see that rescuers may have been at the ready. The problem might be that I didn't give any of these eager heroes the green light because, as much as I wanted it, I confused rescue with invasion, and so had to prevent it. All kidding about old-fashioned notions of princes on white steeds aside, it's probably discovery that I truly want. Here's what I desire: I am in a high tower, the base of which is covered with densely tangled overgrowth, and I am pretty inaccessible. The man reaches the base after bushwhacking his way through the jungle below, and starts hacking away at the vines as he scales the tower. He is unstoppable, and very manly. Best of all, he knows where to find me.

And here's how I feel about Peter: he got to the base of the tower and saw the difficulty of the vegetation and the height of the walls, and he shrugged and walked away.

MY GIRLS HAVE decided they want to make smoothies, so while they get out the ingredients, I go to the pantry to get the blender. Hey, no blender.

"It's here somewhere," I say, bending down to look at the back of the shelves in the cubbyhole. No blender. I go down to the cellar and hunt through the shelves there. No blender. I come back up to the kitchen. Erica stands there next to the ingredients waiting for me to provide the blender. "Where is it?" Alden asks.

"I can't find it. I must have put it somewhere else. Let's look in these cabinets." I dig behind the bowls and plastic water bottles in one cabinet. No blender. My mind begins racing. Finder Mommy kicks into high gear. Did I lend it to someone? Did it break? Am I losing my memory? Then it hits me. Peter. I grab the phone.

"I'm looking for the blender and I can't find it. Did you take it by any chance?"

"Oh yeah, I guess I took it last week when we were having a party."

"Well, next time, call me first, or at least leave me a note so I don't drive myself crazy looking. I just wasted twenty minutes and now we can't make smoothies. The girls were so excited."

When Peter left, he packed a small backpack, dismounted the outdoor speakers I'd given him for his birthday one year, loaded his photo equipment in his car, and left for good. He returned only to take the futon from the spare room that had become my office. He left all that stuff in his walk-in closet, most of his shoes, his toiletries in the medicine chest, the Dopp kit containing, I saw later, the condoms that weren't for my benefit. He left all his mementos and memories, but then, curiously, hasn't hesitated all these months to help himself to things big and small that our household actually needs and uses. One evening, I go down to the cellar to the old au pair's room to get something, and I walk in and I'm in shock. The bed is gone! It's gone.

I go upstairs and call Julia. "I think Peter took it. But he knew we needed that bed to go to Rhode Island when the girls go up to stay with my sister for art school. He agreed to drive it up! I can't believe it. He steals in like a thief when I'm not here and helps himself. It feels like . . . such a violation!"

"What do you mean he comes in when you're not there?" Julia asks. She sounds flabbergasted and calm at the same time. I think she's missing the point.

"He comes in all the time to collect his mail, to take whatever he wants, to pick up the kids—usually three hours earlier than planned."

"But this is your house now," Julia tells me, as if I didn't know I've been paying the huge mortgage myself all this time. "He has his home. He has to be able to see this. Why would his belongings still be in your house? Hasn't it been a year? Even more?"

There's no reason for me to be surprised by what Peter does, I tell myself. That's Peter, and I should not expect any different from him. But now it's time. I'm going to change the locks. I'm going to tell him no. No more. I already told him to stop taking stuff without leaving me a note. Now I'm changing the locks. He's in for a surprise next time he tries to let himself in. I don't know how I can work it so the kids can have their own keys without him just copying one, but I'm doing it. This is my house, and he doesn't belong here. Why did it take me so long? Why have I let him use my house as a storage closet?

ROBERT FROST'S POEM "Mending Wall" keeps coming to my mind these days, especially the line "Good fences make good neighbors." I feel sheepish that I tend to agree with the neighbor that it's good to draw those lines, to know that you'll be raking your leaves on your side of the fence. Sheepish because my mother brought us up with the opposite idea; she'd agree with Frost: *something there is that doesn't love a wall.* It's all about sharing, helping each other, merging—a veritable soup of human righteousness and love. Frost says his neighbor, who mindlessly keeps fixing the wall no matter what, *moves in darkness,* which of course means in small-mindedness or stupidity; Mom would second that. In her view, it takes a big person to give up those silly boundaries.

I needed to build some fences for myself when I was young because, to be perfectly unapologetic about mixing metaphors, I grew up with my personal boundary being nothing more than a sieve. This explains my leakiness as a grown-up around other people. Think of it: I was raised as one of a litter of puppies, indistinguishable from the next. I wasn't supposed to sacrifice the group interest in order to pursue what I needed. I was taught that privacy equals secrecy and secrecy is a punishable crime; whatever I had on my plate, I should share. All very honorable Protestant notions, but they can sure screw you up.

Mom had in some ways forbidden fences, but I needed to keep people out somehow, so I built my fences in a devious way. I became a very diligent worker, very, very busy all the time. That was a fence—"don't bother me, I'm working here." But Mom couldn't critique it, because the thing about Protestants is they have that work ethic. My to-do list has been a fence, a rigid piece of paper that says to others, "this far and no farther" or "not now, I have too much going on." My sense of humor could be a conversational fence, cutting the tension of imminent intimacy and putting it off course. My control, my self-reliance, and my resistance to letting go and to spontaneity—all fences.

Over the years, I lost sight of the fact that I was born like everybody else with my own innate boundaries intact. If those had not been disabled (or rather, punctured), I wouldn't need these rigid fences. I can't see my natural boundaries, but now I know they're there, and I'm sure I can get them to function again. It makes sense; my skin works—why wouldn't my other boundaries work, the invisible ones, the epidermis of my soul? So I think I'll take down my fences, finally, after thirty-five years of determined building and maintenance. I feel no fear, strangely enough. It feels like a dream. If I wake up, I suppose I can get back to the carpentry. Meanwhile, I can say no to people. Just no. I don't have to explain any further. I have my permission. Not angry no, not frantic no, not defensive no. Just a quiet no. A no out of self-respect. There need be no more patrol, no special forces—more like a smile, an exhale.

Unlike locks, boundaries aren't for keeping people out. They're for knowing who you are. If boundaries were for keeping people out, sex would not be fun, at least not for a woman. And now I know: it's not the intrusion itself that feels horrible, it's me giving up myself, being mushy about who I am, that feels the worst. It's this self-betrayal that makes a visit (to my house, or my body) sometimes seem like an invasion. And there's not a fence in the world sturdy or tall enough to help in such a case.

DURING OUR LESSONS, Bill has often asked me to be like a shopping cart. I am inclined to be more like one of those French bags made of string netting, collapsible, lightweight, and easy to store. When I tell Bill about my theory concerning fences, and my ignorance of boundaries, he takes the discussion into our dancing.

"There's a way in which you don't respect your boundaries when we dance," he observes.

"How not?"

"You come inside your own arms," he answers, referring to the circle described by our joined arms, the space between us. I'd expected him to say something about what that does to me, or how bad it looks to have my "chicken wings" sticking out, my elbows too far back behind me instead of in front of me. But no, he says, "When you do that, I feel smothered."

When I give up my boundary, he suffocates? It must be because he's forced to come too far into my space. When I don't maintain my arms, my hands, and my feet in proper relation to each other, he says, it renders his guidance system inoperable. He can't lead.

"It helps to think of a shopping cart," he offers. "You know, it has a handle. And the man pushes that handle and the cart moves forward. Well, with you, when I push the handle, it collapses and I fall into the basket."

Oh dear.

"Funny, it sounds like it's better for me to be more rigid. I always thought rigidity in dance was bad." Like my rigid fences.

"It's about responsiveness, elasticity, not about keeping a stiff frame, but a fluidity or a dynamism. It's as if you enable our power steering. You have a shape, but it should be a responsive shape. When you give that up, we're in trouble."

And so for the first time, life has actually revealed something to me about my dancing instead of the other way around.

ON A CHILLY May evening after a long day at the office, I take the train home and drive from the station to Zinsser Field to watch the second half of Erica's softball game. I walk carefully in my heels over the uneven, gravelly edge of the field to join the small crowd of spectators for her team. As I approach the opponents' bleachers I see someone I recognize. It's been years, maybe about ten, since we last saw each other. I recognize his face, though it is fuller now, and he's put on some weight. It startles me, that he looks a bit worse for wear compared to his fitter self, the one I knew in the eighties, when we both commuted by train and often talked for a few minutes on the platform. I vaguely recall even how he looked when he was maybe ten or twelve years old, because he was in my big sister's class at Hastings Elementary. She had a crush on him then. All the girls did. He was tall, blond, handsome, athletic, and very, very smart.

"Hi, Janet," Greg says. I look at him, pretending he saw me before I saw him. I don't know why I pretend. Maybe all those intervening years have made me shy. Maybe I don't want to say hi first.

"Hey, stranger, where've you been?" I know he and his wife sold their house on Lincoln Avenue, two blocks from ours. The "for sale" sign was out by the curb for some time and I used to see it when I did my power walking around the neighborhood. I wondered where they'd gone. I remember how he'd given me a tour so long ago when they were just moving in and doing a lot of renovation. He was in the construction business in Manhattan and had a huge crew working in the attic.

"I dropped out for a while," he says.

He tells me about his life since the demise of his lucrative business after September 11, when he lost two employees in the towers, and all the people he knew at his main client, Cantor Fitzgerald; and then there was his ugly, five-year divorce.

We talk about our marriages and their endings. I tell him what has happened to mine. "We're still only separated. It's pretty amicable, so I guess there's no rush."

"How's your anger quotient?" he asks.

"I'm learning to get angry at Peter."

He laughs. I enjoy making him laugh. I didn't expect him to have understood my flip remark. Erica comes over to the bleachers after running home from third.

"Mom, you're on the wrong side," she says, grabbing her water bottle.

"I know. Eri, say hi to Greg Lewis. Guess what? We went to elementary school together. He was in Aunt Anna's class."

"Oh. Hi." And she runs off to hang on the fence behind home plate with her teammates.

A few days later, that Friday evening, I come home to find a small white envelope in the mailbox on top of the junk mail. "Janet" is written on the outside. I open it and unfold a small piece of paper. "Janet, I enjoyed our conversation at softball the other night. I would like to see you again. I wanted to call you but your number isn't in the book. Give me a call sometime if you feel like it. Greg Lewis." He'd scribbled his cell number at the bottom.

It feels good to have this little note suggesting that someone out there likes me—someone whom I might actually like back. I do want to be a woman again. And I want to be adored in real life, beyond the dance studio. But of course, it can't be Greg. He is currently unemployed, and probably just looking for a woman to rescue him. That's been my problem—going for dependent guys that I can manage. I'm not going there again.

I tell my mother the next time we speak on the phone. "Oh, Mom, guess who I saw? Greg Lewis. Remember him?"

"Of course. Where? Does he still live in Hastings?"

"I guess so. He was at softball the other night, so we talked. And I got this note from him afterward. It sounds like he wants to go out, but I don't know." I describe his circumstances, and reassure her I'm not going to get involved with any more needy men looking for someone to take care of them. Anyway, even if I'm misjudging him, I still want my Friday nights every other week to myself. I'm too busy!

"Oh, he was so nice, and the smartest boy in Anna's grade," Mom croons. "His whole family was so lovely. He could do worse than to have a friend like you supporting him now after such a difficult time. What a shame. You don't have to date him. You could just be a friend. You could use that, too."

I call him on Sunday just to be polite. Our families have known each other for forty years. How can I ignore his note? That would be mean. Anyway, no harm in a conversation. I liked our first conversation a lot, too.

He does want to get together, have a drink or something, but I avoid that. Instead, we have a few more long phone calls, and we agree to meet at another softball game the following week, when our daughters' teams face each other again. Erica's team wins by a few runs. He walks me to my car, and I decide that's the time to be clear.

"Hey, listen, Greg. I figured I should explain this," I start in, and he stands there at my bumper looking at me. "Not to jump the gun or anything. But I can't have a relationship now. I've really only got time for my work and my kids and keeping my household running. I'm sorry. It's not a good time."

He doesn't look particularly fazed. "That's fine. Just know that when you need to vent or just have a friendly dinner or something, I'm your man." I watch him walk slowly across the empty field in the twilight toward the woods, probably taking a shortcut to town, and find myself wondering if he even owns a car.

IN THE EVOLUTION of my complicated self, this evolution that goes by fits and starts, I presume that treasuring my biweekly alone time is fully justified, but now there's a soupçon of suspicion making itself known in my head: is all that just another fence, and should I be taking it down? I wish I could skip to the answer page in the quiz book, but I haven't found it yet. I've no other choice; I have to keep muddling along.

19 PARING DOWN

DMITRI IS TO my dancing what California Closets would be to my house if I ever let them in. He is eliminating the clutter. "You have a lot of extra stuff in your dancing," he is fond of saying. "We are going to get rid of everything except what is necessary." This reminds me of Bill, who has said, "Nothing is decoration; everything in the dance is functional." It appears that I add too many flourishes—with my hand, for example, as I lift it out to the side in rumba—and I do something weird with my ankle when I'm pointing a foot forward with a long leg. Also, my skittishness leads me to do extra things for no reason, like kinking my rib cage to the right instead of keeping it aligned with the rest of me. I think that's the junk Dmitri is referring to. But also, I try to do too much where less would be better.

I have struggled all my dancing life with balance and stability. It frustrates me that I can't easily do multiple spins, say, in that great disco dance, the hustle, and remain perfectly vertical the whole time. And I envy dancers I've watched at Dance New York who do the seemingly simple forward walks in rumba, wobbling not one bit. I've always remarked on how much more difficult the most basic steps are to execute well, compared to the snazzy advanced ones. When I wear those ridiculous high-heeled Latin sandals that give absolutely no support and try to walk (and every woman blames it on the heels), I lose my composure every few steps. I feel foolish and klutzy. Every Latin teacher I've had in my life has offered me different solutions, to no avail. It's possible that I've specialized in Standard because I get to lean on a partner, which I'm not supposed to do—leaning is the wrong use of your partner because it usually means you're compromising *his* balance, as Bill has said many times—but I still really want to.

I have kept in mind all the things I could do, all the tips I've collected over the years for staying in balance: "Find your center and hold it"; "Step right onto the foot, don't hesitate"; "Place your weight over the center of your foot"; "Look forward, not down"; "Keep your shoulders level"; "Don't rush"; "Don't hesitate"; "Keep some weight pressing on your back foot at all times." That's a lot to remember. One day I walk pretty well, in balance, but the next, or the next week, I'm a teetering mess. I can't rely on any magic bullet no matter how many combinations of instructions I try.

Dmitri has an idea.

"Today, you are having trouble with balance. But you know, it's not as though you are one person one day, and a different person the next. I have mentioned before the stack of books, yes? It's very simple. If you stack one book exactly on top of the other one, and another exactly on top of that, and so on, you can build a very high stack which will not fall down. But if you put one book like this," and he shows with his hands the books looking slightly askew, "your stack will fall down." Listening to him, I begin to stack my insides and imagine keeping them like this when I move.

"When you stack the books vertically, it doesn't matter if it's raining outside or sunny, or if it's early or late, or if you ate a good breakfast. The books will stay; they won't fall."

I'm looking at Dmitri thinking how beautifully simple his idea is, and how convincing. He has taken away the clutter surrounding this one problem, and he looks cherubic as he shares his delight in the logic that promises to be the key to my stability. It is a hallmark of his teaching, this simplifying, and looking at him now, I realize how different we are. I tend to be complicated; I am *complicating*. If my brain were Map Quest, I'd present you with the scenic route along back roads, not the shortest route on the highways. I enjoy the meandering—but now I see that it might behoove me to decomplicate.

It's no help that I have had some lessons with teachers who also complicate things. Oksana, for example, my favorite Latin professional at Dance New York. She moves like a minx, slithers like an otter in her sexy lingerie outfits and fishnets; I have envied her brazen-hussy quality. I booked one lesson with her a few years ago because I wanted a woman to teach me the basic Latin movement. I felt so accomplished in Standard, so rusty in Latin, and shy to writhe. We spent the hour on my hip bones. I wrote down her instructions afterward; it took two pieces of paper. "Move the right front top part of the pelvic girdle forward and then in a circular motion out to the right on the four-one count, keep your lower rib scrunched toward your femur, but keep the back leg straight, the left knee inward and always, the ribs tucked. Settle your weight deep into the right hip socket." And so on. I burned many calories during this lesson concentrating on these ludicrously specific instructions and trying to do as she asked. It was all so arduous. I held my breath trying to locate that front top part of the pelvic bone and make it move forward while the rest of me stayed behind. I felt like a dunce. I treasured those notes, though, and practiced in private at home, convinced at first that it just needed practice, and that one day I'd put all the pieces together and move fluidly. It didn't happen. The notes chided me from my bedside stand, and eventually I moved them to the bookshelf in the spare room. I gave up hoping to become a Latin goddess. I'd just stay where I belonged—in Standard.

"No, no, no," Dmitri said when, in one of our early lessons, I started to explain what I'd been working on. "That's too much. Just walk forward, collect your knees when one leg passes the other, and turn the hip back as far as you can, turn your pants' pocket back to the windows." That and his neat stack of books changed my movement in one forty-five-minute lesson. All the garbage fell away and I did my forward rumba walks, haltingly at first, but soon enough, they were smooth, easy ribbons of Latin lusciousness and I wasn't wobbling. My hips swayed and rotated, my forward motion was confident. For a moment, I could even look at myself in the mirror without shame. I wasn't doing more work better, I was doing less, with far better result.

A yoga master named Erich Schiffman once said: "Love is what is left when you let go of everything that you don't need." Emotional clutter. Now I'd say beauty in dance is what is left when you let go of everything that you didn't realize you don't need, everything that is not joy. The dancer brave enough to be simple is the one who takes your breath away. The beauty is in the necessary movement that remains after all the rest is swept aside. I want to be able to dance like this. And then, we can talk about love.

But for now, I'll settle for clearing the bamboo in my backyard. As a project, this is looking awfully complicated, partly because my hands are full to capacity with basic household maintenance—too much to do—and also because everything looks more complicated if you let it, as I often do when I'm cranky about things, all the burdens and the chaos.

I am looking out my windows at the sprawling stand of bamboo, which for so many years has been a source of delight and serenity for me and others in my home, a single Zen aspect. It's a lovely and constant reminder to me about being delicate, flexible, and strong all at once. So I am bummed, this August morning, that the bamboo has become oppressive. It has grown so tall and so thick that it's now overcrowded, and the tall canes are bowing ominously over the house toward the second-floor bedroom windows, over the once-sunny deck. It's blocking the precious bit of sunlight I used to adore in the sunroom, whose western wall is all windows. On stormy nights in winter, the frozen, icicle-glazed bamboo bends in the wind and scratches along the windows. It's creepy. Time to call Five Brothers or Two Cousins or one of the other numerous landscape outfits in our town.

First to come is a man named Val, who says he'll go up on a ladder and lop off the tops of all the bamboo, make it nice and even and short. I cringe. Sounds like a potential disaster. I'd better research this online. I learn that you shouldn't top bamboo: "It gives an unaesthetic appearance, can lead to rot, and it never grows up again, not like shrubs." That's the end of that. The chat archives recommend thinning instead, by removing the tallest canes.

Next, two landscape experts named Gume and Jorge come to have a look around my property, all one-quarter acre of it, at the bamboo and the gardens. They speak Spanish between themselves for a few minutes and then announce, "Three thousand dollars for a good cleanup and the trees and bamboo." What do they think—I'm stupid? My yard is neither that bad nor that big. I ask Steve and Judy, my neighbors across the street, and learn their yard cleanup is a few hundred bucks. I'll call the brothers or the uncles or somebody else. I make a note on my kitchen counter. More research. Maybe after our vacation in Gloucester, I'll make an appointment. Geez, this is getting to be one of those big deals I don't have time for.

The next morning, I wake up at seven, press the button on the electric kettle, and go outside in my pajamas. I take the saw out of the shed. I look at my overgrown stand of bamboo with love, as if at a poorly trained dog. It only needs some discipline, some good training. I examine on high, settle on the canes bowing the deepest, and saw away at one offender, laying it to rest. Then four or five more. It is really quite satisfying. I haul them over to the moss-covered ground by the shed, and go back to examine. I see what has grown too far to the right and is obscuring my valuable partial river view, so I take three down on that side. I take my time and work gently, out of respect for the bamboo and for my chronically injured elbow.

When we return from our week in Gloucester on Friday evening, the girls go to Peter's house and I go back eagerly to the bamboo first thing the next morning. The canes I cut have dried to a light gray. I step back for a good look and spy the tallest ones in the densest part of the stand; I can't get to them easily, but I am able to pull out some dead canes with my bare hands. I can then reach in with the saw and, despite not much room for maneuvering, saw down the old grandfather canes, the fattest ones that are blocking the most sun. They come down heavy, but I steer them as they fall and they do no damage to the hot tub, the windows, or Unlucky's gravesite. I tear off the juiciest-looking branches and feed them to Ginger, our new Holland dwarf rabbit.

Later that day, I sit at the table in the sunroom to sort the huge pile of mail that the dog walker brought in while we were away. When I look up at around four-thirty, the sunlight is dappling the Italian stone of the dining table, the room is glowing like it used to, and I am filled with a contentment arising from just the necessary bamboo.

As I go along now, I'll try to remember that it's okay to have a complicated mind, as long as I don't allow it to impose complexity in life where there need be none. In my gardening and my dancing, to begin with, I've gotten rid of some clutter and the result is I feel much better. I probably have less to huff and puff and complain about than I thought.

WILL THE REAL JANET PLEASE STAND UP?

I HAD LUNCH recently with my friend Diane, a magazine writer, concert pianist, and psychoanalytic therapist. I told her where I was with my dancing, and asked about her piano, and we got to talking about artistic expression. She told me about the famous bass player Julius Levine, who said something like "When a musician performs and people say, 'Oh, he plays very well indeed,' then you know it's no use." Ah, competence, the kiss of death! Deliver me from my competence!

It looks like it's time. I have been postponing as long as possible. I can tell that Dmitri is not going to let me get away with just being a good student any longer. He is not an intimidating man, or bossy or aggressive. But he has his ways.

"What is the most important thing in dancing?" Dmitri asks.

"Musicality?" I answer.

"No."

"Perfect anticipation?"

"No."

"Communication?"

"No."

"Then what?" I ask, giving up.

"You," Dmitri says with authority. "You can do nothing special if you're not being you in your dance." Sorry, Dmitri, not interested. But of course I'm nodding as if I'll just go right ahead and do as he says. "A lot of my students say they want to be as good as some professional dancer or other that they've seen in competitions. If you want to be as good as Brian Watson, then you are just a copy of Brian Watson. How interesting is that, when we can see the real Brian Watson? What we want to see is . . . you."

I am standing there for a bit looking out the window, pretending to hear what he is saying next, but I am in this train of thought and it is major. I've been so busy pleasing others, I forgot to be authentic. It's been so long, I don't remember how, but I have to find a way to be who I am, not who I think they want me to be. Why am I dancing? Dmitri's right: I shouldn't bother trying to emulate some ideal. I'm not out on the floor to convey sexy; I'm here to convey Janet-sexy. The thing is, I don't have any idea yet what that is exactly. Where will I look for it? I only know (because I find metaphors irresistibly logical) that a person's dancing must be like her smell, a distinctive and lingering impression. That's not much to go on, but it's a start.

And there's Dmitri, doing a better job of faking being me than I do. In demonstrating my part, he is being more of a woman than I am, damn it. He's more alluring, looking all slinky and seductive in his cargo pants and long-sleeve gray T-shirt as he stretches into the sit-lean pose in our routine, his eyes looking down at his gorgeous body, his hands liltingly feminine as they punctuate a movement. Fortunately, any sort of physical attraction is blessedly absent for me in our lessons. Not because he's not attractive, or because I'm old enough to be his mother, but because I have some boundaries in place now, and so does he. Not interested. Not part of the dancing. But it goads me, his knack for womanliness. I *am* a woman. I ought to do that better than he does. What's stopping me? Why do I feel shy or incompetent in the art of feminine seduction when I have what it takes, which is precisely and nothing more than two X chromosomes? I even have geisha training.

I guess I think people will laugh at me if I try to show the "real me" or to be Janet-sexy; or, worse, I imagine they'll take me seriously and want to go straight to bed, daft as that sounds. Maybe I have to start acting like an actor. Or is it that I have to stop acting and just be me? Oh, I'm getting so confused, this is ludicrous. What the hell is *just me*? Where am I? Am I in a breath of music? In the smile I return to the beautiful young woman on the Seventy-second Street crosstown bus on a sunny day after she has so generously for no reason smiled at me? In the gesture I make in the rumba as I pretend to be sexier than I feel? Is there any possibility in me of anything more, as a dancer, than emulation or banal imitation, or have I reached my level of incompetence already? And am I the same me I was just a few years ago when I competed in that tiny green dress and people believed me? Erica, for one, thinks not. She just last night advised me not to wear it for my upcoming showcase with Dmitri because it's unseemly for a fifty-year-old woman. She actually said that. I cringed. Who am I kidding?

But back to the matter at hand. Fine, Dmitri, fine. I'll be a woman somehow. And I get the point: my desire to do it right is getting in the way of doing it my way. Until I show who I am, I will never know how good I can be. Sometimes I think the whole reason I am dancing is to meet that thrilling stranger.

The trouble is, I resist looking at my face in the mirror; I make Dmitri think I am looking, when actually I'm looking at the plant or the wall or the thermostat. The trouble is, I am afraid. I can strut my stuff across the street in leather pants and feel like a hot mama, but looking in the mirror—that's the moment of truth; that's when I have to decide how I feel about myself.

MOST OF MY best thoughts come to me while I'm driving. I have Post-it pads and a pen handy in the car, so I can write notes as I drive. I know it's a little dangerous, but these thoughts are urgent. I write down leads to my stories, errand reminders, brilliant ideas to save, things to tell Peter or the kids. The car itself seems like the perfect metaphor—it's going somewhere. It's fitting, therefore, that this came to me when I was in the car, driving home from work: everything is going along just as it should. (The *Desiderata* just popped into my head again.)

Seconds before, I had been telling myself I was an imposter, doing more Latin dancing now and less Standard. I am at heart a Standard dancer, after all. But wait. Am I? Says who? Everything is happening as it should. The universe is unfolding like a highway. An aha moment on the Major Deegan Expressway northbound: it may be that I chose Standard dancing first and held to it exclusively for five years not because I'm better at or more suited to Standard, but because it was comfortable and safe. It was, for me, a good stepping-stone to Latin, the more exuberant and revealing style— the next turn in my highway. Standard is indeed very challenging and intellectually stimulating, but the main thing here is that it feels much less scary to me than Latin because I get to hide behind my partner. The two of us plastered at the torsos means that people aren't looking at *me,* they're looking at us. Or at least at him half the time. It's like playing doubles instead of singles in tennis. Less pressure on just you. In Latin there's no hiding. You're out there, on your own, connected to your partner by a pinky finger, a hand maybe, or not at all. People see you, all of you, and you'd better know what you're doing or at the very least enjoy doing it.

As a pas de deux, Standard is also less intimate in one small but momentous way: eye contact. There isn't any between partners because they're looking in different directions. I'm not shy about pelvic contact, hand-holding, or anything else, but ask me to look into a partner's eyes in a hot Latin dance, and I'll deal with the terror of it by quickly reverting to coyness, eyes glancing down and off to the side. Standard has offered me my optimal distance—from the audience, and from emotional intimacy with my partner. This style of dancing was a perfect parallel for the way Peter and I were together but not really intimate; we had our parallel existence around the house, our optimal distance heart to heart.

What will happen if I keep looking? I can look indefinitely into my dogs' eyes, or my children's, but not my dance partner's. Dancing is different.

When I came back to dancing a few years ago, I wasn't ready to confront all the demons all at once. Isn't the psyche clever, how it paces itself? I have segued to Latin, I tell myself, because Dmitri's studio is convenient to my home in Westchester, and because I want to get back in practice, but probably the truth is the time is right. I am ready to try with the eye contact. Before, I was ready only for dancing at the elegant distance.

Well, then, what next? Answer: the last eighth of an inch.

Among yogis, there is a saying: "Yoga is the last eighth of an inch." I get exactly what that means, because I am a seven-eighths gal all the way. Or have been. Each of my teachers has in his own colorful way observed as much. Dmitri doesn't sugarcoat things for me, and I love him for that. One day not long after I started taking lessons with him, he told me, "Dancing with you, it feels like your engine is going but you're driving with the handbrake on." Gee, thanks. I laughed, though. He has a way with analogies, and the images teach me more than the words.

Bill tells me that it feels like I'm bracing instead of swinging. Heck, yes.

"Do you know why you do that? Why seven eighths and not eight?"

"I reserve that last eighth for emergencies," I say. I try to be funny when I don't really have an answer. I suspect, though, that it has to do with fear of death. If I take off the brake, that could be the end.

Fear is such a constant companion, I'm not sure I know what it's like to dance without it. Or do anything without it. In the last few months, I have developed fear-in-retrospect of swimming with stingrays, because Steve Irwin, the Crocodile Hunter, just died after being stung in the heart, and I gulp in horror to think Erica and I swam with the rays when we went to the Cayman Islands. Never again. As for daily life, I fear not finishing and not getting things right. I fear not being perfect in something before I learn it. My fear of letting go is probably the most entrenched. The ultimate letting go is of course death, and so in this case, I have fear of metaphor.

In all fairness to myself, I have come *some* distance from seven-eighths through sheer willpower in my dancing. I've gotten plenty closer to eight-eighths in terms of technique. With enough repetition and taking baby steps closer to that edge, some moves that used to make me all jittery and clingy, like the Hover Cross in the waltz (the move I mentioned earlier that's like being a slingshot), are now thoroughly enjoyable. As for artistry—behaving in a way that has nothing to do with correctness and everything to do with inspiration—I'm holding firm at seven-eighths, if that. Seven-eighths might be putting it charitably. And don't think I haven't thought of this: I sometimes use writing about the dance lesson as a diversion, so that I'm not actually doing the thing and getting to eight-eighths in the way of moving—but I've tucked the notion up in my brain, as if that's the accomplishment.

Along with fear, there's self-consciousness behind my tenacity, although that could be classified as fear of imperfection. I'm shy about going all the way. No doubt the solution is not to focus on the audience in hopes of finding the courage to explore my artistry, but to focus inward and feel myself experiencing something. Anything. There must be a reason they say you have to dig down deep.

Authenticity could be as much about me owning my dancing as anything else. I had given it over to my teachers for all that time; maybe now I've got what it takes. It may be time to decide what kind of dancer I am, what I want to become, whether I want to compete again, or teach, or learn salsa so I can go out on a Saturday night and dance with a variety of men.

For a long time, I have tried to ask myself, "Just how good am I, anyway?" But I haven't known how to consider the question, or even if it's a question to ask. I do know it's not about my skill set, my body's flexibility, the number of hours I've put in practicing, or my results in a competition. I have a pretty good idea the answer has more to do with a decision I will make to be present in my dancing in a way that has been very hard for me. That must be the route to authenticity. Once or twice, I have managed it, and it does seem worth allowing. I like the quiet—some dancers call it a monumental stillness—when I'm moving without my usual effort and noisy roof chatter. It's an escape from the solitary confinement of the ego, when my spirit soars in that quietude, and yet it is a way of coming to myself.

"Do the beginning of our routine, and let me see if I believe you," Dmitri says on a Monday afternoon just weeks before the looming showcase. I know that for him to "believe me," I must be fully involved in my dance and therefore convincing to him.

There's just enough time for me to feel a thud in my chest before he takes my hand and we move to the center of the room, me facing the mirror, he the windows. My left leg points forward, taunting him, my left arm on my thigh, ready or not to seduce. We begin and I say to myself, *Why not? What's the worst that could happen if I let myself go?* I look in his eyes and run the fingers of my free hand up my leg as he moves close to me. I allow his approach by bending my elbows to the max. He is a breath away. I am looking in his eyes (not so bad) until it is time to drive myself back and wrap my arm at the back of my head, down my neck, between my breasts, and then I turn my head to the side with a downward glance before looking back into his eyes and coming to him, close enough to touch, and then I reach up to the ceiling, stretching and curling, to spill forward into the quick, fiery steps leading up to the Fan—POW, and I look at myself in the mirror with a dare. A defiance of my own resistance. *I will do this.*

"What did you like about that?" he asks me when we stop after the Hip Twist. But I am afraid to say. He goes ahead with an eagerness, so I listen, expecting, frankly, to have failed, because I didn't do so much that was different.

"I liked the beginning the most," he says. "I really believed you. Then when you did the Fan, I didn't believe you. You came out of it then."

He's talented. Or else, I'm not as good a faker as I thought. Or else, the subtle difference between giving something of myself to my dancing and not giving it is all the difference. I did feel better in the first part, less self-studious. And it was easier to do than I thought it would be.

"You know," Dmitri launches into another train of thought with his chin up, running his hands through his longish brown hair. "You don't have to tell the story of *War and Peace*. It can just be one arm moving like this, and one small idea." He does a few steps and speaks an imaginary inner monologue as if it's inspiring his dancing. "This is my new hairstyle," as he drapes his arm over the top of his head and lets it slither down and around his neck. "I have been going to the gym, see how fit I am?" as he caresses his thigh.

"And you can be looking out that window when you do your Crossover and see a tree. You don't have to see someone in the audience out the window. See the tree, but really *see* it and maybe say, 'Nice tree.' You can look at the exit sign over there when you do the spin. You don't need to be seeing a handsome man in Rio de Janeiro."

Slowly it sinks in that, contrary to what I'd been thinking for the past couple of weeks, I don't have to lose myself in an intricate fantasy to express myself in our dancing. And to find my sense of myself as a dancer, it doesn't need to be as complicated as I thought. It can be just one arm. One moment. In this moment, I love the movement I can make with this arm, now that hip. I don't have to do past-life regression therapy to find who I am. I can let a few small, concrete images tell my story in the present.

"So if you are looking at the exit sign over that door, and really seeing it, the audience will not know it's only the exit sign, but they will believe that you are seeing something that captures your attention."

"And I can let them have their fantasy about what I'm seeing?"

"Yes, exactly. Let them think it's the man in Rio de Janeiro."

"Meanwhile, I'm being honest. I'm not faking anything!"

We dance the same section of our routine again, this time to music. It's harder for me, because the real music is faster than the imaginary music of our dancing in silence. I'm anxious, but at the same time, I'm trying to see the tree, the exit sign, and let these trigger something fuller in my artistic expression. In the turn called Natural Top, I notice Dmitri is smiling. I ask, "Why are you smiling?"

"I'll tell you later," he answers, and on we go to the rest of it. When we stop, he says, "I was smiling because you seemed tense. I could feel you trying to get everything right, worrying that you didn't do that right, the next thing, the next. It's not like this is the space shuttle. But you were pushing the buttons," he's imitating me again at the control panel, and this time I look frantic. "Pushing every button, trying to get the shuttle to take off."

Damn.

I laugh. "It's amazing you could feel all that. I can't lie to you."

"Yes, that's the thing about dancing. I'm not saying you didn't do better. You are much better as a dancer than you were four months ago. But it would be nice if you could be more careless . . ." He dances my part now to show me a woman unconcerned about timing or getting on to the next thing. I suspect that in an ideal partnership, she is not being stupidly careless, she is trusting in her partner. "You can enjoy yourself there until I lead you forward. If we are late after the Opening Out, just remember that it is my fault." I am both frustrated and amused that my sense of responsibility detracts so much from my dancing. If only I could be more selfish. If only I could not give a shit about the future.

I want to be just like Erica when I grow up. My little girl wakes up with this look of lust for life on her face: What's in it for me? Where's the fun around here? I want some of that. Let's do it. She is selfish in the purest sense of the word—owning her self. A relatively uncontaminated child, she knows what she wants, and she says it, without shame or fear of consequence, without dressing it up to be palatable or acceptable. I know it is easier to read a person who is selfish like this. She can be hard to live with, but the priceless beauty is we know who she is and where she stands. How can I get some of that?

THREE DAYS PASS, Saturday, Sunday, Monday, and I have done no practicing because I went away to visit my writer friend Barbara upstate for the weekend. I have been negligent. But at my lesson Monday afternoon, I am different. My movement is more elastic and settled in the earth, possibly even careless. Dmitri says, "Whatever track you were on over the weekend, stay on it." To think all that practice I do at home on the floor, rolling up rugs and examining myself in the windows at night, repeating steps, memorizing routines, is not as productive as simply thinking as I speed up Route 22 to get there before dark.

After a tough week at work, I arrive for my next lesson on Sunday afternoon feeling a bit anxious because I still haven't practiced, have barely even thought about dancing since my last lesson, and no wonder, because I had a plumbing disaster in the basement and Erica had a dental crisis. Oh well, I think, maybe that's what it means, to be in the moment. Cope with each problem as it arises. So up the stairs I go to see Dmitri. And today, I decide, the point is not whether dancing brings me joy, but whether I can bring my joy to my dancing. And my anger, humor, eccentricity—all of it.

21 · LEAVING PROVIDENCE

I TAKE ONE Friday in August 2006 off from work to drive to Stamford and catch the train to Providence, where Alden, Erica, and their cousin Sarah are taking summer art classes at Rhode Island School of Design. Erica wants me to see her in the play her theater class is staging on the last day. "I'm not sure if I can, honey. I wish I'd known ahead of time."

"But I'm the lead, Mom," she argued on the phone two days ago. Peter might be able to be there, since he is scheduled to pick up the girls Saturday at the end of their three-week stint of classes. But I won't know for sure; as usual, he can't commit further than "Let's see what happens." I'd love to see her play, but I just last week took a day off to go to Providence for Alden's birthday and I'm feeling guilty about work.

"How can you not come?" Erica asked. "Anyway, you'll always have work, but you'll only be able to see me in this play once." That did it. I booked the 8:46 a.m. Amtrak Acela and charged up the video camera. She's right, and preposterously persuasive for a kid. Get your priorities straight. I don't want to miss her play, or Alden's sculpture presentation at her last Clayworks class for that matter. I can bring my laptop and work on the train.

My half-sister Hannah picks me up just after eleven. We drive to the RISD area, park on Benefit Street, walk down to Washington Street and into the Design Center. The first stop is Sarah's photography class. Anna is there with her video camera. Alden and Erica come in just after I do, and they rattle off their important news to me as we look at the photos. We have time for lunch before Erica's play. Out on the street, we run into my mother, who is looking for us. "Hi, Gamma Helen!" Erica chirps. Hugs all around. Then we find an Italian deli and take our focaccia sandwiches out to sit on stone benches by the river. I can tell already that this will be one of those unforgettable family days: my daughters so happy and proud to be at RISD doing art for the summer; their grandmother driving from Gloucester to be there, enjoying her adventures still at the age of eighty; my sister, Anna, helping get everyone organized despite the absence of need for organization; and Hannah, hosting our daughters at the rented Purple Shack, as we call it, today showing her nerves, frayed from the experience of having gone from being the mother of a single toddler to surrogate mother of a whole gaggle of girls, including a teenager.

With a half hour to spare, we wander back to the Design Center and take the big, slow elevator up to the third floor to get seats in the classroom serving as a theater. I hold a few metal chairs in the front row and a few in the second for everyone, including Peter, who has called Alden to say he is on his way. At five minutes before showtime, he saunters in wearing a short-sleeved shirt and jeans, carrying nothing, traveling light as usual. He greets Anna, whose affection for him has survived our split. He gives my mother a more awkward greeting, smiling at the floor, head tilted to one shoulder, no body contact. He sits in the second row, though I thought he might choose the first and man the video camera. He says he prefers just to watch. Our exchange is friendly, but he's keeping his distance. Erica comes in and beams when she sees him, runs up to give him a hug, her cheek pressed to his chest, her arms wrapping around his waist, much trimmer now since we've been separated. She hands me one of the two programs she's made, one for each parent. The other kids just made one program each.

The play, about a girl who goes through a manhole and travels through time, is adorable and somewhat incoherent, but magical, and Erica plays confidently opposite the male lead, a younger Indian boy at least two heads shorter. Next, we see Alden in her sculpture class. Her teacher, Bruce, makes comments about each student's work. He says it's amazing how prolific Alden was in the three weeks, and he particularly admires the elephant she made for me (elephants are my favorite animal). Peter helps Alden pack up everything but the elephant in newspaper and carefully places them in cardboard boxes for the trip home. The elephant will stay for the student show in September.

At afternoon's end, it feels odd to say good-bye to them all on a street corner and go on my way solo to catch the five p.m. train back to Stamford. We normally travel in a pack, my family, like wolves. But it's nice to see Alden and Erica cheerful as usual and excited to be going home. First, Peter is going to take them back to the Purple Shack so they can throw all their clothes and stuff in duffels and help Hannah clean up for the owners' return.

I'm going to walk the few blocks to the station, but Peter offers to give me a ride. "It's okay, I have plenty of time to walk," I demur.

"It's a straight shot for me," he says of his home turf. "Come on, you're in heels. I'll drop you." I go ahead and soak up that bit of tenderness, and climb into the high truck's backseat behind Alden, who's in the passenger seat, and next to Erica, who is staring at me, I think because she's never seen me in her dad's new car. To my horror, when I glance forward, I notice Peter's forearm and his hand on the steering wheel. They look really elegant and masculine, a perfect combination of physical qualities, and I feel that positive attraction I used to feel with him. I always admired his skill as a driver, his finesse. *God, no, don't feel that. You're not supposed to now.*

He's not your husband anymore. Well, technically he is still, you're not divorced yet, but he's not your man. You have a new life. You can't go back. Still, I wonder if he has had enough time away from me to remember why he used to like me. I wonder if at times he wants to come back to our life. I am aware of my own recklessness here, as though in allowing these thoughts, I have skated dangerously close to the edge where the ice melts into water.

Julia warned me on the phone yesterday morning when we spoke about my disastrous blind date with a creepy guy named Michael—I'd met him on Perfectmatch.com and he looked great on-screen—that I might have some kind of reaction to the frightfulness of the date. "He was so old and gross, completely wrong for me," I told her. "Too bad, because he's a millionaire, but I know I can't bring myself to choose a man for his money. He was so slight-shouldered, not manly at all, with fingers red and inflamed as if from eczema, and he kept scratching his chest and closing his eyes when he pontificated over the foie gras and pretended to be humble—but he was really a blatant show-off about his money." Julia laughed and moaned at the appropriate points in the recounting, then warned me that I might, in reaction to my revulsion, find myself thinking that Greg, my old friend from elementary school in Hastings, was pretty attractive. Instead, here in the Honda pickup, I've gone all the way back to Peter.

We have arrived at the station, and he pauses in front. I say thank you and gather my things to get out. "Bye, Mom," each daughter says sweetly. "I love you," I say, then step onto the curb in the bright sunlight, a pretty scene after the rain and clouds of the first part of the day. I watch as Peter and the girls drive off—my family. Why are they going off without me? And I feel that tug of sadness again. Why am I here and not with them? Why are we not packing up Camp Carlson together? The answer, duh, is that I chose this. My sorrow is overwhelming and time stops at that moment to allow me to absorb the full force of it—the pain of this loss of which I am, in part, the architect. Have I made a grave mistake?

I feel an awful aloneness. My mind whirls as I attempt to remind myself what it is about Peter that drove me away. *Quick, list the negatives, name his faults, the ways he hurt me beyond forgiveness.* But standing on the sidewalk in the glare, I do forgive him. There is no sense in not forgiving. *Will he forgive me? Has he already? Is he going to drive back to this station and pick me up so we can go on to the Purple Shack and pack up our girls together, drive them home? No, he is not. What if he knew I was crying in the rotunda of the station? No, it's not for him to know. I will get over it. Keep moving.*

But even as my emotions thrust up from such a deep place and make a mess of me, overflowing my neat bounds—the ones implied by my fashionable shoes, nice haircut, and competence with Map Quest and a tote-on-wheels—another part of me feels strangely fine about splitting up with Peter. And I'm okay with experiencing the enormous grief that comes in unpredicted aftershocks at inconvenient times. I walk tall toward the benches at the center of the train station with tears in my eyes and choose a seat next to an attractive man, thinking maybe he's the one for me, the one to rescue me. But he doesn't even look up. I take out my BlackBerry and immerse myself in the trail of e-mails needing reply.

There is time, here in the station and later during the train ride, for me to reflect on how hard the past year and a half has been—trying to stay afloat financially and spend more time with my daughters while working and keeping the household running—regardless of the fact that I am turning out to be up to the task. And to think I am privileged compared to the single working mother in Harlem with two jobs, no medical coverage, and three children. She keeps it together; she goes to church on Sunday and thanks the Lord for her blessings.

I USED TO always be able to neatly skirt the scorched and treeless land of regret and find another way around. That barren territory held nothing of interest. But recently, for me, regret has become an immensely useful though not a comfortable experience. I no longer believe that dumb adage "No regrets." I believe in its opposite. In allowing my regret its free rein for the first time, I feel myself released from a trap, like a fox that has gnawed off its foot to survive.

I am sitting alone on our deck, staring at the arbor vitae that conceal it from passersby; the ungainly shrubs have grown tall and scrawny at their bottoms since we bought the house thirteen years before. The deck is handsome, if petite, nicely weathered to gray, and it is the only spot on our property that gets any real sun. I sit at our wrought-iron table and reflect. I have been analyzing my relationship with Peter for years now, and even though it is more or less officially over, I continue to study it, review the ways in which it fell apart. I wonder now, fingering the smooth handle of the bone china mug from which I sip my tea, letting the sad late-afternoon sun seep into me to my bones, whether it is enough for me to feel blameless. For years, that was enough—that was everything—feeling justified and righteous in the battle over the dishes and all the rest of it, but today something falls away while I stare into the middle distance of our yard, overgrown in the back because no one has been tending it, not even me. At this moment, it doesn't seem that blamelessness is enough.

What might I have done to cause this? Although there were plenty of times during arguments with Peter when I considered whether I had caused him to shut down, many times when I may have brought my bad mood to the table and later apologized, times when I knew I was stubbornly sticking to my opinion and ought to have backed down, this is different. An unfamiliar feeling has come over me because of the sunlight dappling the dogwood and the bamboo, and perhaps because it is time. Something has ripened in me, and like a piece of fruit, the pulp of my spirit has softened; I am ready.

For the first time now, I look at my faults in a neutral way, without shame. There they are. They exist in me; they belong to me. I drove Peter away. I won every argument and lost the love. I got into the habit of loving to be right, instead of loving to be loving, and my marriage was the casualty lying now at my feet on this splintered deck. I failed my marriage.

It doesn't matter to me anymore about Peter, what I might prove with my ironclad anecdotes about how he was hurtful and cold and careless. Peter is not my business. All I know is that I have a regret deeper than any regret of my life. That I can give up my need to be blameless. I was wrong. I was responsible for this marriage ending. Yes, Peter shares responsibility for our failure, but I will spend not one more ounce of energy working out the percentage. I know only that I regret. There was something there between us in the beginning, and I didn't do enough to help us keep it alive. The regret is a hiccup wracking my chest; I have to cough before it chokes me. Why was I blind all those years? Embracing this darkness is the very thing that releases me from it. The tension of defending myself falls away and to my utter amazement, it really does feel better to accept my failure than to pretend I have not failed. At last, I feel wonderful, like after having a good cry—only I'm done with crying now.

22 CHANGE PARTNERS, DANCE ANOTHER DANCE

I T HAS BEEN about two years since Peter moved out, and when I
look back I can hardly believe how far away from our old life I
feel. I remember fondly certain moments like cooking dinner for
friends and deciding where to put the new Ikea cabinet, and I remember us with our children, from diapering all the way through to
the first run down a ski slope. But the connection between us has
quietly and nearly completely withered. It's as if we never kissed,
never made love, and never whispered softly in the darkness of night
about our hopes or fears.

The girls have had to get used to packing up on Wednesday afternoons to spend the night with their dad, and they've had to remember their math books and cell phone chargers, going and
coming. And while they were startled, in the beginning, when every
other Friday they faced spending the weekend in a different house,
on the upside, they trilled about the fun of having two bedrooms
and maybe having their dad all to themselves.

Except they don't very often, because Peter has a new girlfriend.
I learned of her existence in an offhand way, from Alden and Erica.

"We went to a dude ranch this weekend, Mom. It was really fun. Alli is so nice."

"Who's Alli?"

"Dad's friend."

I wasn't entirely happy that Peter was imposing his new love interest on our children so early on, but he was adamant that it was a good thing. Alden and Erica mentioned things occasionally, like "Mom, Alli looks like you, only younger" and "Look what Alli bought me at Nordstrom." Finally, I met her one day. It was easy. Handshake, smile, a little chitchat in my front hall. You're welcome to him; I don't want him anymore, no hard feelings. Well, all right, maybe I was a little nervous. And I did hate her for not having a single wrinkle on her face, and for her great cheekbones—the kind of face that looks good in any style of sunglasses.

IT IS LATE SUMMER. My daughters and I have just returned from a week's vacation in France—the girls' first trip to Europe. They're set to spend this next week with Peter and Allison at their new house in Irvington. Summer break is winding down, and Alden and Erica love to spend some time before school starts just hanging around. It'll be a nice week for me, too. I love that it's still light for a couple of hours when I come home from work. One evening, I arrange to have dinner with an executive from the Estée Lauder Companies, a woman named Lynne Greene who also lives in Irvington.

I get off the 6:58 and walked across the overpass to the river side of the tracks, past the tennis bubbles, to Harvest on Hudson, a Tuscan restaurant right on the river. It's too hot to eat outside, so I sit inside in the reception area waiting for Lynne. Within minutes, I see her walk in the door, but I am distracted by a quick movement to my right. I look over as a young girl bounds up to me. Erica! My own daughter! "Erica!" I exclaim. "What are you doing here?" And then I see Ivan, Alli's two-year-old son, and Alli herself, who comes up to plant a big kiss on my cheek and take Ivan's hand just as Lynne tries to greet me. What fun! Peter and the girls are obviously having dinner at the same place, and even in the confusion of the surprise, I manage introductions. "Lynne, meet my daughter Erica, and this is Ivan, and, uh, Allison." There are handshakes and smiles, and I explain to Lynne, who knows nothing so far of my impending divorce, that my daughter's father is at their table, and perhaps she wouldn't mind if we stopped to say hello on our way to ours.

We trail Erica to a big round table where Peter looks up and I see a flicker of surprise on his face; then Alden sees me and, unguarded for a fleeting instant, breaks into a big smile. "Mom, what are you doing here?"

"I'm having dinner with someone I work with. This is Lynne Greene. Lynne, this is Peter, my soon-to-be ex-husband. Alli is his partner, and this is Anna, her daughter, and you've met Erica. This is Alden, our elder daughter."

Lynne doesn't miss a beat. She and Peter shake hands. When I mention that Lynne lives in Irvington, too, they have a nice chat about the town. I hear a bit about Alden's and Erica's swimming accomplishments earlier in the day in Peter and Alli's pool, and then Lynne and I go along to our table.

Well, that was pleasant, I'm thinking. *Not so hard, my first public explanation of my new extended family.* Maybe it's easier than I expected, because I've more or less given Peter up, don't feel attached in a romantic sense anymore, or maybe because I am determined to keep divorce amicable for our daughters' sake in a way that it wasn't for me forty years ago. As the song says, "Change partners and dance"; I'm reinforced by the simple logic of this protocol. So I choose to be amicable not just with Peter but also with Allison. As time goes on, we will offer each other a glass of wine in our kitchens while waiting for children to pack up; we will plan vacation schedules, chat about books, and act practically like regular girlfriends. I'll occasionally wonder if people have noticed that my husband's girlfriend and I are this friendly—I have to say, she is very nice and so I count myself among the fortunate—and will they find that strange or wonderful? To me, it's the only choice. That doesn't mean it's always going to be easy, of course.

As far as I'm concerned, a person can never have too much love, and that goes especially for my daughters. But a few weeks later, I have a lapse in my slightly too-good-to-be-true equanimity when I feel competitive and hurt at back-to-school night. In Erica's classroom, I read her cute little illustrated bio posted on the wall: "I have two dogs, one sister, a father and two mothers." Two mothers? You have ONE mother and that's me! *See? You're not as cool as you pretend to be.* Still, never too much love, I remind myself. I override my feelings. Then, shortly after this, I hit a bigger stumbling block on the path toward enlightenment: the goddamn Halloween party.

It all started maybe ten years ago when Peter and I decided to welcome people into our house on Halloween night for cheese and crackers and hot apple cider. The next year, I made chili, too, and more people came. It grew from there. Every year people asked for my chili. Then we added music, because the adults in costumes were outnumbering the children, and while kids looked over their candy and traded for favorites, the grown-ups danced. Then Alden and Erica decided to institute a costume competition, and they were the judges. One year, we sent out the invitations using our kids' photo from the previous Halloween. The next year, we put the whole family on the invite. After that, we had to rent a tent for the yard because our house couldn't contain everybody. We encouraged people to bring a dish because we couldn't cook for 150 people. It became the party of the season. People in town talked about it, asked for their invitation, eagerly planned their costumes. The party then grew so big that Peter arranged for us to have it at his boat club on the river, a downmarket sort of place that smelled of cigarette smoke and beer, but would work fine. We got a Brazilian band, and our guests went wild, dancing in costume to a samba beat.

By the time Peter and I were estranged, the party was less my cup of tea, and more suited to adults than kids, but still, it was our tradition, so I happily made my chili, now in four vats, with Japanese rice cookers cranking out the rice. Our neighbors and friends didn't need to know we were having problems; we'd pretend to be together for the party. We didn't dance together, we coexisted as cohosts and that was that.

But this year, Peter and Allison have invited *me* to the party. The party that used to be our party and is now their party. I'm Miss Congeniality, so of course when I stop at their house one day in late September to drop off Erica's soccer shirt, they have me sit and meet their guests on the deck and eat a hamburger. It seems very important to Erica that I sit and eat a hamburger, so I do. It is a beautiful end to a beautiful fall day and once I sit, my hunger catches up with me; I haven't had a decent meal yet today. I haven't finished my errands either, but so what. We chat. And Alli says, "We're thinking eighties this year." I don't know what she's talking about. Then I realize. Oh, the Halloween party.

"I mean the party theme. What do you think? We thought maybe eighties dress, but is that too gruesome?" She seems to genuinely want my opinion, but I don't know what to say. I stifle a dull ache in my chest. It only occurs to me later, when I'm in the car alone, to answer her, "Hey, give me a break! Don't you realize I don't want to hear about that party? That was my party; I created it, with Peter and our kids. That was our party for years and years, and now I'm excluded. Do you have any idea how that feels? I don't give a flying fuck what theme you pick." But I give my opinion instead, while she is looking at me expectantly as a kind of authority, I guess, as a magazine editor: "Oh, I think since the eighties just recently had a comeback in fashion, it almost seems unoriginal as a party theme. I don't know."

"Yeah, I agree with you. The other theme we talked about was 'anything but clothes.' " Oh, that's a good one.

ONE OF MY absolute favorite self-help books is *Passionate Marriage* by Dr. David Schnarch (pronounced as though you were stifling a big sneeze), a sex therapist and marriage counselor in Evergreen, Colorado. Schnarch says that you don't work on your marriage; your marriage works on you. "Marriage is a people-growing machine." It took me a while to get that. He literally means that the partnership entity can cause each person to evolve, if they're lucky. The marriage is like the grain of sand provoking the oyster to make the pearl, or it's a thorn in your side spurring you on to better things within yourself, usually by inducing some kind of self-confrontation. And in Schnarch's view, two people in a relationship can forget about merging, becoming one, and all that nonsense. Two people find the deepest intimacy, he contends, by *not* losing themselves or letting go, but by holding on to themselves, and standing on their own two feet. Dr. Schnarch would likely make a fantastic ballroom dancer.

Partnership dancing has worked on me like marriage according to his theory. It has led me to confront and ultimately understand myself better. It grew me up, and in a direction that Peter wasn't headed. When people ask if dancing is why Peter and I split, I say yes, but it's not what they think; it's not that I found more attention or titillation or love in the studio (although that's partly true)—it's that dancing taught me what I could expect in a partnership, and I didn't want to settle any longer. I saw that Peter and I weren't ever going to get there. Best to give it up.

I also realized that dancing couldn't save my marriage because I am a gardener. My perennial woodland garden is all shade plants—

astilbes, hostas, hellebores, Solomon's seal, toad lilies, brunnera. A couple of years after we bought our home in Hastings, I convinced Peter that we should get rid of the scruffy old juniper bushes lining the driveway and put in this beautiful garden with a little walkway through it leading to the unkempt back area we hardly used because the bushes were a barrier. Plus, they always ran my pantyhose when I got into the car on the driver's side. He agreed, and I found Kate Goodspeed, an army-boot-wearing, dirty-fingernailed landscape designer who hates that pretentious phrase and calls herself a gardener. One day, the three of us put in the garden together. Peter wielded a spade and also laid the stones along the path. And when it was all planted, full of promise, I learned how to tend the garden. For years, through spring and summer, I'd go out at the crack of dawn on Saturdays and Sundays with my cup of tea and I'd weed, clip, water, and study my plants. I got to know them. I watched some thrive, some wither and die despite my ministration.

One thing all gardeners must learn if they're going to cultivate a healthy, vibrant garden is to divide their plants. Dividing means taking a shovel and a pitchfork to a plant that's grown too big for its space and hauling it out of the earth, then hacking it right down the middle in order to replant the two halves. For many people, me included, it is hard at first to do this violence to a cherished old friend. But if you don't do it, the plant languishes and your garden suffers, so up and out it is, for dividing. A good gardener knows how to administer tough love. She also learns to accept death. How do you know when a plant is too far gone and is going to die no matter what else you do? It has that look: weak and withered despite proper watering, and more brown than green now. It's a percentage of brown, roughly measured by the loving eye, that tells a gardener this plant is dying and cannot be saved. Gardening teaches an essential appreciation of the life-death-life cycle.

When Peter and I first split up, I resisted, in myself and in other people, the idea that this was a failure. The way I looked at it was that marriages have a half-life. Ours happened to be seven years. Think of all the good that came during the span of our marriage. Two wonderful children and albums full of good memories. So who says marriage should be forever? I don't believe that. Relationships last as long as they last. Sometimes, dividing is necessary. Maybe we're not meant to be married for life as the vows would have us believe; but society tells us that's how it is supposed to be, and so we feel deficient and blame ourselves when our relationships end instead of celebrating them for what they were when they were in full bloom. Peter and I thrived for a time, and now that time is over.

I used to feel a little nervous about my unconventional thoughts, as though I might be punished or thought ill of because of them, but now I find notions like this one about marriage keep me moving forward toward a certain cheerful faith. I know what's coming will be good, so I can let this go. It's kind of like letting go the hand of a man at the end of a dance. The fun isn't over yet. Another song is starting, another dance, and I can't wait.

23 THE GOOD SOLDIER STANDS DOWN

EPTEMBER HAS PASSED into October and something is changing. It's a subtle change. For whatever reason, I feel a load on my shoulders lighten as the days grow shorter. It's puzzling, because there is still all the usual work to be done. I just feel less weight pressing down on me.

As I drive upstate late one Friday afternoon to visit my friend Barbara, who is renting a country house where we will do some writing, make meals, sip tea, and catch up, I call Greg. I don't know why I have the impulse to call. I have recalled once or twice my mother's words of compassion—"he could use a friend now." The last time I saw him, I think, was in July, when he left a beautiful fine-art note card in my mailbox telling me he'd gotten the job he'd hoped to get, and wanted to celebrate—would I call him? I did, that Friday evening. He was at Blu, a restaurant by the river, at the tennis club. I changed, let the dogs out to pee, and went down to join him. We sat at the bar and had Pinot Grigio and shared an entrée. At the end of the evening, he asked if he could kiss me, but I said no. With my official new boundaries in place, I was pleased with myself in that very moment for saying just "no" to him, while to myself I gave the long version of the excuse. I'm not ready; I don't know you well enough. Yet.

"Hello?" he answers his cell now.

"Hi, Greg, it's Janet Carlson." One beat of hesitation from his end.

"Oh, hi. How are you?" He sounds friendly, not at all miffed that we'd been out of touch for months because I'd rebuffed him.

"I'm good. I called to say hi. What are you up to?"

"I'm driving to Providence." Hmm, I wonder if he knows, probably he does, that Providence means divine guidance. "I'm going for my high school reunion," he continues. "I'm going to be late, though. The traffic on ninety-five is really bad. I'm glad you called. How've you been?"

We talk for an hour at least, until Verizon Wireless decides to cut us off. *What am I doing?* I ask myself, but I feel no urge to find an answer.

Six days later, on Thursday, I call Greg again, this time from a taxi on my way to an appointment. I invite him to the annual Oktoberfest party some friends are having in Hastings on Saturday afternoon. He accepts. It seems a safe time of day for this kind of date: tentative. I dress carefully: tight jeans, a black cashmere pullover, my short-waisted camel suede jacket, boots. I park at his house because he lives only a street away and he suggested we walk across the street to the party together. We both know the small town will take notice of us arriving together, or at least our friends will— we know many people in common, having both grown up in Hastings and made our families here. I feel myself not giving a hoot what people know or don't know about me. I'm doing this for me. And what am I doing? Breaking my rules, ignoring my strict schedule, that's what I'm doing. Bad dog. But something is not quite the same.

The following Monday, Columbus Day, I take Erica to New

York, to Dr. Marc Lowenberg's cosmetic dentistry office, to have her front tooth repaired. The poor girl has put up with the repeated discoloring of the front right tooth, which was bonded by another dentist; an endodontist we consulted told me she needed a root canal because bonding killed the tooth. Peter and I felt terrible that we'd allowed this to happen. This is the kind of situation we handle well together as coparents. We both worked the phones. And now here Erica and I are at Lowenberg's. The tooth is fine. He fixes in twenty minutes the problem that has plagued her for months. I am entering into jubilance on her behalf as he polishes and trims the new bonding and my cell phone rings. "Hey, Janet, it's Greg. What's up?"

"Hi, Greg. I'm in New York with Erica at the dentist. We'll be home by about three. Want to come walk the dogs?" I am only a little nervous about Alden and Erica objecting to an intruder on our Monday afternoons home alone together. And a little nervous about myself morphing into some alien creature.

"Sure. What a beautiful day it is. What time?"

"Anytime after three."

A COUPLE OF hours later, the bell rings. I am down in the basement trying to figure out why the clothes in our expensive new dryer aren't drying properly. Normally, I'd be quite cranky about this, but, gee, what a good mood I am in!

"Mom, someone's here," Alden calls down to me. "It's Greg Lewis." She and Erica know of him because of his numerous (four) children in school. Plus, his ex-wife happens to be Alden's English teacher this year.

"I'll be right up."

I walk up to him and we kiss on the cheek. He's obviously already said hi to the girls. I introduce him to Anna's kids, Ted and Sarah, who've come by to hang out for the afternoon.

"Who wants to walk the dogs with us?" I am relieved that none of the kids is the least bit inclined. They want to stay indoors on this sunny, cloudless day and play Erica's PlayStation games. Fine with me! Alden probably has lots of homework to do as usual. They won't even notice my absence. Things are looking up.

We walk side by side, Greg holding Cookie's leash, me not holding anything, because Rizzo walks beside us untethered as a rule. I am his alpha human, but now there is this hulking, tall man with me. Will Rizzo be obliged to recalculate and defer to Greg? What might Rizzo have decided already that I haven't? Dogs are so admirably intuitive. He lifts a leg and pisses loudly and forever on the neighbor's bush.

"I feel so unencumbered," I say as we pass the mailbox at the end of Cochrane Avenue.

"Good," Greg says, and I can tell he is pleased to be of help.

The sunlight in the woods is achingly pretty on the leaves that will be turning brown soon but for now are green and gold. The air is warm, probably seventy degrees. We are without jackets. I feel super self-conscious—and excited—to be walking alone in these woods with Greg. He takes us on a route I'm not familiar with. When I come alone with the dogs, we always follow the same route. Today, I am happy to defer to Greg. He is perhaps walking the three of us. I hope he notices my butt. Thank goodness my children took me shopping a few months ago for these hip Lucky Brand jeans. I want to be a woman again. We talk as we walk for an hour. When we get home, we sit on my front porch. The dogs gulp water from a dirty yellow plastic bowl. I get us some water, too. Greg doesn't notice the mess in the yard. Or if he does, he doesn't care about it. I don't think he cares.

We walk around the side of the house to the deck. I show him my hot tub, my oaks, my special place for thinking. We sit on the iron chairs on the deck and talk the afternoon away. I feel occasional jolts of surprise that the kids inside continue to amuse themselves. I keep expecting interruption, complaints, but none come.

"There aren't a lot of interesting people in Hastings, I don't think," Greg says, leaning back in his chair, his arm resting on the table, his hand wrapped around his water glass, his shoulders looking powerful at rest. "But you are interesting. You're very intelligent." I writhe with the ticklishness of being complimented so baldly.

"I had a bit of a crush on you twenty-five years ago," he says, looking right at me.

"Really? I'm so flattered. I didn't have a clue. You mean when we commuted together?"

"Mmm. Do you remember we bumped into each other at that deli in New York on Fifty-fifth? I recognized you as a Carlson even standing behind you in line. We had lunch together after that, I think at Bill's Gay Nineties. I knew you were special. But I was married. I had to stay away from you. It would have been wrong."

"I'm not special, I'm ordinary. But I think ordinary is good."

"No. You're special." Here's another person, like Bill, like my mother, insisting I'm special. Will somebody please tell me, when is this going to be resolved once and for all?

"No, I'm not. Or maybe special is in the eye of the beholder. I don't know."

"Okay, so you're special to me. You're not like anybody I've ever known."

It feels good to have him sitting there being so direct and sure of himself and coming after me. It's such a contrast to my coyness. "Thank you. That's nice to hear. I'm sorry I'm so aloof."

"You're too hard on yourself. I don't think you're very aloof—in fact you're not at all. But you're taking your time. You've been nibbling at my bait. Just nibbling. Come on, take the hook."

That's much too direct for me and I blush, cover my eyes.

"Why?" I ask, shamelessly coy again.

"Because it would be fun." His confidence—I see it as male swagger—bowls me over and doesn't fool me one bit.

"Oh no, not *that*," I say.

"Don't worry. I can wait," he says, and my little heart leaps up, thrilled by the respect in those three words, and the determination. "I'm not going anywhere," he says, then laughs at himself, a small, nervous laugh, as if he were aware that he might sound pathetic. He doesn't realize how sexy his patience might be to me. "But sometimes, it's a matter of timing. If the time is right, sometimes the best thing is to go for it. Life is short."

The afternoon passes into evening, and we go inside. He sits on the brown leather couch while I help Alden with her science homework. Then I notice the time.

"Would you like to stay for some dinner? Nothing fancy."

"Okay."

I can't believe what I've just done—I haven't been to the grocery store. *Holy crap, what am I going to make?* I open the fridge and begin pulling things out. There's the pork loin I roasted yesterday, that was good. Asparagus, snow peas. I can make Alden's favorite vegetable dish, with sesame seeds and soy sauce. Tofu on the side for her. Salad. Linguine with tomato sauce. Boring but serviceable. What else? Strawberries for dessert. Good enough. I get to work in the kitchen, pour some wine, hand Greg a glass, take a gulp of mine to find calm in the midst of this craziness, making dinner, spending all day with this man.

There is no recognizing me; I don't fuss and get crazy with panic about the messiness of the house, the dining room table covered with my work papers. I don't go into my usual high gear. I light some candles, put water on to boil, microwave and chop and steam, but not like a madwoman. More like a woman who is not mad anymore.

I am no longer concerned about Alden and Erica wondering who the heck this man is hanging around all day and all night. They don't seem to be paying attention. I keep going, enjoying a sense of good things coming. Greg comes in from time to time to help chop an onion, wash the lettuce. *How long it's been. This does feel good. Thank God for someone to chop the onion. It always makes me cry.*

"Do you know how I usually chop onions without crying?" I test Greg, giving the answer before he has a chance to guess. "With swim goggles on."

"Erica, honey, could you finish setting the table?" I call out, with no real hope of her compliance. I have cleared my work and put out place mats. She adds candles. I think Greg has taken out the forks and knives. *Why don't we eat at the table more often? This isn't so hard.*

Now is the critical time. I have four burners fired up, four pans on them, which I am variously tending, stirring, and seasoning at a fast clip. I glance to my left and see Greg standing in the doorway to the kitchen watching me with a look on his face that stops me from my busyness. I think it is a peaceful appreciation of my juggling the pots on the stove, our dinner. He smiles at me.

"The food is ready to go. I should heat serving dishes."

He comes toward me. "No, let's just put the pots out. Fewer dishes to wash." Ah, the dishes. Somehow I knew they would not be a problem tonight.

"Alden, Erica, let's eat." I don't have a prayer of getting them to the table, I know. Homework, TV, resentment of the intruder. But within seconds, they both come into the dining room and sit at the oval table made of Italian stone, glowing in the candlelight and covered with all the various things I've prepared, plus the multicolored miniature glasses Erica likes.

I sit without exhaustion. I sit and behold my family, or some version of it, gathered around the warmth of this long-lost ritual: dinner on a school night. I sit next to Greg, and look across the full table at Alden and Erica piling food on their plates, passing things. There is conversation, about what I don't recall, the stuff of the day.

All my expectations of my children punishing me for this unex-plained change of routine, with unfamiliar company no less, are dashed. Coming to this meal, they come to life before my very eyes.

Erica stands after we've finished and asks, "Can I put out the candles with my fingers?" She licks them with high hopes.

"Yes," I say, watching her zero in on the first.

"Ouch!" she says with a smile, pulling her hand away, a little afraid but mostly enchanted to be playing with fire with permission. She tries again. No hiss, nor darkening of the wick. Her eyes shine as she goes in for a third time. This time, her finger catches a bit of wick or something aflame, and it rides on her finger in the air as she sweeps her arm in a sideways arc. We laugh at Erica-with-a-fiery-fingertip. She extinguishes that, giggling at her exciting mishap. Alden stands and does the deed on her first try, naturally. But there is no fight between rivalrous sisters.

"You have to get your fingers wetter," Alden says.

Erica licks. Greg offers a gentle suggestion: "Try just opening your fingers after you press them closed. Don't pull them away first; just open them."

That works. Erica relights the candles to do it all over again.

I haven't looked at my watch for hours. Alden says, "I know it's late, but I'm so dying for Cold Stone Creamery." The popular ice cream shop just opened ten minutes away, in Ardsley. I've been want-ing to go there with the girls.

"Call them," I say.

"Really? Now? It's eight-thirty."

"Yes."

She flies to the computer, googles until she finds the phone num-ber. As usual too afraid to speak to a stranger on the phone, she hands it to me. We hear the recording on speakerphone. Open until ten.

"Are you serious?" Alden asks.

"Yeah, I am. Hey, you've been indoors all day doing homework.

I think you could do with getting outdoors once, even if it's in the dark."

"Mom, it's *so* not you!" she says, sounding ready to suspend her disbelief anyway. But it *is* me, I'm sure of it; it has just been so long.

We clear the table. Greg does the dishes, or most of them, before his son calls to be picked up in Bronxville, and I get my car keys.

I HAVE SINCE called that day mystical Monday, because of the quiet ease of it, and the distinct hum between Greg and me. We both noticed it throughout the evening, but we don't speak about it until the next day. It is a too-good-to-be-true thing, meaning it was too good not to be true, this buzz in the air. Was it love tiptoeing in unannounced, sitting silently in the room, not waiting to be acknowledged and introduced, but expecting to be recognized after a bit? I'll take my time about it, either way. Can you blame me? Even with the fantastically apt metaphors in dance to spur me on, I haven't yet dared to feel optimistic about partnership in real life. It has taken a long time for me to start being glad again, and willing to see my dance lessons bear such fruit. Just this first luscious hint, though, is worth the wait.

I can't get over how nice, willing, even chatty, my girls were at the dinner table. It amazes me. I've spent the last nearly two years giving them what I thought they needed, or wanted, which was me, Mommy, all to themselves. Just us three girls in our cocoon. But they were so incredibly happy and animated at that dinner, and I can't help thinking it was because Greg was there. That made it a complete family set or something. How ironic, my children got instantly happier when I stopped trying to protect them from my happiness.

"I don't think it's me being there," Greg says on the phone when I mention this. "I think it's you, a change in you. They're picking up on that."

Maybe I've stopped protecting *me* from my own happiness, now that I think of it. Maybe eight-eighths isn't death like I thought—maybe eight-eighths is life. I can tell I've moved from seven-eighths to at least fifteen-sixteenths and there's no telling what might happen next.

I REJECT EVERY single rumba tune Dmitri plays for me during our next lesson. It's only a week or so until the show that I still don't quite believe we're going to do, and we need to choose our music. Each tune is either ersatz or bland, not sexy enough, not percussive enough. Or the singer's voice isn't for me, or the words are too corny. We listen to all the others, try dancing to some, and they're frankly soporific. Dmitri trudges back to the sound system and tries another, looks at me for my approval. I am amused he cares so much whether I like the music, as if he counts on it to give inspiration to the student performing.

"Wow, you are difficult to please," he jokes as he walks across the room again to stop the music after about the twentieth rumba, his head hanging in mock defeat.

"I like the Eagles," I say.

"What? Oh, yes. What's the song? I think we have that."

" 'Hotel California.' I have it in my car. The live version from *Hell Freezes Over.* Shall I go get it?"

"Yes. Because time and music are running out."

We dance to the live version, but it's way too slow.

Then I play the cut before "Hotel California" on *Hell Freezes Over.* "Tequila Sunrise." A rumba! A fantastic rumba! Dmitri likes it, too. And so it is decided: this will be our song. I'm happy that in dancing in a ballroom to the Eagles, a band I grew up with, I can briefly merge my ballroom and my civilian lives.

In the days before the show, I wonder how my performance anxiety will affect me, how "real" I will manage to be in those three minutes. I decide nervousness is about wanting to be better than you are, and I can forgo that and just be as good as I am. What a shame it would be to let nerves detract from how good you actually are. Nevertheless, I am nervous.

For the first time, I wear my hair not in a tight French twist, but loose and curly instead, with one shiny silvery clip with a rhinestone heart pulling it off my face. Yes, this is how I want to be now. No unbudgeable architectural structure; I will let my hair down. And the barely-there green dress is just right, despite Erica's misgivings. My girls help me change into it after the dinner in the vast ballroom of the wonderful old Polish Center in Yonkers. It's time for me to perform. I try to believe what Bill once told me, "Every practice is a performance, and every performance is just another practice." Alden dusts me with sparkly powder, my collarbone, my arms, my back, while Erica, hopping around on one leg due to a soccer injury, inspects my new fishnets.

I say bye to them at our table at floor's edge and walk over to wait on deck by Dmitri—he's looking sharp in a black catsuit and white shirt with puffy sleeves with his hair slicked back. The other students about to dance, John and Eviva, are nearby, shifting nervously from leg to leg and stretching necks, calves; we wish each other good luck, but otherwise don't speak. And now it's time. The couple before me and Dmitri leaves the floor to applause. Then their applause wanes, but it may be that I've suddenly become deaf rather than that the audience has stopped clapping. Everything goes surreal; it is our turn. My mouth is parched, but I can still feel my legs. I put my hand in Dmitri's and smile at him, as if I were ready to go out and do this.

We walk out to the center of the floor to the opening lyrics. *It's another tequila sunrise, starin' slowly across the sky* . . . I know that by the time I hear—if I hear—the phrase "take another shot of courage," we will be well into our routine. This is just a song, a brief song, so you may as well enjoy it.

Dmitri turns and stops in his dramatic ready pose and I turn to face him, come closer and place my right hand in his with a slight tease, point my left foot at him. He looks into my eyes. I look back at him and give him a come-hither hint of a smile, and it is not altogether forced. I look down at my thigh, letting my hand play on my leg, my hip, then lift out to the side. I am a woman again. I look past my outstretched fingers and make love to the exit sign beneath the huge clock over the double doors. *She wasn't just another woman, and I couldn't keep from comin' on.* I flirt with that exit sign—but I do not leave. I look back at Dmitri on two, the back break, and he is smiling in wonder at me. Maybe a little surprised that I can play a vixen after all, or that I am finally showing my pleasure. I stay until he signals our coming together on three.

Acknowledgments

I write alone. No three words are falser than those. I loved *being* alone when I sat down to write this book at my dining room table on weekends while my children were still asleep or visiting their dad. But hovering close to comfort and guide me at key moments all along were the following people, without whom this book would not exist, and to whom I am extremely grateful.

Julia, my friend who, in addition to being a mother and a wife, is a yoga practitioner and teacher, a breast-feeding consultant, and a sometime unofficial preacher at her church, could also rightfully hang out one more shingle: editor. She read and offered valuable insights and critique on nearly every chapter as I wrote it, and because she knows me probably better than anyone, she helped point me in the direction of my honesty. Plus, she has a better memory for some of the events and experiences in my life than I do (see amnesia, page 79), so I have her to thank for some of the key scenes that actually made it into this book. But most important of all, Julia is a dedicated reader and a superbly clear thinker, and I am indebted to her for giving so much of her time, brainpower, and heart to this book over the last two years.

I think the heavens were smiling on me when they brought me Ann Campbell, my editor at Doubleday/Broadway Books. Ann trained her remarkable wisdom, clarity and story-telling radar on my manuscript when it was still nebulous and she gave it shape. With admirable persistence, she reminded me to think of the reader as I put on paper what was in my head. Because of Ann, I think it's fair to say that *Quick, Before the Music Stops* is actually a memoir rather than a mere public display of self-therapy.

I also thank three Amy's. In chronological order: Amy Gross, editor of *O, The Oprah Magazine,* who said "yes" so fast when I pitched (that is, whispered to her in the elevator at Hearst Magazines) my idea for a ballroom dancing piece in her magazine. Second: Amy Williams, my agent at McCormick Williams. Her spare but somehow encouraging email message to me about how lousy my initial proposal was ("it needs more love") made it possible—and imperative—for me to start fresh. Bless her for her instinct, her fearlessness, and her smarts, which have served me and my first book so well. If not for Mandy Aftel, who took out her cell phone and called Amy about my book idea right then and there in our meeting at *Town & Country,* I wouldn't have found my way to this stellar agent. Third is Amy Hertz, my original editor at Morgan Road Books. I love Amy for loving salsa and my book proposal, and for having had the vision to go for it.

I am fortunate to have these writer/editors as friends who generously gave me their advice and shared their expertise: Nina Judar, my colleague at *Town & Country,* who listened and read patiently and offered fabulous criticism, Heather Bracher Severs, and also these seasoned pros who've written books: Val Monroe, Barbara Ascher, and Kate Lardner.

My often shown but rarely articulated gratitude goes to my teachers of ballroom dancing—to Bill Davies, Dmitri and Svetlana Ostashkin, Darius Mosteika, Sergei Shapoval, John and Cathi Nyemchek, John Adams and the late Virginia Gross: your teachings and devotion to dance have immeasurably enriched my life beyond the four walls of the ballroom. Thank you for showing me the way back to myself.

There is no way for me to thank my two daughters, Alden and Erica, enough for the way they so cheerfully and lovingly supported me in this process, for sleeping late, for showing interest, for being proud of me, for bringing open minds and wonderful ideas and criticisms to this project, and for somehow knowing when and how to enjoy quite a few weekend hours without my full attention. I have so appreciated Alden's wisdom and sensible point of view, and Erica's optimism and indomitable spirit. How much I have learned from both of them! And I am thrilled that they have finally started walking our two dogs without complaint.

The rest of my family—Alison, John, Anna, Bill, Rob, Elizabeth, Hannah, Charlie, Julia, Joe, Carol, and many nieces and nephews—all buoyed me with grace. And I owe special thanks, with love, to my mother, Helen Garland, for whom much of this book will be new (and possibly difficult) territory and who I know loves me despite that. As I love her. And to my daddy, Robert Carlson, my best dance partner ever. I have been touched by his appreciation of the writing process, and his faith in my love.

To Peter and Allison: I couldn't have done this without you—and I don't mean that only in jest. Thank you for embracing the whole ball of wax that is the modern extended family, and for being there for our children.

And last, I am grateful to two people I wish I had the honor of knowing personally: Clarissa Pinkola Estes, author of *Women Who Run with the Wolves*. She showed me Wild Woman (and gave me hope that Wild Man is out there somewhere) and reassured me that the life-death-life cycle is a wondrous thing. Don Henley gave me strength through his song "Heart of the Matter," in particular with this lyric: ". . . my will gets weak, and my thoughts seem to scatter, but I think it's about forgiveness." I think he's right.